Routledge Revivals

A Theory of Group Structures

First published in 1976, A Theory of Group Structures is a study of the aggregation of individuals into groups, which cuts across many different social sciences. Volume two examines a sequence of twelve experiments and reports empirical tests of the theory presented in volume one. The result is a major revision of existing research into problems of group structure and a case study in paradigm development. This book will be of interest to students of all social sciences.

A Theory of Group Structures

Volume II: Empirical Tests

Kenneth D. Mackenzie

First published in 1976
by Gordon and Breach, Science Publishers Ltd.

This edition first published in 2016 by Routledge
2 Park Square, Milton Park, Abingdon, Oxon, OX14 4RN
and by Routledge
711 Third Avenue, New York, NY 10017

Routledge is an imprint of the Taylor & Francis Group, an informa business

© 1976 Kenneth D. Mackenzie

The right of Kenneth D. Mackenzie to be identified as author of this work has been asserted by him in accordance with sections 77 and 78 of the Copyright, Designs and Patents Act 1988.
All rights reserved. No part of this book may be reprinted or reproduced or utilised in any form or by any electronic, mechanical, or other means, now known or hereafter invented, including photocopying and recording, or in any information storage or retrieval system, without permission in writing from the publishers.

Publisher's Note
The publisher has gone to great lengths to ensure the quality of this reprint but points out that some imperfections in the original copies may be apparent.

Disclaimer
The publisher has made every effort to trace copyright holders and welcomes correspondence from those they have been unable to contact.

A Library of Congress record exists under LC control number: 75029594

ISBN 13: 978-1-138-65941-4 (hbk)
ISBN 13: 978-1-315-62020-6 (ebk)
ISBN 13: 978-1-138-65944-5 (pbk)
ISBN 13: 978-1-138-65950-6 (set hbk)
ISBN 13: 978-1-315-62015-2 (set ebk)

A Theory of Group Structures

Volume II: Empirical Tests

KENNETH D. MACKENZIE

*Edmund P. Learned Distinguished Professor,
School of Business,
University of Kansas*

GORDON AND BREACH SCIENCE PUBLISHERS
New York   London   Paris

Copyright © 1976 by
    Gordon and Breach, Science Publishers, Inc.
    1 Park Avenue
    New York, N.Y. 10016

Editorial office for the United Kingdom
    Gordon and Breach, Science Publishers Ltd.
    42 William IV Street
    London W.C.2.

Editorial office for France
    Gordon & Breach
    7–9 rue Emile Dubois
    Paris 75014

Library of Congress catalog card number 75-29594. ISBN 0 677 05320 7. All rights reserved. No part of this book may be reproduced or utilized in any form or by any means, electronic or mechanical, including photocopying, recording, or by any information storage or retrieval system, without permission in writing from the publishers.
Printed in Great Britain.

Volume II is also dedicated to my wife, Sally, who is my best friend.

TABLE OF CONTENTS

VOLUME II

PREFACE — xi-xv

CHAPTER 11   A METHOD FOR STRONG INFERENCE — 266-277

  A Procedure for Using Strong Inference — 269-277

CHAPTER 12   SOME BASIC RESULTS — 278-314

  The Faucheux-Mackenzie Experiment — 280-299
  The Berkeley Eight-Hour Experiments — 299-313
  Revised Strong Inference Tree — 313-314

CHAPTER 13   CHANNEL PREFERENCES — 315-344

  The Berkeley Channel Renting Experiment — 317-325
  The Carnegie-Mellon Channel Renting Experiments — 325-344

CHAPTER 14   GROUP PREFERENCES FOR TYPE OF STRUCTURE — 345-374

  The Waterloo Circle Experiment — 353-357
  The Waterloo Lutheran Chain Experiment — 357-362
  The Waterloo Lutheran Channel-Renting Groups — 362-374

CHAPTER 15   EX ANTE TEST IMPLICATIONS OF THE THEORY — 375-397

  Waterloo Structural Adoption Experiment — 380-394

  Appendix 15.1   Confederate's Answer Sheet, Normal and Delay Times — 395
  Appendix 15.2   Persuasion Messages Used by Confederates — 396-397

CHAPTER 16   A TEST FOR THE VALIDITY OF THE AXIOM OF CONSUMMATION AND A MODEL FOR INTERPERSONAL HOSTILITY — 398-438

  Hostility — 403-404
  A Model for Changes in Levels of Interpersonal Hostility — 404-418
  Axiom of Consummation Experiment — 419-436

  Appendix 16.1   The Questionnaire Administered After the End of the Experiment for the Mackenzie-Beynon Experiment — 437-438

CHAPTER 17	SUMMARIZING THE EMPIRICAL WORK	439-479
Part A	Basic Theoretical Laws	442-446
Part B	Channel Renting Experiments	447-449
Part C	Problem Complexity, Difficulty of Organizing, and Some Voting Behavior	450-453
Part D	Structural Preference	453-457
Part E	Learning, Multiple Structures, and Stability of Hierarchies	458-462
Part F	Adoption Processes and Mapping Functions	462-466
Part G	Controlling Group Structures	466-470
Part H	Axiom of Consummation, Structural Change, and Hostility	470-474
	Some Limitations of This Work	474-479
REFERENCES		480-491
AUTHOR INDEX		492-493
SUBJECT INDEX		494-499

TABLE OF CONTENTS

VOLUME I

PREFACE	xi–xviii
CHAPTER 1 INTRODUCTION	1–14
Introduction	1–2
Basic Commitments	2–6
What We Observe	7–8
Social Processes	8–13
Plan of Volume I	13–14
CHAPTER 2 DEFINING GROUP STRUCTURES	15–37
Introduction	15–17
Concepts of Structure	17–33
Theoretical Differences Implied by the Concepts	33–37
CHAPTER 3 MEASURING GROUP STRUCTURES, STRUCTURAL CENTRALITY AND TOTAL EXPECTED PARTICIPATION	38–55
Introduction	38–39
A Concept of an Experiment	39–43
A Search Heuristic for Conducting Investigations	44–47
Measures of Group Structure	48–55
CHAPTER 4 TASK PROCESSES, STRUCTURES, ROLES, LEVELS AND EFFICIENCY	56–97
Concept of Milestones	58–60
Reaching, Timely, Untimely and Redundant	61–63
Structures and Task Processes	63–64
Milestones and Roles	64–74
Levels	75–81
Roles and Efficiency	81–85
Description of A and B Problems Used in the Laboratory Studies	85–90
Appendix 4.1 Problem Solving Processes for A and B Type Problems	91–97
CHAPTER 5 A PROCESS BASED MEASURE FOR THE DEGREE OF HIERARCHY	98–118
Introduction	98–102
A Concept of Hierarchy	102–116
Hierarchy and Efficiency	116–118

CHAPTER 6 MAXIMUM SPAN OF CONTROL	119-143
Introduction	119-125
Maximum Span of Control	125-130
Procedure for Estimating $\hat{T}_{oT}^*$ For A and B Problems	130-141
Some Effects of Changes in Maximum Span of Control	142-143
CHAPTER 7 TWO BEHAVIORAL CONSTITUTIONS FOR CHANGING A GROUP'S ROLE MATRIX	144-186
Introduction	144-146
Hedonic Formulations	146-154
Behavioral Constitutions	154-155
Definitions	155-163
Axioms for Constitution	163-167
Some Results and Implications	167-168
Determination of a Group Structure	168-169
Multiple Issue Voting	170-177
Axioms for Milestone Voting	177-178
Critical and Dependent Milestones	178-181
Adoption and Consummation Processes	182-184
Discussion	184-186
CHAPTER 8 A CONCEPT OF CHANGE AND A MODEL FOR THE RATE OF CHANGE OF GROUP STRUCTURE	187-208
A Concept of Change	188-198
Models of Change	198-201
Change Processes	203-208
CHAPTER 9 A MODEL FOR PREDICTING THE OCCURRENCE OF A CHANGE IN GROUP STRUCTURE	209-223
A Mapping Function for Predicting the Occurrence of Structural Change	213-223
CHAPTER 10 SUMMARY AND TEST IMPLICATIONS OF THIS THEORY	224-265
Some Preliminary Notions	224-241
The Mapping Function	241-243
The Diffusion Model	243-244
Preference Functions for Channels and Structures	244-263
Examining the Models	263-265
REFERENCES	x-x+8
AUTHOR INDEX	y-y+1
SUBJECT INDEX	z-z+5

PREFACE TO VOLUME II

In the Preface to the Series in Volume I, I tried to express my many debts of gratitude, present a short history of these researches, state my purposes, and describe the division of labors represented in the several volumes. It is difficult to see how it would ever be possible to repay those who have helped me. If the reader is reading this volume's preface before the one in Volume I, I invite him to go back and read the earlier one, especially the section where I thank my many benefactors.

I thought that because this volume covers the series of empirical tests of the theory, models, and methods presented in Volume I, I should write this preface as a preview of the experiments. I have tried to be faithful to the commitments made on pages 2 - 3 of Chapter One. The chapters in this volume demonstrate the utility of these commitments and report many results that offer tentative judgments about the theory and measures presented in Volume I.

I begin this volume with a statement about the process of strong inference in Chapter 11. As strong inference is the prime inferential procedures for the analysis of the different experiments reported in Chpater 12 - 16, I thought that it would serve to explain it more fully than I did in Chapters 1 and 3. I believe that any theory, including mine, is ultimately wrong, and that results lying outside those predicted by the theory are dut to incorrect theory. Given these positions, I conclude that instead of trying to prove my theory correct, I should try to improve it. I believe that the best source of clues about my theory's deficiencies is the production of counterexamples. Thus, I seek test situations where the theory, as stated, should result in a rejection. Further, instead of using the rhetoric of accept-reject, I find it more satisfying to use "not no, yet" and "no." This leaves the door to future tests ajar and serves to indicate starting points for subsequent attempts to reject the theory. I see strong

inference as an active process and explicate a procedure for employing it
in Chapter 11.

Chapter 12 contains a reanalysis of data from an earlier experiment
(Faucheux and Mackenzie, 1966) that was conducted before I began to use strong
inference. I also check out a number of models presented in Volume I. I
demonstrate the existence of multiple structures. I use the concept of task
processes in Chapter 4, the structural measures in Chapter 3, the index of
the degree of hierarchy of Chapter 5 the maximum span of control model of
Chapter 6, the behavioral constitution of Chapter 7, the model for the rate
of adoption of a structure of Chapter 8, the mapping function of Chapter 9, and
the learning models of Chapter 10. In addition, I compare indices of hierarchy
with measures of efficiency and effectiveness and with other measures of
structure such as structural centrality. Two additional experiments are
reported in Chapter 12 to check out alternative explanations. One important
conclusion is that actual groups can solve the more complex network problems
(cf. Chapter 5) in either a wheel or an all-channel network. The analysis
of solution times provides additional evidence for the basic reasoning about
task processes presented in Chapter 4.

A basic tenet of the theory of group structures presented in Volume I is
that structures represent need satisfying patterns of interactions. While it
is difficult to measure needs and to determine what exactly is meant by
satisfaction, it is possible to derive several simple inferences that are
testable. Arguing that if structures represent need satisfying interaction
patterns, there should be a preference function for the use or non-use of
any given half-channel. I guess at the form of such a function and use it to
derive a number of conclusions about what would be the effects on the structures
selected by subjects if its various terms were systematically manipulated. I

vary the costs of using certain channels, I vary the benefits, and I even vary what we could call obnoxiousness. These are sequentially and, in some cases, cumulatively employed to alter the chosen structures. There are four separate experimental conditions used. In addition, I use the data to check out a number of the measures and processes introduced in Volume I. One interesting result is that the type of incentive can alter the problem solving processes of a group.

Experiments reported in Chapter 14 investigate other features of the channel preference formulation. Results up to this point suggest that subjects prefer either the wheel or the all-channel structures for solving problems. I attempt to rank order the preferences among the wheel, chain, circle, and all-channel structures using the paradigm employed in Chapter 13. There are three experiments reported in Chapter 14. The results of the first two support the findings of Chapter 13. The third, called the Waterloo Lutheran Discussion Experiments, varies the procedure of the previous experiments by requiring consensus about group structure prior to beginning each problem. The results are used to test various conclusions from the theory and to rank order the wheel and the all-channel. Data suggest that the all-channel is not preferred to the wheel. The common finding that groups select all-channels is seen to be a decision not to decide about structure rather than as a preference for the all-channel. Subsidiary analysis was made on the various measures of structure, efficiency and effectiveness.

The experiment reported in Chapter 15 is very different from those in Chapter 12 - 14. Taking the mapping function of Chapter 9, the behavioral constitution of Chapter 7, the change model of Chapter 8, and the maximum span of control model of Chapter 6, we systematically cause structural changes. Using the simple A problems (cf. Chapter 5) we cause a confederate to be chosen as hub. Then we cause him to be replaced by another confederate as hub. Then we cause him to be replaced by another confederate as hub. Finally, we cause the group to switch back to the original confederate as hub. These manipulations provide a strong inference test of portions of the theory. We also investigate the effects of status on the gross adoption rate of structure.

There were two possible counterexamples to the theory following the experiments reported in Chapter 16. The procedures used in the experiments of Chapter 16 were believed to have inadvertently created a violation of the axiom of consummation of the behavioral constitution. Reasoning that such a violation is also a norm violation, the behavioral sequences may have caused hostility to arise which changed the conditions of the earlier experiment. A theory and model for the formation of interpersonal hostility was formulated. We then sought to explain the two counterexamples and to test one aspect of the behavioral constitution. Results strongly suggest that the reasoning is not incorrect and that the model for interpersonal hostility formation provides a strong predictor for the level of interpersonal hostility.

At each stage of the empirical tests, I attempted to construct and fit together a strong inference tree for the whole theory. These are brought together in Chapter 17. Chapter 17 summarizes the reasoning of the theory and the results of the many empirical tests. Consequently, Chapter 17 is the most complete summary of the theory of group structures embodied in Volumes I and II.

The present form of this theory of group structures raises many new problems to be solved. My students and I have been working on some of these for the last two years. These extensions include turnover of group members, a structural theory of leadership effectiveness, a beginning of a theory for the formation of committees, and a structural theory of interpersonal processes

of attraction and hostility. In addition, there has been development of
new mathematical results for the degree of hierarchy and group design.
Every time I take a close look at the theory I see new tests and extensions.
I invite the reader to take on this theory by formulating a new result and
conducting a strong inference experiment to reject at least a portion of
the theory.

                              K.D.M.
                              Lawrence, Kansas

CHAPTER 11

A METHOD FOR STRONG INFERENCE

Platt (1964) introduced a procedure for empirical research called strong inference. The idea of strong inference is described in Chapter 1. A commitment to employ strong inference was made in Chapter 1. The concept of an experiment and a procedure for conducting investigations was introduced in Chapter 3. Chapters 12-17 of this book report results from investigations and experiments using strong inference. In order to understand how these experiments and investigations were conducted and to integrate strong inference and the concept of experiment and investigation, more specific explanations of the manner in which I use strong inference as a search heuristic to improve theory in is order. The emphasis is on improving rather than justifying a theory.

The basic idea of strong inference is: Given a theory, form an experimental question, and then devise an experiment that has the strongest chance of rejecting the theory.[1] The criterion for rejection is a result that is contrary to the prediction of the theory. A result capacle of rejecting the theory will often be a single counterexample. There may be many cases that do not infirm the theory, but if there are any clear cut counterexamples, we judge the theory, as written, to be incorrect. Incorrect theories require reworking. Failure to reject does not confirm the theory; it just means that at the present stage of its development and given the existing data, we have not been able to reject it. Failures to reject are followed up by more attempts to seek rejection.

The use of strong inference, then, is a heuristic strategy for conducting a sequence of research efforts. It is an active process. The previous paragraph describes one step. While I hold that this is a step in the right direction,

---

[1] Logically, it is difficult to know what is false because of the difficulty in knowing truth. However, counterexamples to a theory can be generated. These are inconsistencies to the theory as stated. These inconsistencies can exist because of incorrect theory and because of measurement errors. I use two criteria for counting a datum as a counterexample: (1) After allowing for measurement error, a datum is a counterexample if it still lies within the set of results that disconfirm the stated result, and (2) it is possible to replicate the conditions producing the counterexample in order to produce more of them.

an attempt should be made to describe a strong inference process that
guides the sequence of steps in terms of my concept of an experiment and
investigation.

Following Hempel (1966) I should like to distinguish between "internal"
principles and "bridge" principles. "The former will characterize the basic
entities and processes invoked by the theory and the laws to which they are
assumed to conform. The latter will indicate how the processes envisaged by
the theory are related to empirical phenomena with which we are already acquainted, and which the theory may then explain, predict, or retrodict" (Hempel, 1966, pp. 72-73). A strong inference tree is constructed from sequences.
Each sequence consists of a set of "internal" principles or general laws,
a set of "bridge" principles or assertions about particular facts, a conclusion
or explanandum sentence or hypothesis to be tested empirically, and the outcome
of the empirical test. Each new experiment involves another sequence. A strong
inference tree is constructed out of these sequences.

In the description that follows of the strong inference process, I compress
these sequences to the hypothesis and the outcome of an empirical test. This
is done to emphasize some main steps in a strong inference process. The other
portions of the sequences are assumed. When I actually draw strong inference
trees in Chapters 12-17, I include the whole of each sequence.

The completion of the analysis of one experiment leads to steps for
a second, etc. The results of these steps are the creation of a strong
inference tree. The base of the tree is a relatively crude statement of
the theory. If the result of the first experiment is not inconsistent
with this theory, one has more specific information about the theory. As
a result, the theory can be made less crude or more fine. If the result
of the first experiment is not inconsistent and the experimenter feels that
he can still reject the theory using a different experiment, he should try

it. If this new experiment does not infirm the theory, he now has two branches coming from the base of the tree. If the results are inconsistent with the theory, the theory must be changed. After the change, he repeats the steps to construct the first branches out of this new base. These branches on the same level are called <u>outward</u> growths. Those branches leading from other branches due to subsequent follow up attempts to reject the theory are <u>upward</u> growths. The process of strong inference starts at the base and proceeds upwards and outwards into more specificity about the theory or its mechanisms. A rejection at a higher level always calls into disrepute the failure to reject at the lower level. Rejections are used to prune the strong inference tree. Pruning consists of cutting back "dead" branches from the strong inference tree. In the process of pruning, it may turn out that the branch in question has been allowed to grow from a conceptually incorrect branch. The result is a weeding out of other growths from the tree. Weeding and pruning often result in a reorganization of the tree.

A failure to produce a rejection allows the tree to grow outward and upwards. Less is learned by such failures than by success in producing a rejection. A failure to reject adds a twig or a leaf. A success in producing a rejection allows one to chop off branches. The goal of strong inference is to improve a theory. This is best done by pruning and weeding because it is wasteful to expend resources following clearly false leads, no matter how attractive they may seem.

In one sense, strong inference is counter to the "success ethic" whereby researchers act as if they are "piece workers" grinding out a quota of "successes" per unit time, with bonuses for above average productivity. One attempts to produce rejections instead of "successes." A virtue is made out of success in producing rejections. The error of working on the wrong problem (examining twigs on a dead branch) is considered more serious than accepting a false hypothesis (calling a twig "alive" when it is not). The most trivial of errors is the rejection of a true hypothesis (calling a twig "dead" when it is alive). Because the error of working on the wrong problem (a type 3 error) is rarely mentioned, even in conversations, and because conventional statistics does not treat this important error, strong inference is likely to be efficacious in generating better theory. It would seem that "piece work" based upon producing rejections is potentially better paid than "piece work" based upon producing "successes," assuming of course that the goal is to seek truth and not merely a larger number of publications.

A PROCEDURE FOR USING STRONG INFERENCE

A concept of an experiment was presented in Chapter 3. An experiment, E, is defined by

$$E = \langle \{\tau_0, \tau_1, \tau_2, \tau_3, \tau_4, \tau_5\}, (T,R), (T', R') \rangle.$$

τ_0 is the transformation selecting an experimental environment, Ω_E, from the universe of potential observations, $\{\Omega\}$. τ_1 describes the selection of recorded observations $\{D\}$ out of Ω_E. τ_2 is the coding of these recorded observations into raw data, $\{D_R\}$. τ_3 is the transformation that converts recorded observations to measures, $\{M\}$. The transformation τ_4 converts $\{M\}$ into data ready for hypothesis testing, $\{D_{HT}\}$. Finally, τ_5 is a hypothesis testing procedure that yields results, R or R'. The transformations $\tau_0, \ldots, \tau_5$ are consistent with respect to both theories T and T'. An experiment consists of the application of the $\{\tau_j\}$ to determine a result. If R obtains, we reject T' and if R' obtains, we reject T. The rejection of T does not imply the acceptance of T' and the rejection of T' does not imply the acceptance of T. With respect to a theory, there are always two possible outcomes of an experiment: (1) rejected, and (2) not rejected yet.

If all but one of these transformations is known, the procedure is called an investigation. Explorations occur when the transformations are not known. The purpose of explorations and investigations is to produce experiments. The purpose of experiments is to improve theory. Strong inference is a procedure to generate improvements in theory by producing rejections of inadequate theory by means of crucial experiments.

Two basic propositions are made when one uses strong inference: (1) theory T is incorrect and (2) any inconsistencies in the results of research are due to a failure of the theory. The commitment that theory T is incorrect is a recognition that theories, no matter how good at explaining a set of phenomena, will undergo modification over time. I am aware of no counter-examples to this proposition. The fate of the better theories is to become explanations that hold for some phenomena in some limited conditions. Most theories are eventually rejected outright or ignored. The proposition that T is incorrect and that any subsequent T is incorrect implies that the strong inference process never ends. The second proposition that inconsistencies between theory and results are due to inadequate theory has two purposes: (a) to focus attention on the theory rather than the transformations and (b) to be critical of petty excuses and eclecticism. The transformations should be defined with respect to the theory. The proper place for the burden of proof is on the theory and not upon the astuteness of the experimenter in _ex post facto_ data manipulations. Rummaging through pages of computer output may provide clues as to probable reasons for rejection.

Speculations for the causes of failure are encouraged to suggest the next step but should not be used as rationalizations. The conduct of research that does not provide clear cut evidence for the rejection of a theory causes many problems. The second proposition is the main reason why one should seek unambiguous criteria for rejection of a theory. The example of amoeba movement in Chapter 1 is a good illustration of this principle.

It is difficult to take the first step in constructing a strong inference tree. It is difficult to make successive steps, especially after rejections occur. The fuzzier the theory, the less precise the instrumentation, the less agreement about measures and models, the more difficult the steps. However, a simple action checklist can be provided for taking a step:

(1) Think of a way to reject the theory.

(2) Select an experiment, E, that you think has the best chance of producing a successful rejection. This involves the selection of τ_1, τ_2, τ_3, τ_4, τ_5.

 (a) Select the Ω_E (τ_0).

 (b) Select the data to be recorded and the code (τ_1 and τ_2).

 (c) Select the measures and models (τ_3 and τ_4).

 (d) Determine decision criteria for rejection (τ_5).

 (e) Apply the τ_j.

(3) Analyze the results of the experiment in order to begin planning for the next step.

Action (1) presupposes a theory that one is seeking to reject. For underdeveloped, myth encrusted, and value laden issues it is not necessary to posit a very fancy theory. Keep it simple here. For example, a good beginning of a study of group structure is to determine whether or not structure is static or dynamic. As one progresses upwards and outwards on the strong inference tree, action one becomes more contingent on previous steps. As the theory becomes more articulated and finer, so does the care taken in action (1). Action (2), selecting the experiment, depends on action (1). Action (2) consists of selecting the transformations, $\{\tau_j\}$. These are subdivided into 4 groups for convenience. Action (2a) is the choice of the experimental situation that is believed to be capable of implementing action (1). Failure to produce a rejection of T in a previous step may lead to the choice of another Ω_E that may produce a rejection. Such outward growths of the tree that seem plausible ought to be tried before further upwards growths, because the closer one is to the base when a rejection occurs, the more one learns. Action (2b) is the selection of the data from Ω_E that is recorded and the selection of the coding scheme. Action (2b) determines the data that are analyzed in the later actions. Action (2c) is particularly important because different sets of measures and models can be applied to the same raw data. Thus, the same raw data can be used for several steps in the same strong inference tree. A "clamping down" of successive transformations from τ_1 can be used when conducting investigations, a procedure explained in Chapter 3. It is possible to take many steps with the same τ_0 and τ_1. For example, given τ_1, one can vary τ_2. Given τ_1 and τ_2, we can vary τ_3, etc. Two experiments are different if at least one of the τ_j differs. Many experiments can be conducted with the same data. This is why the "clamping down" procedure explained in Chapter 3 typically begins with τ_2 or τ_3. Each successive τ_j is constrained by the outcomes of the preceding τ_j's. Action (2c) is often very difficult. The models and measures of Chapters 3-10 are examples of this type of action.[2]

---

[2] In the case of investigations and explorations, one proceeds by working backwards from the expected results to determine the transformations. The action sequences in (2) are the forward steps described in Chapter 3. The analysis of strong inference in this section is for experiments. Extension to investigations is made by including actions for working backwards from expected results to define the transformations. Then one performs action (2).

Action (2d), the determination of decision criteria, is crucial. It must yield clear decision outcomes. It is at this action where the scientist must be hardnosed and unsentimental. It is here that the propositions (1) and (2) are most necessary. No matter how overwhelming the evidence for not yet rejecting the theory, the existence of clear counterexamples are the data that should receive the greatest scrutiny for action (3). It is useful to employ the technique used in accounting of separating the functions of collecting money, reporting, and auditing cash flows. As it is very difficult to not become emotionally involved with one's own theory, it is helpful to separate the functions of collecting the data, performing the analysis, and judging the results. This may be done by using assistants for different phases and employing rewards for finding faults, discrepancies, etc.[3] Action (3) leads into a new action (1), etc.

There are many options the experimenter can take on each step. There is more than one type of step to be taken for different outcomes of a step. We can move upwards, outwards, downwards on the strong inference tree; we can reorganize the tree by rearranging the branches; and we can conduct subsequent experiments with the same data by clamping down on successive transformations. I need to introduce a few definitions before launching into the discussion of the dependency of a step on prior contingencies.

In an experiment, T predicts R and T' predicts R'. There are two outcomes of a step: "no" and "not no yet." The outcome is "no" when the result of E is R'. The outcome is "not no yet" when the result of E is R.

---

[3]The "piecework ethic" of producing non-rejections has spread to the assistants. Experience suggests it takes approximately two years of work with an assistant before he becomes converted from a "success" producer to a rejection hunter. It is very upsetting to them to report to their professor that his theory has been rejected. The professor may also be upset. He has to be rather Spartan about these rejections, for they are in his own best interests.

"No" corresponds to reject and "not no yet" corresponds to "not yet rejected."
Each step must include an experimental question and a decision criteria
that results in either "no" or "not no yet."

There are five basic options that an experimenter can take in generating
the strong inference tree:

(1) <u>Keep T and Change</u> Ω_E. This is the procedure of outward growths. It
is the attempt to reject T by selecting another experimental situation for
which he believes he has a good chance of rejecting the theory.

(2) <u>Keep T and change the</u> $\{\tau_j\}$. There is usually not a one-to-one relationship
between the theory, T, and the set of transformations, $\{\tau_j\}$. This is used
in "clamping down" procedures that use one Ω_E to generate a sequence of
experiments by fixing a τ_j and allowing $\tau_{j+1}, \ldots, \tau_5$ to vary.

(3) <u>Change T by making it finer</u>. A theory T is made finer by making the
conditions and variables of Y more specific for which a "no not yet" outcome
is obtained. T is made finer by upward growths of the strong inference tree.

(4) <u>Change T by making it coarser</u>. A theory T is made more coarse by
making the conditions and variables of Y less specific for which a "not no yet"
outcome is obtained. T is made coarser by pruning the strong inference tree.

(5) <u>Change T by reorganizing it</u>. A theory T is reorganized by rearranging
the dependencies of conditions and variables. Often outward and upward growths
have occurred at the wrong level in the strong inference tree. For example,
the nature of the group problem may be considered a more basic variable
than the structure of a milestone in an earlier step. Later steps may
indicate that it is the instrumentality of the milestone structures that

determine the effect of the type of group problem. The earlier strong inference tree would have to be rearranged to illustrate such dependencies.

These five options open to the experimenter refer to the selection of actions (1) and (2) of the next step. Recalling that action (3) is the analysis of the results of the experiment for planning the next step, the choice of which option is exercised on the next step depends upon the option selected on the previous step and the outcome of the experiment. These contingencies among option taken, outcome of the experiment, and option to be taken are a part of action (3) decision making. These contingencies are summarized in Table 11.1.

Refer to Table 11.1 (Page 276)

An outcome of "not no yet" represents a failure to produce a rejection. There are always the three options in such an event: (1) keep the theory but change the experimental situation, Ω_E; (2) keep the theory but try clamping down on $\tau_2 - \tau_5$ in the attempt to produce inconsistencies; and (3) change the theory by making it finer. The outcome of "no" represents a success in producing a rejection. The response in this case depends upon the option taken previously. There is always the option of reorganizing the theory (option 3). If any of the first four options were taken, there is always the option of making the theory more coarse. However, if the

TABLE 11.1 EXPERIMENTER OPTIONS CONTINGENT UPON PREVIOUS
OPTION AND EXPERIMENTAL OUTCOME

Option Taken in Experiment	Outcome of Experiment	
	No	Not No Yet
1. Keep T, change Ω_E	3,4,5	1,2,3
2. Keep T, change $\{\tau_j\}$	3,4,5	1,2,3
3. Change T, making it finer	4,5	1,2,3
4. Change T, making it coarser	4,5	1,2,3
5. Change T by reorganizing it	5	1,2,3

theory was unchanged and the experimenter tried a new Ω_E (option 1) or new τ_j (option 2), the information gained may suggest ways in which the conditions and variables of Y can be made more specific. Hence, for a "no" outcome following options (1) or (2), there is the option of changing T by making it finer. It should be noted that there is no option of quitting research on the problem, which follows from proposition one that T is incorrect. Proposition two that inconsistencies ("no" outcomes) are due to theory is reflected in the entries of the "no" column of Table 11.1. A "no" outcome always results in an attempt to alter the theory.

Strong inference, as described here, is the main method of inference used in conducting the experiments and investigations reported in this book. Chapters 12-17 constitute both empirical support for a theory of group structure and a case study for the employment of strong inference. We know that the theory is incorrect, but it is certainly less incorrect than its predecessors.

The empirical chapters are a report using hindsight of the various studies. Results did not come effortlessly. The actual progression was, to say the least, less orderly than its presentation. The author's batting average is approximately 19 ideas and procedures that were rejected for every 20 he proposed. Because most of the bad ideas were proposed by him, the actual number of steps is much larger than those contained in Chapters 12-17. For the sake of brevity and not wishing to be a complete boor, only the more "significant" steps are reported. I am confident that the future will demonstrate that 19 out of 20 was too low a failure rate. While his high rate of ill-formed, incomplete, and outright stupid ideas may reflect inherent limitations on intelligence plus a Celtic persistence in adversity, it is certainly clear that, for him at least, strong inference was necessary.

CHAPTER 12

SOME BASIC RESULTS

This chapter reports several early experimental situations for testing a theory of group structures. The first is a reexamination of earlier work reported by Faucheux and Mackenzie (1966). The second and the third present an analysis of data taken in Berkeley, in which the network decomposition problems were given to groups who worked on them for an eight-hour period. Each experimental situation provides many growths on a strong inference tree for structural change. The strong inference tree has its base in the Faucheux and Mackenzie experiment. The two Berkeley experiments provide additional branches and twigs on this tree.

After presenting a condensed theoretical introduction, I shall draw the portion of the strong inference tree under investigation. The discussion of the results proceeds by considering the data that is relevant to each portion of the tree. The tree, of course, is a summary, using hindsight, of the lengthy analyses that actually took place. Most of the steps are reported as "not no yet" outcomes. The many outcomes of "no" that went into forming the strong inference tree are not presented. For brevity and for the purpose of displaying the results to date, the pruning, weeding, and reorganizations of it that actually occurred can only be inferred from examining the tree itself. For the sake of compactness, measures and procedures used are not reintroduced, as they are described in the earlier chapters.

The Faucheux-Mackenzie experiment was conducted in 1965. At that time I did not know about strong inference. Consequently, this early experiment had a more traditional "split-half" design. There was also no clear theory to guide even that "design." The spirit was to try varying the problem and then look at what would result. I felt that group structures ought to change and that how they changed would depend in part on the nature of the problem being solved. It seemed to me that there was insufficient concern with the problems being solved in the communications network experiments.

The original paper illustrates the *ad* *hoc* spirit with which we did the work. From the vantage of the passage of nine years, I would not do this experiment today the way that we did it. I have taken the liberty of recasting the analysis in the form of movements in a strong inference tree. In this way I believe the main results can be easily integrated with those following in the next five chapters.

Despite the shortcomings of the original design, the main results and the secondary analyses of the data using tools developed after 1966 are theoretically relevant. They constitute a core of basic results about structural change. The closer reasoning about why these results occurred and the more detailed analyses and implications of structural change came much later. I have tried to present these basic findings as directly as possible and in such a manner that the later experiments can build upon this base.

One immediate casuality is the use of words like "tend" rather than more precise language of strong inference. Another is the complete reworking of the trees of Figures 12.2, 12.4 and 12.5 when writing the summary in Chapter 17. The strong inference trees of this chapter lack the detail and precision of later strong inference trees. Nevertheless, the results and arguments used in the analysis set the stage for later chapters.

There are also extra results in this chapter. These extra results are not always very significant theoretically but they do provide some validation to the studies by reporting certain findings in the language of earlier work. In short, while providing some basic results, the reanalysis of this earlier experiment also provides a bridge between the pre-strong inference and the post-strong inference method of examining these data.

THE FAUCHEUX-MACKENZIE EXPERIMENT

Method

The experiment reported by Faucheux and Mackenzie (1966) has been described in Chapter 4 and in Appendix 4.1. Briefly, we used a communications network paradigm using two types of group problems. One group problem is the minimum list of symbols (or A) problem. The other is the network decomposition (or B) problem. Half of the 14 experimental groups did a sequence of eight A problems followed by four B problems. The other half began with the same four B problems and finished with the same eight A problems. All problems of the same type are presented to the group in the same order. Subjects were paid six dollars to complete the 12 problems and answer a questionnaire. Subjects were told that since the pay is constant, the faster they could solve the problems, the more pay they would receive per hour. By this means, we attempted to have each group member act as if his goal was to minimize time per problem solved. Thus, we encouraged each group to be as efficient as possible in solving these problems.

Theory

Recalling that I assume that group structures represent need-satisfying interaction patterns, I conclude that structures will change if they are not able to satisfy the needs of the members. Structures that are capable of satisfying these needs, on the other hand, will not change. At minimum one should expect that structures can and do change; they are not static, as is assumed in most models and implicitly in most structural studies. Furthermore, those structures that are no longer satisfying will be changed to become more satisfying.

Each group problem involves group milestones, and different types of problems involve different milestones. A solution to a problem represents an edge progression through a process graph (cf. Chapter 4). This edge progression of reaching these milestones is the task process of the group. I assume that groups learn to solve these group problems and develop task processes as they gain experience. Each milestone has a group structure. Different structures may be satisfying for different milestones. A problems involve fewer milestones than the B problems, and the difficulty of reaching the group milestones for the B problems is much greater since they require the formation of patterns, subsolutions, and agreement upon the total solution. I assume that the less complex the nature of the problem, the easier it is to see how to organize the task processes to solve it. The easier it is to determine the task processes, the easier it is to see what milestone structures or group role matrix is required. Because all members had to have the same answer in the same order for the A problems, there are clear and easily perceived benefits for forming a hierarchy or centralizing. The necessity for having all the subsolutions for the B problems should also encourage the formation of a hierarchy; however, the greater complexity of these problems make this more difficult to accomplish. Voting on structures to change task processes is assumed to occur the greater the expected benefits of changing relative to the "costs" of changing.

It is expected that voting on structures will occur rarely on the earliest problems for each type and that voting is more likely to occur for the A problems than for the B problems. Accordingly, if the goal is efficiency, groups working on the A problems will be more likely to vote, and the result of the voting process will usually be wheel structures on both the data-sharing and answer-forming phases. Thus, we expect hierarchies to occur for the A problems but not necessarily for the B problems. For the B problems there should, however, be a trend towards forming a hierarchy. They just may not reach it by the end of only a few problems.

Most, but not all, groups working on A problems will centralize their structures. Those that eventually centralize will vote more than those that don't. Those groups that do centralize will tend to remain centralized and will cease voting after centralization. The mapping function of Chapter 9 and the voting processes described by the behavioral constitution of Chapter 7 will explain departures from this rule. If groups form structures that are need-satisfying and if the goal is efficiency, centralized groups that form will be more efficient and more effective. In addition, the correlation coefficient between the index of centrality and satisfaction will be strongly positive for A problems. While for the B problems the group is usually decentralized, the average centrality of the first B problem following the completion of the A problems may be greater than for the first B problem not following the A problems. However, the changes and non-changes in structure should be explained by the mapping function.

The adoption model given by Equation (8.27) (cf. Chapter 8) for the rate of adoption of structure will give good predictions for the actual adoption rates based upon the relative intensities of favorable and unfavorable votes. The estimates of complexity for each problem given in Chapter 6 and the procedure for determining the maximum span of control (Equations (6.18) and (6.19)) are used to calculate the capacity for change (variable 7 in Equation (9.1)) of the mapping function. The mapping function will predict the changes and non-changes of the group structure for data and answer phases for all 12 problems of every group.

A typical group beginning with A problems will have low degrees of centrality that tend to increase up to the beginning of problem 5, when it "abruptly" becomes 1.0 (cf. Chapter 3). Centrality remains at 1.0 until the first B problem. At that point the group structures will become non-centralized and will exhibit no significant trend towards centralization. The adoption model implies that this is not an abrupt change, but is rather one that takes place over a number of problems because of voting. The change in centrality only appears abrupt because of the sensitivity of the index of centrality on the closing of the last few non-wheel half-channels. The "sudden" decentralization when the group performs the first B problem is due to a change in capacity caused by increased problem complexity. The ups and downs of the index of centrality are followed exactly by the mapping function. They are illustrated in Figure 12.1.

Refer To Figure 12.1 (Page 284)

The strong inference tree for this study of structural change is

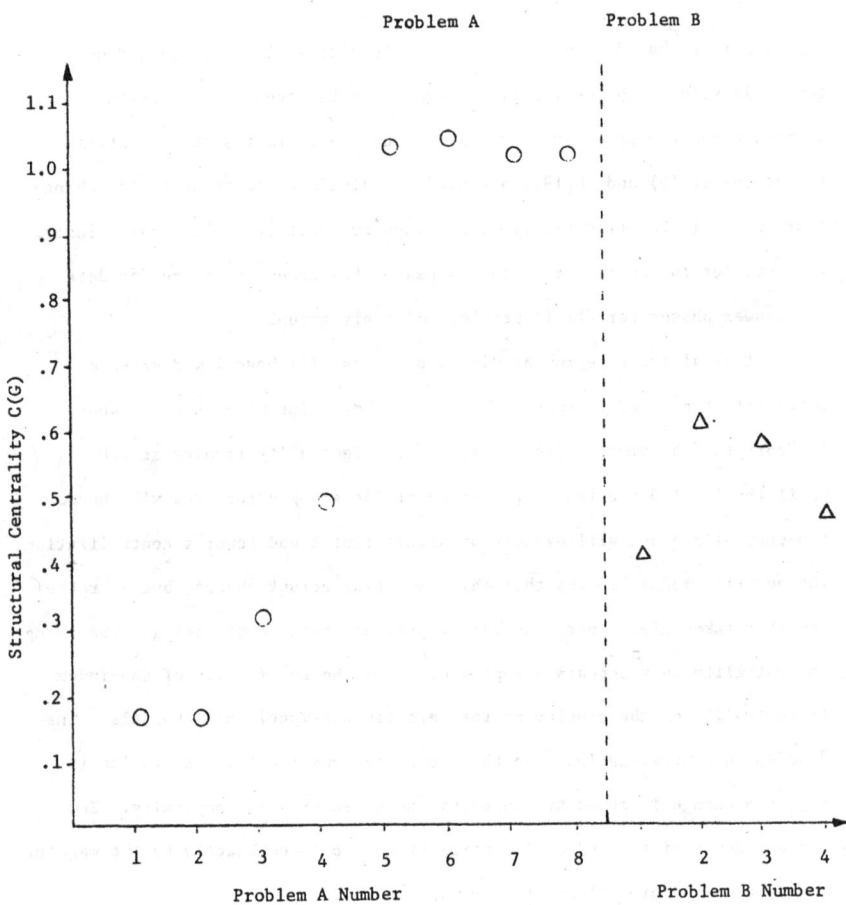

Figure 12.1 Structural Centrality as a Function of Problem Number for a Typical Group on Problems A and B for Task-Oriented Communications.

presented in Figure 12.2. Each decision represented in Figure 12.2 is a
result. Data for these results are presented in the next section.

Refer To Figure 12.2 (Page 286)

Results

Let us proceed up the strong inference tree by first taking the left hand branch and continuing to the top twig. Then let us do the right hand branch from the bottom to the top. The first question is the rejection or non-rejection of the statement "structures can change." Every one of the fourteen groups for both the data and the answer-forming phases exhibited changes in structure. Most changed from an all-channel to a wheel on the A problems. Centralized A problem groups usually changed back to an all-channel. Aside from these major changes, all groups exhibited changes in both incidence matrices (cf. Equation (2.7)). There is no example of a group whose incidence matrix did not change over the 12 problems. Stated another way, these data reject the convenient assumption that structures are static.

The next two questions concern the tendency of groups to form hierarchies on the two types of group problems. Unfortunately, these questions are less precise because of the use of the word "tendency." Given the facts that different wheel groups centralized at different rates and implemented a wheel structure on different problems, that the presence of errors reduces

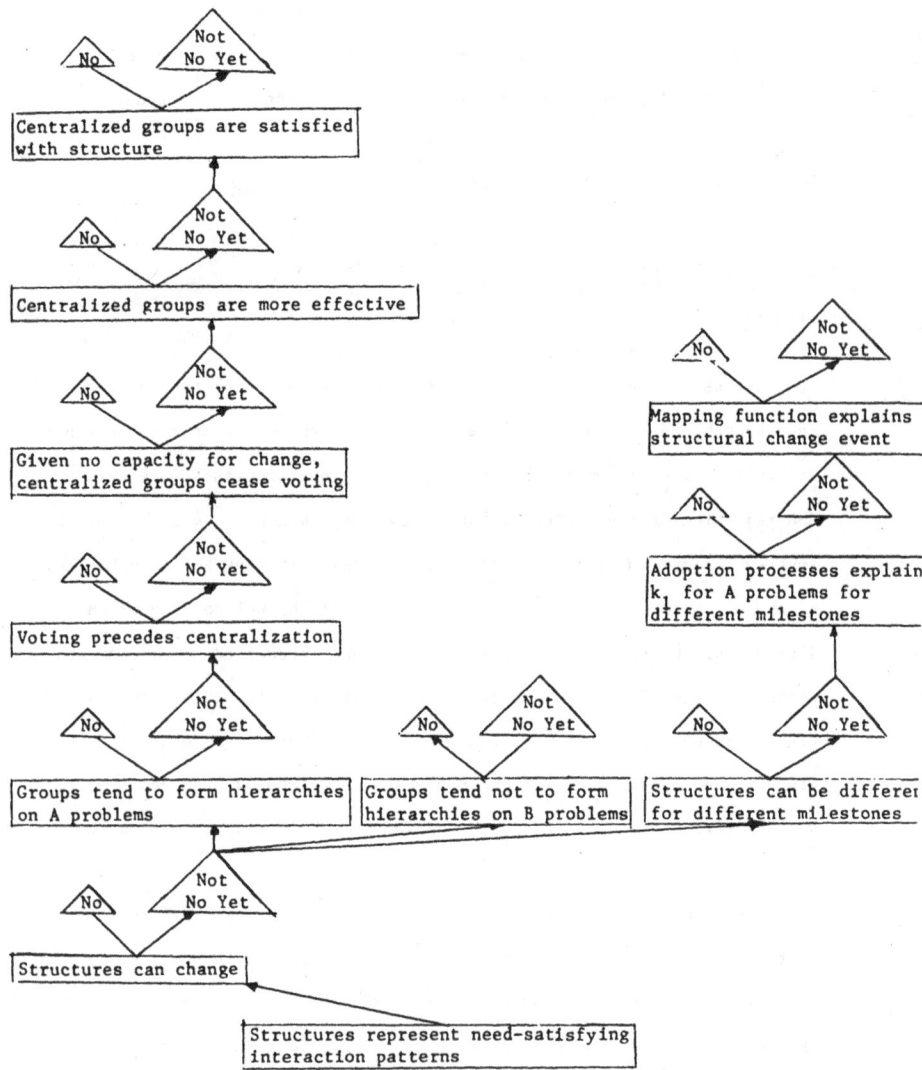

Lines with arrowhead are those supported by the data. Lines without arrowheads are those rejected by the data.

Figure 12.2 Faucheux-Mackenzie Experimental Strong Inference Tree

the degree of hierarchy, the fact that three groups (N, I, and J) did not complete all of the A problems and two (I and J) did not centralize, and the fact that the questions in Figure 12.2 inquire about a trend, the correlation between the degree of hierarchy (cf. Equation (5.4)) and problem number only suggests a tendency.[3] For all 14 groups the correlation coefficient between degree of hierarchy and problem number is +0.647 ($p < .01$, d.f. = 101) for A problems and +.034 ($p > .50$, d.f. = 54) for B problems respectively. The correlation coefficient for the A problems can be subdivided into those groups performing the A problems first ($p = .642$, $p < .01$, d.f. = 54) and those performing the A problems second ($p = .665$, $p < .001$, d.f. = 45). The three groups not completing the complete set of A problems did the A problems second. Since groups performing A problems tended to centralize, the correlation coefficient for these groups (for the A problems) should be less due to the exclusion of these later values. The correlation coefficients between hierarchy and problem number for the B problems present an interesting pattern. For those performing the B problems first, the value is +.416 ($p < .05$, d.f. = 26). For those performing the B problems second, the value is -.205 ($p > .10$, d.f. = 25   Thus, we can reject a hypothesis that groups tend not to form a hierarchy with B problems. We must tentatively not reject the hypothesis that groups tend to form a hierarchy with A problems. There is additional evidence to support this conclusion.

For such small groups, the index of centrality is closely related to but not equivalent to the index of hierarchy. We can examine changes and trends in changes of the value of the centrality index to track the formation

---

[3] Once a group centralizes and is pure hierarchy, the correlation between degree of hierarchy and problem number should be close to zero. The actual value is 0.031 ($p > .10$, d.f. = 28). This is another reason why $\rho(H,T) < 1.0$ for A Problems. A correlation between the degree of hierarchy and trial number is not a very good test for tendency to form a hierarchy, especially for the B problems. This problem of tendency will be proved more delicately later.

of a hierarchy. Ten out of the eleven groups completing all eight A problems centralized both phases. The eleventh centralized the answer-forming phase. One out of the three groups that did not complete all eight A problems centralized. There were two groups that did not centralize who failed to complete all eight A problems. One completed four and the other completed five. These data for those completing the entire eight A problems do not provide a counterexample to the proposition that groups centralize the answer phase on the A-type problem. All but one centralize both phases. However, there is only a tendency to form a hierarchy, despite the fact that the number of uncle and cousin relationships (cf. Equations 5.2 and 5.1) in all eleven groups (answer phase) is small. It is the number of untimely behaviors (due to errors) that destroys the precise conclusion that groups form hierarchies on A problems. For the purpose of the strong inference tree, I shall ignore the errors and focus on the number of uncle and cousin relationships to conclude "not no yet" on the hypothesis that groups tend to form hierarchies on the A problems.

We must consider additional evidence, too, about the hypothesis that groups performing B problems do not form hierarchies. Groups O (problem 4), S (problem 1), T (problems 2, 3, 4), and group W (problem 2) are centralized for the answer phase on B problems. Group S has cousin but no uncle relationships on problem 2. Thus, we have two clear counterexamples (if we disregard untimely messages) to this hypothesis. Hence, using the criterion of strong inference, we reject this hypothesis.

There is no strong effect of order of presentation of the type of problem on the structures formed: the analysis of Faucheux and Mackenzie

(1966, p. 368) indicates that there is a task dependency of organizational centrality. While the trend is very strong statistically, using strong inference one must reject the conclusion that the nature of the problem determines the type of structure. A and B problems can and have been solved in both wheel and all-channel groups. The effect of the type of problem lies more in the milestones, problem complexity, voting processes, and capacity for change in structure. The stimulus "problem" does not cause "structures." Rather, there is a set of processes that intervenes between the presentation of the first group problem and the implementation of a set of group structures.

Failure to reject the statement that groups tend to form hierarchies on A problems leads directly to attempts to understand how such changes take place. The assumption of Chapter 7 that the members exchange influence efforts to affect the outcome led to a formulation of a calculus of influence efforts called a behavioral constitution. The mapping function also depends upon voting. Because all A groups begin in an all-channel, the theory assumes that voting must occur before centralization of the structures. A single group centralizing without a vote would mean that voting processes are not necessary in all cases. A very simple check, then, is to see if one can reject the hypothesis that voting precedes centralization for the A problems. Because every group performing the A problems engaged in some voting, we conclude "not no yet."

Since a structure represents a need-satisfying interaction pattern, voting occurs when at least one member is dissatisfied (there must be a recall to start up a voting sequence), because a vote is an attempt to alter a structure. A member who is satisfied (all other alternatives have positive opportunity costs) has no reason to vote and alter the structure. If the group forms a hierarchy and centralizes in order to achieve maximum efficiency, and if the network that it forms is a need-satisfying one, voting should cease unless there is a change in capacity. That is, post-centralized groups should cease to vote unless there is a capacity for change due to a failure of the person in the top level to perform within the norm time allowed for that problem. This hypothesis that centralized groups cease to vote (unless a capacity for change develops) cannot be rejected at this time. We conclude "not no yet."

A subsidiary check on this reasoning is to determine whether or not centralized or hierarchical groups are more efficient. This question can be examined in several ways. Looking at measures of effectiveness presented by Faucheux and Mackenzie (1966, p. 370), following centralization the mean number of messages sent within the group dropped from 32.6 to 10.4, the mean time per problem dropped from 10.5 to 4.0 minutes, and the mean number of errors per problem dropped from .32 to .13. Clearly, centralized groups are, on the average, more effective than non-centralized groups. This average improvement also extends to the differences in average effectiveness measures for each group, comparing pre-centralized with centralized data. Efficiency, defined by Equation (4.5), is not the same as effectiveness. Recalling that the A groups form hierarchies, an examination of the relationship between hierarchy and efficiency would provide more information.

Figure 12.3 is a plot of these two measures for A problem data. The correlation is 0.96 with 101 degrees of freedom.

Refer To Figure 12.3 (Page 292)

We can tie hierarchy and effectiveness more closely by noting that for the A problems, the correlation between hierarchy and the number of messages is $-.758$ ($p < .001$, d.f. = 101), between hierarchy and time per problem is $-.594$ ($p < .001$, d.f. = 101), and between hierarchy and the number of errors is $-.419$ ($p < .001$, d.f. = 101).

A final check on the relationship between structure and satisfaction with the structure is given by Faucheux and Mackenzie (1966, 371-372). There is some difficulty in using these calculations for a strong inference test because the experimenters used a questionnaire given at the end of the 12 problems to assess satisfaction in different ways. For example, perhaps the satisfaction reported for the A problems was not affected by the experiences on the B problems, and vice versa. There is also no direct link between the centrality on a given problem and the satisfaction for the whole set of problems. However, there is a correlation of 0.817, $p < .05$ between average centrality (mean of post-centralization problems or the mean of all trials if the group did not centralize) and mean group performance evaluation of the A problems. There was a negative correlation of $-.365$, $p > .05$ for the B problems. Because forming a hierarchy requires each member to do specific subtasks, there should be a strong relationship between the assessment of

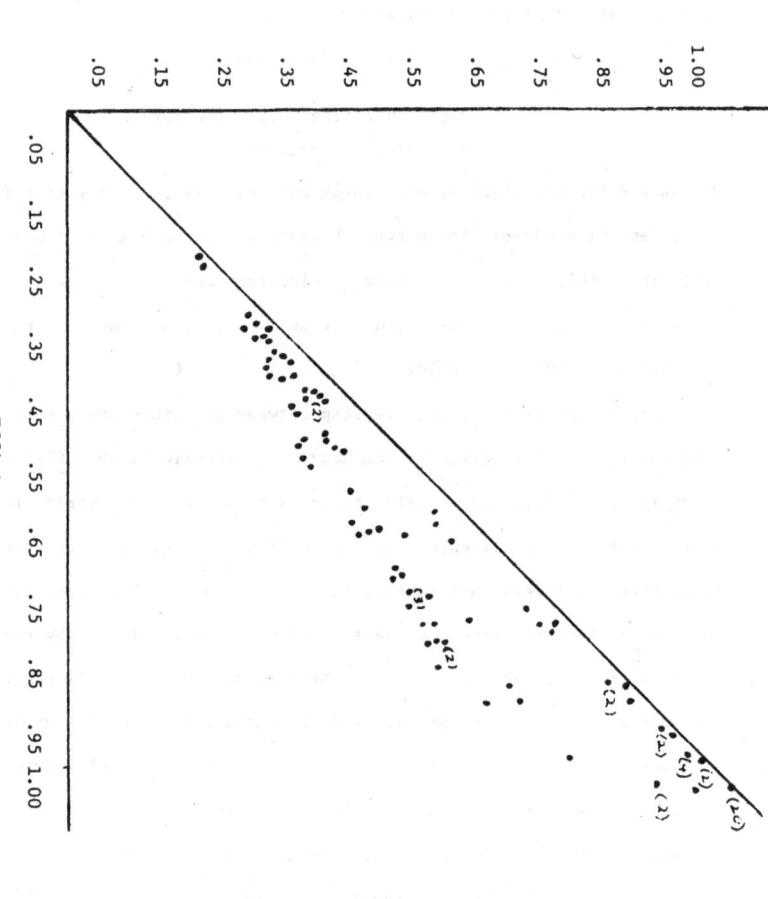

Figure 12.3. The plot of the degree of hierarchy and efficiency for the Faucheux-Mackenzie A problems.

whether group members took appropriate roles as needed and the evaluation of group performance. The results are $+.702$, $p < .05$ for A problems and $.687$, $p < .05$ for B problems. Furthermore, for A problems the correlation coefficient between role fulfillment and group centrality is $+.852$, $p < .05$. There is, as expected, no corresponding significant finding for the B problems ($+.076$, $p > .50$).

These results provide no reason to reject the hypothesis that centralized groups are more effective; that more hierarchical groups are more efficient; and that centralized groups appear satisfied with the structures for A problems. The results also indicate that different roles were expected (on the average) for the two types of problems.

We have yet to check out the right hand branch of the strong inference tree of Figure 12.2. The first step is determining whether structures can be different for different milestones. This occurred many times. In one case mentioned earlier, the data phase was completed using a decentralized structure and the answer phase was completed using a centralized structure. Thus, the outcome is "not no yet." This finding of different structures occurring for different milestones indicates that the multivariate stochastic concept of structure presented in Chapter 2 is probably the most valid and general of the six concepts of structure.

The location of the next decision was placed one step above, even though it involves an analysis of voting processes and a change model introduced in Chapter 8 (Equation 8.30). It is placed here because we shall perform an analysis of the rate of adoption for both the data phases and the answer-forming phases of the A problem groups.

Using the behavioral constitution and the definitions of adoption, the favorable and unfavorable half-channel votes for data phases and answer-forming phases were determined for each group. These were divided by the adoption time to form the intensities of favorable votes, V_F, and unfavorable votes, V_U. The slope of the structural adoption curve, k_1 of Equation (8.29), was estimated from the half channel adoption curve for both phases for each group on the A problems.[4] The result for the data phase is

---

[4]The time of the ith adoption of a half-channel, t_i, should be proportional to $\log \frac{i}{20-i}$ because of Equation (8.29). k_1 is estimated by seeking the best value of k_1 for

$$t_i = \frac{1}{k_1}\left[\log \frac{20-4}{4} + \log \frac{i}{20-i}\right]$$

where there must be four half-channels open for each phase if centralized. One essentially has an estimate of k_1 for each adoption. We minimize

$$\sum_{i=4}^{19}\left[t_i - \frac{1}{k_1}\left(\log \frac{20-4}{4} + \log \frac{i}{20-i}\right)\right]^2$$

over all k_1. Taking the derivative of the above expression with respect to k_1 and setting it equal to zero, one can show that the best estimate of k_1 from the adoption curve is

$$\hat{k}_1 = \frac{\sum_{i=4}^{19} \log\left(\frac{4i}{20-i}\right)^2}{\sum_{i=4}^{19} t_i \log\left(\frac{4i}{20-i}\right)}$$

The value of k_1 we call the "actual value" in Table 12.1.

$$k_1 = .393 + .015\, V_F - .163\, V_U \qquad (12.1)$$

The t-statistics of the significance (of being non-zero) of the coefficients of V_F and V_U are 4.37 and 2.00 respectively. The adjusted R^2 (fraction of variance in k_1 explained by the model) is 0.762. The F-statistic is $F(2,7) = 11.23$. The correlation between V_F and V_U is .042. The result for the answer phase is

$$k_1 = .037 + .09\, V_F \qquad (12.2)$$

The t-statistic for the significance of the coefficient of V_F is 18.4. The adjusted R^2 is .976 and the F-statistic ($F(1,8)$) is 338.5. The better fit for the answer phase is probably due to the dependency of the answer phase structure upon the data phase structure when the data phase is centralized.

Equation (12.1) is not as good a fit as one desires, but Equation (12.2) is probably too good. The actual values of k_1 and the values of k_1 predicted by the models are given in Table 12.1.

Refer To Table 12.1 (Page 296)

Note that the values of k_1 for the same group differs for the two phases, often markedly. This is further evidence for the utility of considering a group as having more than one structure.

The decision of whether or not to reject the assertion that the rate of structural adoption is explained by the model for k_1 of Equation (8.30) is not as clear as are most steps in the strong inference tree because the

TABLE 12.1 ACTUAL AND PREDICTED SLOPE FOR STRUCTURAL ADOPTION FOR DATA SHARING AND ANSWER FORMING PHASE FOR A PROBLEMS

Group	Data Sharing Phase		Answer Forming Phase	
	Actual k_1	Predicted[a] k_1	Actual k_1	Predicted[b] k_1
K	.28	.35	.11	.12
L	.10	.22	.12	.13
N	.13	.15	.70	.69
O	.72	.35	.72	.72
Q	.25	.43	.62	.61
R	1.15	1.10	.39	.40
T	.12	.15	.12	.06
U	.13	.02	.39	.39
V	.31	.23	.22	.26
W	.15	.34	.12	.14

[a] Using Equation (12.1)

[b] Using Equation (12.2). Here V_F is the intensity of favorable implicit votes.

results are statistical. The data do not provide a perfect ($R^2 = 1.0$) fit, but they are a reasonably good fit. Knowing the data and the imprecision due to the difference between adoption and implementation (especially for the data phase, where one may have to wait until the next trial to have implicit votes complete the election), I believe we should conclude that it has not yet been rejected.

The next step is determining whether or not the mapping function (Equation (9.1)) described in Chapter 9 is capable of predicting the changes and non-changes in structures on the next problem, based upon information available from the previous problem. Using the groups that perform the A problems first, we have the more interesting data. Many of these groups centralized for A problems and then decentralized for B problems. The prediction is whether or not for each phase the structure is centralized or non-centralized. A single "stray" message can cause a prediction of centrality to be wrong. There are 29 predicted changes and 99 predicted non-changes using the mapping function. Twenty-five out of the 29 predicted changes and 97 out of the 99 predicted non-changes are correct. The result is 122 out of 128 correct predictions. The six incorrect predictions are due to five messages out of approximately 5,000. The six incorrect predictions were correct on the next problem. These predictions and the actual events are summarized in Table 12.2.

Refer To Table 12.2 (Page 298)

TABLE 12.2   TIMING OF STRUCTURAL CHANGES FOR FAUCHEUX-MACKENZIE EXPERIMENT EXPLAINED BY SPAN-OF-CONTROL AND ELECTION PROCEDURES

	A1 - A8		B1 FROM A8		B1 - B4		ALL COMBINED	
	DATA	ANSWER	DATA	ANSWER	DATA	ANSWER	DATA	ANSWER
Number of Changes	6	5	5	5	1	7	12	17
Number of Changes Predicted Correctly*	5 [1]	5	5	5	0 [3]	5 [2]	10	15
Percent of Changes Predicted*	83	100	100	100	0	71	83	88
Number of Non-Changes	33	36	1	1	17	11	51	48
Number of Non-Changes Predicted*	31 [4]	36	1	1	17	11	49	48
Percent of Non-Changes Predicted*	94	100	100	100	100	100	96	100
Percent of Correct Predictions	92	100	100	100	94	89	94	97

*A correct prediction is made when the predicted change (or a non-change) takes place (or does not take place) when it was predicted.

[1] Group K, problem A-5 caused by vote implementation delay on A-4. (cf. footnote 4).
[2] Group R, B-4, and Group W, B-2. Group R due to one message opening a channel but not voted to recall except by message.
[3] Group W, B-2 reason is unclear due to a delay in implementing vote.
[4] Group R, B-3, exchange of data outside Y-network.
Groups K, A-4, and V, A-3. Seems to have been a delay in implementing vote.

-298-

Strictly speaking, the six incorrect predictions using strong inference reject the conclusion that the mapping function explains the occurrence or non-occurrence of structural change. However, there are 122 out of 128 correct predictions and the six incorrect predictions became correct on the next problem. Remembering that these data come from five-person human groups where each person has absolute control over the usage of his half-channels, perhaps one should require more evidence before rejecting the mapping function. For the time being, then, I have decided to judge the outcome as "not no yet." In later chapters we shall consider two more sets of evidence about the mapping function.

THE BERKELEY EIGHT-HOUR WHEEL EXPERIMENTS

The Faucheux-Mackenzie data provide evidence for rejecting the hypothesis that groups tend <u>not</u> to form hierarchies for the B problems. The rejection follows because of several counterexamples. The correlations between hierarchy, efficiency, and effectiveness are very high for the A problems, as reported in the last section, but they are of the same magnitude for the B problems. The results are summarized in Table 12.3.

Refer To Table 12.3 (Page 300)

The B problem data in Table 12.3 suggest that further experiments are required. The data suggest that if the group has a goal of increasing

TABLE 12.3 CORRELATION COEFFICIENTS BETWEEN DEGREE OF HIERARCHY AND MEASURES OF EFFICIENCY AND EFFECTIVENESS FOR A AND B PROBLEMS[a]

Type of Problem	Pair of Variables				
	Hierarchy and Efficiency	Hierarchy and Time Per Problem	Hierarchy and No. of Messages	Hierarchy and No. of Errors	Degrees of Freedom
A Problems	.958	-.594	-.758	-.419	101
B Problems	.986	-.704	-.768	-.518	57

[a] There are 103 observations for the A problems and 59 for the B problems. For the A problems, then, if the absolute value of the correlation coefficient is greater than 0.31, it is statistically significantly greater than zero at $p < .001$. Similarly, for the B problems, if the absolute value of the correlation coefficient is greater than 0.41, it is statistically significantly greater than zero at $p < .001$. All values in this table are statistically significantly different from zero at $p < .001$.

efficiency or effectiveness, it can do so by increasing its degree of hierarchy. We are thus interested in why groups working on B problems do not centralize more often. This breaks down into the questions of (1) whether or not the B problems could be solved as effectively in a wheel as in an all-channel, and (2) whether or not groups tend to form hierarchies for B problems as they gain more experience. In addition, we should ask whether centralization is the same thing as hierarchy. The learning model of Chapter 10 needs testing. It will be used to determine whether or not timely and untimely processes are different with respect to a learning model. The strong inference trees to be examined using the Berkeley eight-hour data are given in Figures 12.4 and 12.5.

Refer To Figure 12.4 (Page 302)

Refer To Figure 12.5 (Page 303)

Method

Subjects were chosen from the summer school population at the University of California at Berkeley to work for eight hours on B problems. Each was paid $16 to participate. There were two coffee breaks, and a dinner was served after approximately four hours of work. These groups were asked to work as many B problems as they could within the eight-hour period.

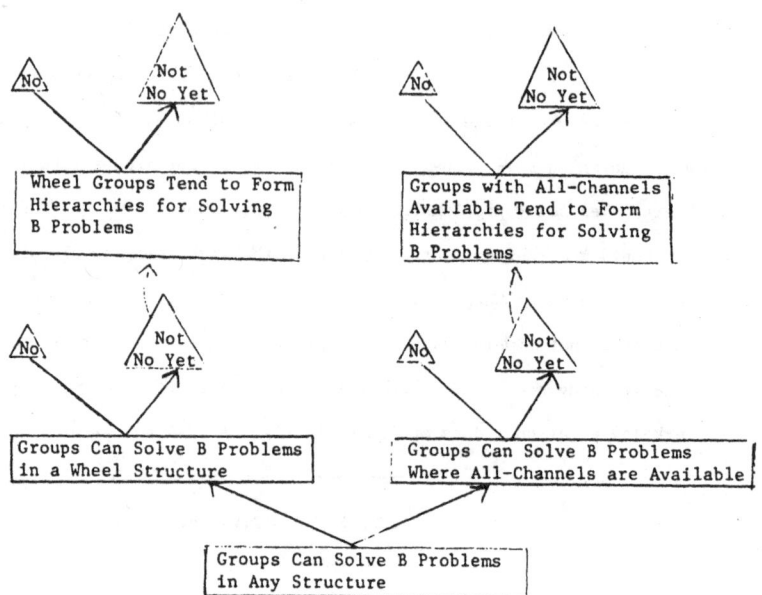

Figure 12.4 Berkeley Eight-hour Experimental Strong Inference Tree #1

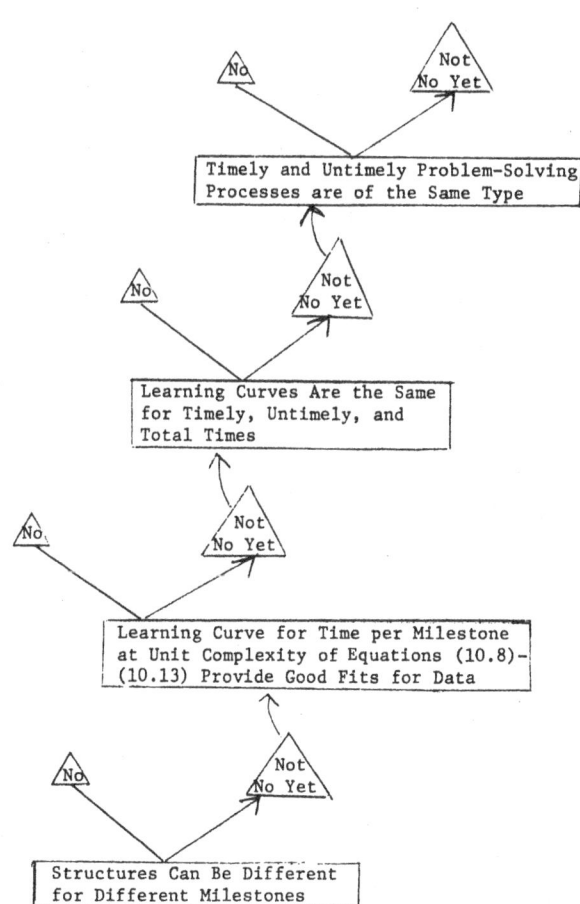

Figure 12.5 Berkeley Eight-hour Experimental Strong Inference Tree #2

Thus, they were encouraged to work as rapidly as possible. The first four B problems were the same as the four used in the Faucheux and Mackenzie experiment. Every problem was different in terms of the distribution of information but some networks reappeared on later problems.

Five groups began in an all-channel communications network and three groups were restricted to working as a wheel group.

Results

There are three groups that performed in a wheel imposed by the experimenter for the eight-hour period. There is no data to reject the hypothesis that groups can solve B problems in a wheel. In fact, except for a smaller number of messages, the performance of groups in wheels is remarkably similar to performances of groups with all-channels available. Performance data for the Berkeley eight-hour groups is summarized in Table 12.4.

Refer To Table 12.4 (Page 305)

If anything, the enforced wheel groups would appear to be slightly superior to those having all-channels available. These data are for the whole set of problems. Because structures and processes become altered with experience, these aggregate figures may not be the same as what one would expect on the first four problems. For the first four problems, the average times and average number of errors are similar for the two conditions (34.8 vs. 30.6 and 0.33 vs. 0.42 respectively).

TABLE 12.4 PERFORMANCE OF BERKELEY EIGHT-HOUR B PROBLEM GROUPS BY EXPERIMENTAL CONDITION

Condition	Average Time per Problem	Average Number of Messages per Problem	Average Number of Answer Sets per Problem[a]	Average Number of Timely Milestones per Problem	Average Number of Untimely Milestones per Problem
Enforced Wheel (54 Problems Solved)	18.74 (15.10)[b]	45.67 (21.63)	1.17 (.47)	7.76 (1.36)	1.13 (2.64)
All-channels Available (70 Problems Solved)	21.37 (11.02)	70.50 (28.34)	1.39 (.57)	7.93 (1.25)	2.59 (3.15)
All Eight-Hour Data Combined	20.23 (12.96)	59.69 (28.37)	1.29 (.54)	7.85 (1.30)	1.95 (3.02)

[a] The number of answer sets minus one is the number of errors.
[b] The number in parenthesis is the standard deviation of the set of numbers whose mean is directly above the parenthesis.

The main problem becomes the one shown as step two in the strong inference tree of Figure 12.4: We must determine whether or not groups tend to form hierarchies when solving the B problems. By examining correlation coefficients between degree of hierarchy and performance measures, we can see that there is at least a trend toward the formation of hierarchies. These correlations are reported in Table 12.5.

Refer To Table 12.5 (Page 307)

The presence of untimely processes and cousin relationships due to the difficulty of solving the B problems makes it hard for the group to install a hierarchy. As there is no algorithm (except complete enumeration) for solving B problems, it is difficult for a top level person to be able to solve each problem within the time allowed by the group norm. Failure to solve the problem creates untimely and cousin relationships. Two of the five groups beginning in an all-channel evolved hierarchies and two of the three enforced wheel groups evolved hierarchies. One must therefore reject the hypothesis that groups do not form hierarchies to solve B problems. However, we shall tentatively not reject the hypothesis that there is a tendency for groups to form hierarchies to solve B problems, whether in enforced wheels or in formations where all-channels are available.

We turn now to the strong inference tree of Figure 12.5. The first question is whether or not the learning curve formulae of Equations (10.8) - (10.13) provide good fits for the data. The basic data for the calculations are given in Table 12.6

Refer To Table 12.6 (Page 308)

TABLE 12.5 CORRELATION COEFFICIENTS BETWEEN DEGREE OF HIERARCHY AND MEASURES OF PERFORMANCE FOR B PROBLEMS

Condition	Hierarchy and Efficiency	Hierarchy and Problem No.	Hierarchy and Time per Problem	Hierarchy and No. of Messages	Hierarchy and No. of Errors	Hierarchy and No. of Untimely Milestones
Enforced Wheel (52 d.f.)	.940	.413[a]	-.736	-.813	-.488	-.534
All-channels Available (70 d.f.)	.895	.261	-.718	-.624	-.517	-.484
All Eight-hour Groups (124 d.f.)	.911	.382	-.604	-.601	-.481	-.500

[a] Every number in this table except these two is significant at $p < .001$. These are significant at $p < .05$.

Table 12.6 Summary Performance Data From Eight-Hour Berkeley Groups

Problem	Groups Solving It	Relative Complexity of Problem[c]	Average Time/Problem	Average No. Timely Milestones	Average Untimely Milestones	Average Total Time per Unit Complex Milestone	Computed Value of Z(T) Using Equation 11.5
1	6[a]	.39	43.4	8.17	2.40	9.62	9.42
2	7[a]	.48	30.0	7.57	3.75	6.72	6.36
3	7[a]	.75	29.0	8.14	2.00	4.18	4.68
4	7[a]	.88	30.8	9.29	3.83	2.55	3.75
5	7[a]	.39	15.6	7.00	2.50	4.13	3.25
6	8	.39	11.3	7.88	2.25	3.33	2.97
7	8	.43	10.5	7.75	1.00	3.03	2.82
8	8	.43	9.3	7.50	1.33	2.70	2.73
9	8	.75	20.9	7.38	3.75	3.00	2.69
10	8	1.07	31.9	8.50	4.00	2.16	2.66
11	8	.75	21.5	8.00	3.33	2.92	2.65
12	8	.56	17.1	7.75	2.50	3.20	2.64
13	7[b]	.64	15.3	8.29	2.50	2.48	2.64
14	6	.69	13.0	7.50	1.00	2.55	2.64
15	5	.60	13.2	7.80	3.00	2.82	2.63
16	4	.66	15.5	7.50	6.00	2.43	2.63
17	2	1.07	24.5	8.50	3.00	2.03	2.63
18	2	.48	7.0	7.00	0	2.18	2.63
19	2	1.07	---[d]	5.00[d]	0	---[d]	---[d]
20	2	.56	9.5	7.00	0	2.38	2.63

[a] One group started with the second problem by mistake. One group did the first five out of order. That is why number of groups on these early trials is less than eight.

[b] These numbers are the number of groups completing this many problems. Only two groups did 20.

[c] Problems 1 and 6 have the same network. Problems 7 and 8 have the same network. Problems 10, 17, and 19 have the all-channel network. Problems 12 and 20 are the same. Dinner break began after problem 7.

[d] This was the third occurrence of problem 10. It was done by rote memory. Problem 19 is not included in the learning curve calculations.

Total time to solve each problem was divided into timely and untimely time. These times were adjusted for the number of milestones and the relative complexity of the problem. It is assumed that the greater the number of milestones and the more complex the problem, the longer it would take to solve it. The variable is changed from time per problem to time per unit complex milestone. The results are:

a. Timely Time Per Unit Complex Milestone

$$X(T) = 11.60\ e^{-.54T} + 2.54, \quad R = .967 \quad (12.3)$$

b. Untimely Time Per Unit Complex Milestone

$$Y(T) = 10.53\ e^{-.60T} + 2.73, \quad R = .901 \quad (12.4)$$

c. Total Time Per Unit Complex Milestone

$$Z(T) = 12.38\ e^{-.60T} + 2.63, \quad R = .969 \quad (12.5)$$

A plot of the values of $Z(T)$ from Equation (12.5) for each problem is presented in Figure 12.6. The average values of $Z(T)$ from the actual data for all Berkeley 8-hour groups are represented by the dots in Figure 12.6. It is clear that Equation 12.5 provides a fairly good fit to these data. It is also clear that the fit could be better.

Refer To Figure 12.6 (Page 310)

The apparent uniformity of the total time per unit complex milestone is sharply contrasted with the seemingly "chaotic" average total time per problem data presented in Figure 12.7. The adjustments for relative complexity and number of milestones in $Z(T)$ smooths out the average time per problem data. The data for Figures 12.6 and 12.7 are presented in Table 12.6.

Refer To Figure 12.7 (Page 311)

-310-

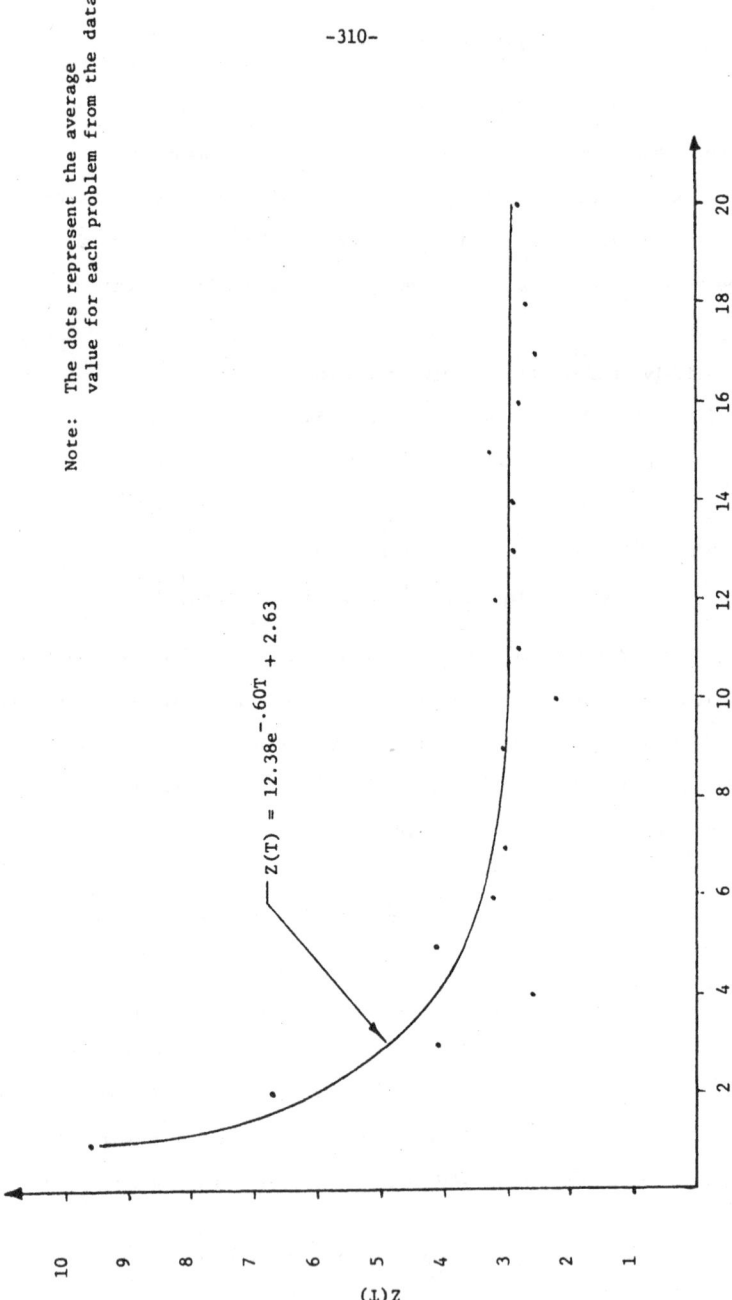

Figure 12.6 Plot of Total Time per Unit Complex Milestone versus Problem Number for Berkeley 8-hour Groups

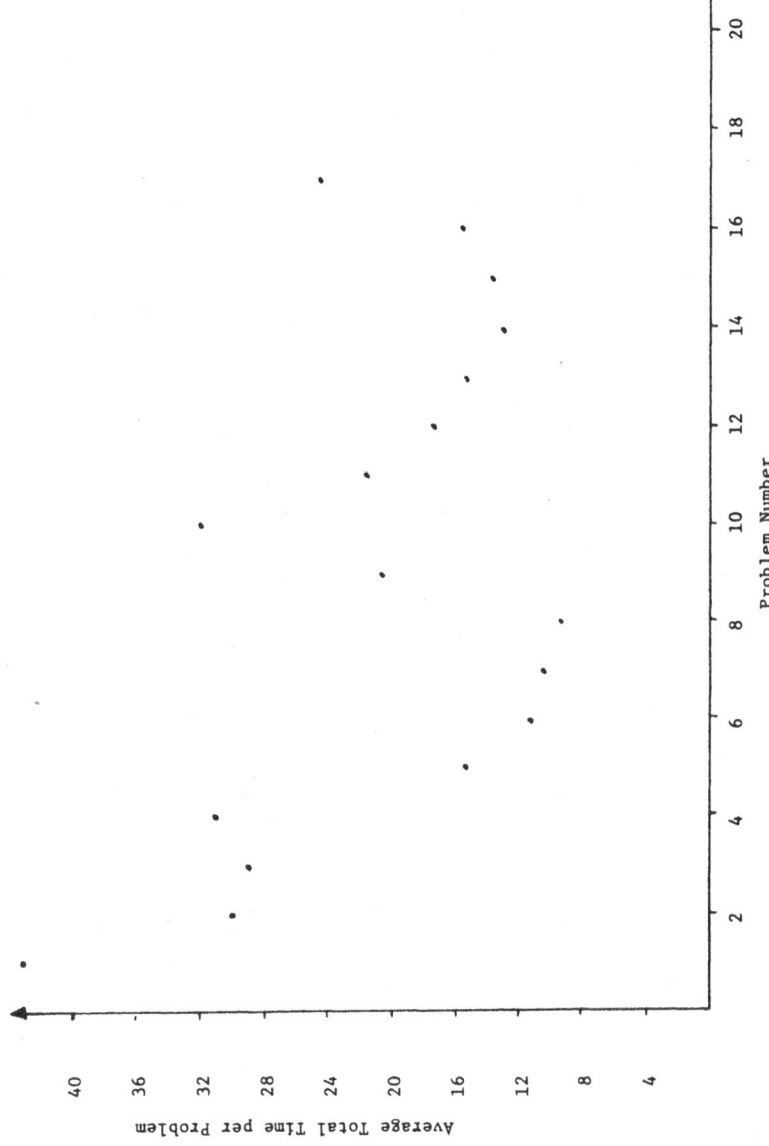

Figure 12.7 Plot of Average Total Time per Problem for Berkeley 8-hour Groups

Supplementary calculations to fit a linear learning curve of the type $Z(T) = \alpha - \beta T$ resulted in $Z(T) = 5.63 - .24T$, where the standard errors of the constant were at 3.09 and the coefficient was 0.0319. The value of R^2 is .57 with an $F(1,122)$ of 57.5. This does not compare favorably with the $R^2 = .94$ for $Z(T)$ defined by Equation (12.5).

A learning curve of the exponential type $t(T) = Ae^{bT}$ where $t(T)$ is the time per submitted solution was also tried. The number of submitted solutions is the number of errors plus one. Time is the total problem solving time. The variable $t(T)$ does not incorporate problem complexity and assumes the number of milestones is the same per solution, a patently false assumption (but the one usually made implicitly). The result is

$$\log t(T) = 23.3 - 5.6T$$

where $R^2 = .26$ and there are 58 degrees of freedom.

Learning curves of total time per problem were computed for a linear learning curve and a simple exponential type. The results are poor. The R^2 for the linear model is .20. The R^2 for the exponential type is .20.

Equations (12.3) - (12.5) provide reasonably good fits for the times taken. Thus, we do not yet reject the hypothesis that Equations (10.8) - (10.13) are good models for time taken. The three equations are remarkably similar in value. In fact, using one to predict values of the other still yields good fits. That is, one can use the equation for $X(T)$ to make accurate predictions for $Y(T)$ and $Z(T)$, $Y(T)$ to make predictions for $X(T)$ and $Z(T)$, and $Z(T)$ to make predictions for $X(T)$ and $Y(T)$. Thus, we do not yet reject the hypothesis that we are dealing with only one basic learning curve for the B problems. Further, the similarity of the learning curves for timely and untimely processes leads me to not yet reject the hypothesis that timely problem-solving processes are similar to untimely problem-solving processes for the B problems. These results are not inconsistent with the reasoning used to develop the type of task-process analysis presented in Chapter 4.

REVISED STRONG INFERENCE TREE

Figure (12.8) compiles the strong inference trees of the Faucheux-Mackenzie and the Berkeley eight-hour experiments. There remain many more steps. We have yet to provide an adequate model for the formation of a hierarchy, to investigate the mapping function, to investigate the preference for certain structures, and to validate the behavioral constitution.

Refer To Figure 12.8 (Page 314)

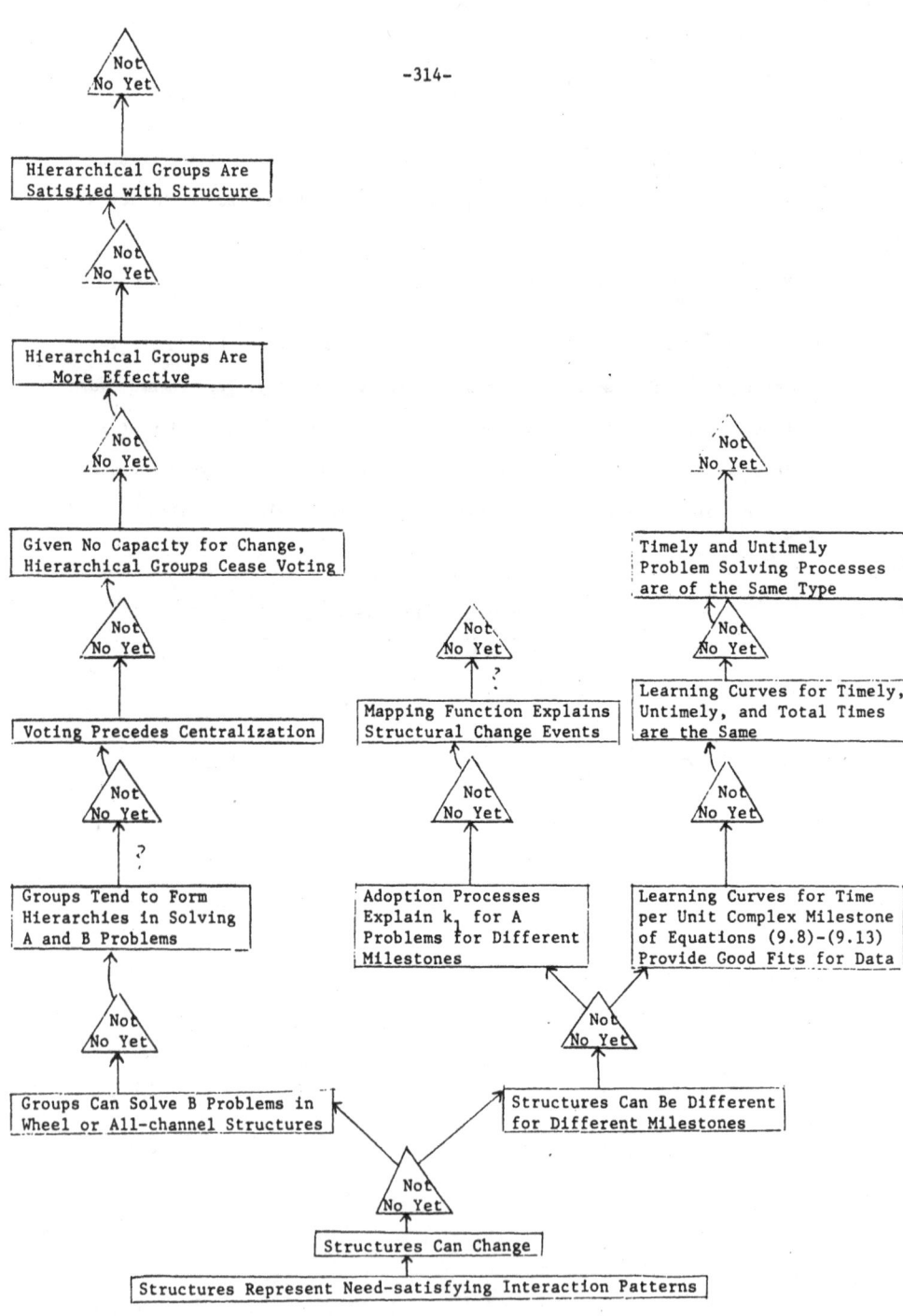

Figure 12.8 Current State of the Strong Inference Tree

CHAPTER 13

CHANNEL PREFERENCES

Given the premise that structures represent need-satisfying patterns of interaction, there should exist a preference function for the use or non-use of each particular channel. This conceptual preference varies with the individual, the overall network of which the channel is part, the performance of the group, the type of incentives and costs (whether monetary, emotional, peer pressure, etc.) and can change during the group's life history. For reasons stated in Chapter 10, I am unable to describe and measure the time-dependent preference function of each member for each channel. However, by assuming that a group acts as if each member has such a preference function, it is possible to formulate a crude model, derive a few consequences, make a few predictions, conduct some experiments, and then compare the results with these predictions as a weak test of the theory. It must be made clear at the outset that the uniqueness of the model, its functional form, and its values are highly questionable. It is merely a heuristic device for drawing implications of what would be likely to happen if certain conditions were present.

Assume that there is more than one kind of benefit. These benefits have magnitudes $B_1, B_2, \ldots, B_k, \ldots, B_m$ where each B_k is non-negative. Associated with each B_k is a value, r'_{kij}, which is the net value, given a unit of B_k, to a decision maker, x_i, if the ij^{th} channel is opened. The net benefit to x_i if the ij^{th} channel is opened is U_{iij} where

$$U_{iij} = \sum_{k=1}^{m} r'_{kij} B_k + a_{oij} \qquad (13.1)$$

where a_{oij} is the value of U_{iij} when all the values of B_k are zero. There may also be a net benefit for a subject for any channel, such as U_{i12} for the channel between x_1 and x_2. The benefits can include costs of using channels, costs of opening the channels, the perceived benefits of direct access between two members, etc. I assume further that there is a value for U_{iij}, U_{iij}^*, which, when exceeded, will make x_i want to open the ij^{th} channel. Conversely, if $U_{iij} < U_{iij}^*$, x_i will not want to open the channel

The model of Equation (13.1) could have been written in many other ways. At this stage the precise form of the model is unimportant. What is important is the claim that, <u>ceteris paribus</u>, if some B_k is increased, the value of U_{iij} will increase if r_{kij} is positive, decrease if r_{kij} is negative, and have no change in value of $r_{kij} = 0$. In such a case, if r_{kij} is positive, the increase in B_k will tend to increase U_{iij}. This may raise U_{iij} above U_{iij}^* and, if the channel is not already open, increase the likelihood that it will be opened. If the ij^{th} channel is already open, the increase in U_{iij} will not decrease the likelihood that it remains open. If, on the other hand, r_{kij} is negative, <u>ceteris paribus</u>, the increase in B_k will decrease U_{iij}. This may reduce U_{iij} below U_{iij}^* and decrease the likelihood that x_i will want the ij^{th} channel open. If it is already open, it is more likely to be closed. If it is closed, it is less likely to be opened. If r_{kij} is zero, <u>ceteris paribus</u>, there should be no effect at all on the opening or closing of the channel. Thus, given a model like Equation (13.1), I conclude that if one benefit is increased, all other benefits and coefficients remaining the same, the result will depend upon the value of r_{kij}: if $r_{kij} > 0$, the likelihood is increased that the ij^{th} channel is or will be opened. If $r_{kij} < 0$, the likelihood is increased that the ij^{th} channel is or will be closed. By systematically changing the B_k one should, then, be able to manipulate group structures.

This chapter describes two sets of experiments in which we manipulated group structures by controlling special types of benefits for channel usage. The benefits included (1) money costs for channel usage, (2) time costs for channel usage, (3) bonuses to encourage more direct access, and (4) obnoxious behavior of a "confederate" to encourage members to purchase alternate channels and bypass the obnoxious one. The strong inference tree for this chapter is given in Figure 13.1. The specific hypotheses are indicated by the arrows to the "not no yet" decision nodes in Figure 13.1.

Experiments were conducted at Berkeley and Carnegie-Mellon University using B problems in a communications network paradigm. These experiments are reported separately. The Berkeley experiment is the left branch and the Carnegie experiments are the right branch of Figure 13.1.

Refer To Figure 13.1 (Page 318)

THE BERKELEY CHANNEL RENTING EXPERIMENT

Method

Thirty-eight groups of five undergraduates completed a series of four B problems, presented in the same order as in the Faucheux-Mackenzie experiment.

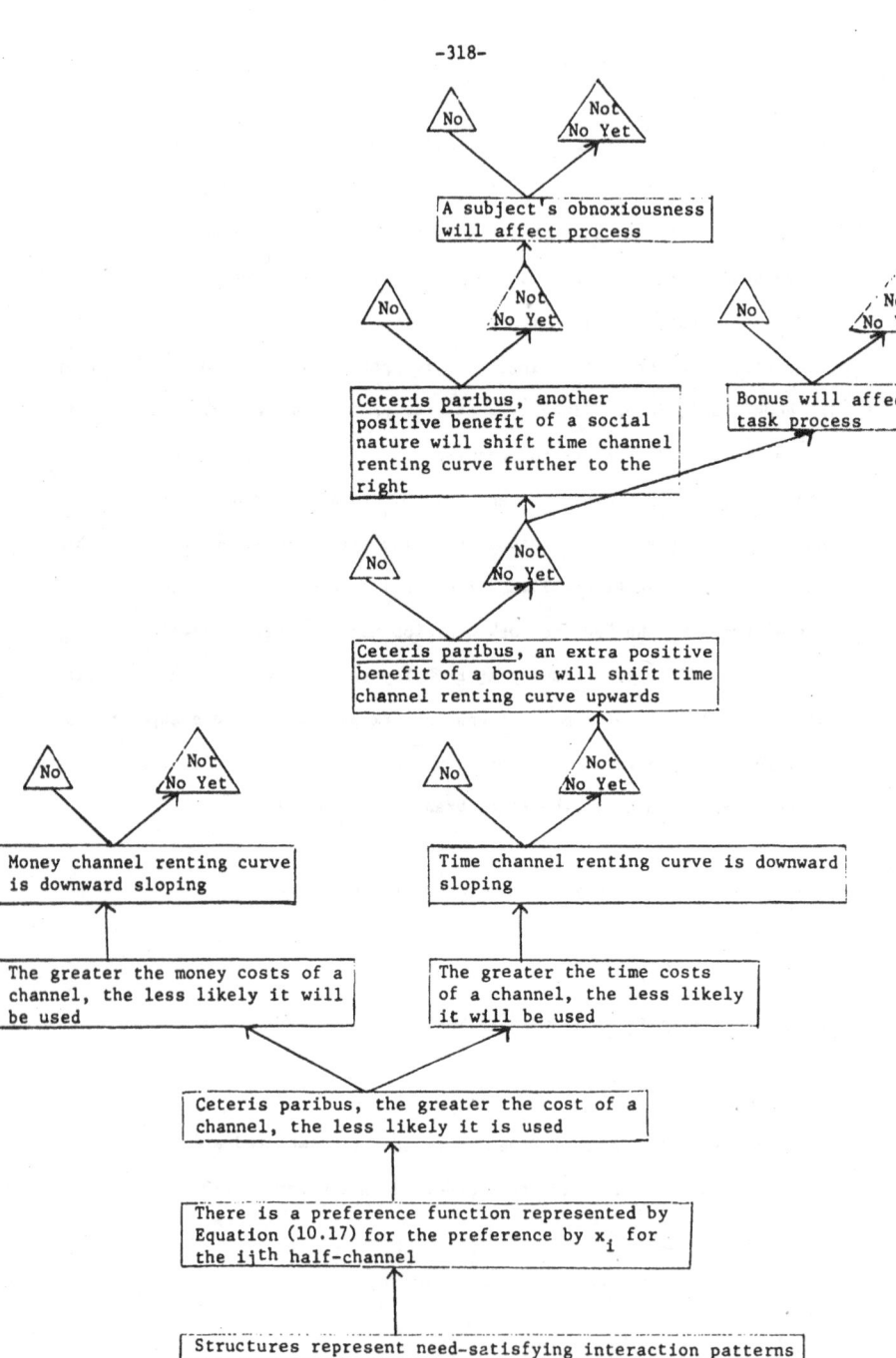

Figure 13.1 Strong Inference Tree Explored in this Chapter

Each group is given the usual instructions for solving the B problems.
Each group member is identified by a color. They are told that unless they
rent channels, using the six dollars paid by the experimenter, they are
restricted to interacting only with Pink. That is, unless they rent extra
channels, the group structure is a wheel with Pink as its hub. The decision
to rent or not rent any of the six extra channels (There are 10 possible
channels in a five-person group, but only 4 are used in the wheel formation)
is to be made at the beginning of each of the four problems in the following
manner: The price is the same for each problem for a group. The members
are assigned to cubicles where they are visually, orally, and tactilly
isolated. Before the start of a problem, each receives a channel rental
form that lists the free channels and the six optional channels. The subject
checks off those "he feels the group needs." The price per channel is
indicated on this form. These are then sent back to the experimenter, who
tabulates the separate decisions. If any one person checks off a channel
to be rented, it is rented by the entire group, regardless of what the others
decide. Each person's decisions are binding upon the others. For example,
if two persons out of the five rent the same channel, all five must pay
for it. If one person rents all six and the others rent none, every member
must pay for all six. Each member makes his decisions anonymously and without
consultation. No one is told which member has rented what channels. During
a problem there are no restrictions of any kind on the types of messages.
In particular, the group has this chance to remove restrictions on to whom
a message may be sent. For example, members can vote on the group structure

for the next problem, but they can only use the channels to Pink and those rented for the voting process.

Different channel charges are used for different groups. The charges are 25¢, 10¢, 5¢, 1¢, and 0¢. Because there are six channel rentals possible and four problems, each group can rent from 0 to 24 channels. If all channels are rented at 25¢/channel, there will be zero take-home pay for solving the four problems. The take home pay will be $3.60 for 10¢ channels, $4.80 for 5¢ channels, $5.76 for 1¢ channels, and $6.00 for 0¢ channels. Four groups were run without the channel-rental option.

A questionnaire was administered at the end of the experiment.

Results

Plotting average percentage of available channels rented on the abscissa and cost of channel in dollars on the ordinate, the result is shown in Figure 13.2. The average percentages of channels rented by each channel cost for the four problems are presented in Table 13.1.

Refer To Figure 13.2 (Page 321)

Refer To Table 13.1 (Page 322)

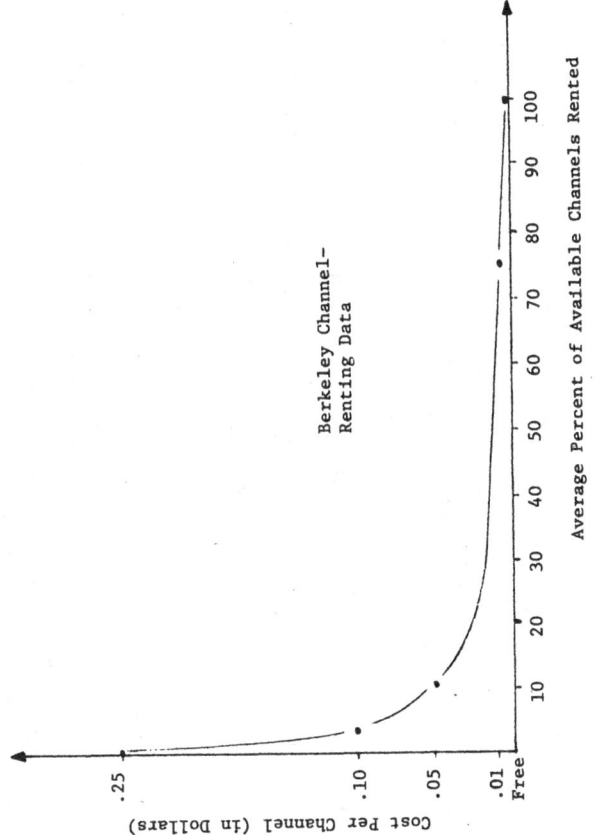

Figure 13.2 Berkeley Experiment Channel-Renting Curve

Table 13.1 AVERAGE PERCENT OF CHANNELS RENTED BY CHANNEL COST FOR BERKELEY EXPERIMENT

Percent of Available Channels Rented

Condition (Channel Cost)	Problem 1	Problem 2	Problem 3	Problem 4	All Problems
.00	100.0 ($\frac{24}{24}$)[a]	100.0 ($\frac{24}{24}$)	100.0 ($\frac{24}{24}$)	100.0 ($\frac{24}{24}$)	100.0 ($\frac{96}{96}$)
.01	85.2 ($\frac{46}{54}$)	90.7 ($\frac{49}{54}$)	55.6 ($\frac{30}{54}$)	57.4 ($\frac{31}{54}$)	75.7 ($\frac{156}{216}$)
.05	21.4 ($\frac{9}{42}$)	4.8 ($\frac{2}{42}$)	9.5 ($\frac{4}{42}$)	7.1 ($\frac{3}{42}$)	10.7 ($\frac{18}{168}$)
.10	1.9 ($\frac{1}{54}$)	5.6 ($\frac{3}{54}$)	1.9 ($\frac{1}{54}$)	1.9 ($\frac{1}{54}$)	2.8 ($\frac{6}{216}$)
.25	0 ($\frac{0}{24}$)	0 ($\frac{0}{24}$)	0 ($\frac{0}{24}$)	0 ($\frac{0}{24}$)	0 ($\frac{0}{96}$)
8	0 ($\frac{0}{24}$)	0 ($\frac{0}{24}$)	0 ($\frac{0}{24}$)	0 ($\frac{0}{24}$)	0 ($\frac{0}{96}$)
Total	36.0 ($\frac{80}{222}$)	35.1 ($\frac{78}{222}$)	26.6 ($\frac{59}{222}$)	26.6 ($\frac{59}{222}$)	31.1 ($\frac{276}{889}$)

[a] The fraction in the parentheses is the number of channels rented divided by the maximum number of channels that could have been rented. The denominator divided by 6 is the number of groups in this condition.

Clearly, the money channel curve is downward sloping. There is no discrepancy that would violate this conclusion from these data. Hence, we have failed, at this time, to reject the downward sloping hypothesis.

Discussion

Based on equation (13.1), this experiment differs from the Faucheux-Mackenzie experiment only in the value of B_1, which is zero for the Faucheux-Mackenzie experiment. For both experiments, all other benefits are held constant. In this experiment, only B_1 is manipulated. It is assumed that $R_{1ij} < 0$ in this case because money is a commodity (subjects generally prefer more to less), and loss of money due to channel-renting would reduce U_{1ij} for each person. The greater the channel charge, the greater the value of B_1 and the smaller the value of U_{1ij}. Hence, on the average, ceteris paribus, we would expect fewer channels to be rented the greater the channel charge. This conclusion is not rejected by the data.

The value of having a channel open is different for each person. Because it only takes one person to decide to open a channel, the channel is opened whenever there is at least one subject whose value of U_{1ij} exceeds U_{1ij}^*. The evaluation of the advantage for opening a channel may change with experience. The change in evaluation means that at least one of the benefits or the evaluation of a benefit has changed. There seems to be a trend towards less channel renting on problems 3 and 4 than on problems 1 and 2. Across all conditions, 36% were rented on problem one, 35.1% on problem two, and 26.6% on problems 3 and 4. This may indicate that the model of Equation (13.1) does not have constant values.

Across all groups, the correlation coefficient between hierarchy and efficiency is .960 ($p < .001$), between hierarchy and problem number .226 ($p < .05$), between hierarchy and time per problem $-.603$ ($p < .001$), and between hierarchy and the number of messages $-.741$ ($p < .001$). There are 148 observations for these correlations. These data indicate that there is a trend towards forming hierarchies and that hierarchy is related to effectiveness. Assuming that a group desires to be as efficient as possible, the formation of a hierarchy would reduce the benefits associated with those channels not in the hierarchy. Hence, it is possible that experience has caused a reduction in the evaluation of the benefits of opening extra channels.

The renting of every channel at 0¢ replicates the findings from the Faucheux-Mackenzie experiments for the B problem. The renting of almost all the channels (75.7%) at 1¢ cost and the relatively rare occurrence of renting at the 5¢ (10.7%) and 10¢ (2.8%) costs may indicate that the channel renting curve is more of a threshold phenomenon than a continuous "demand curve" phenomenon. That is, at some very low price (about 10¢), channels are no longer rented. The cost of 10¢ is just enough to curtail the renting of channels.

Since the subjects make these decisions anonymously, this is a remarkably mild cost for gaining conformity to a wheel structure. The channel cost is a form of the extent of social pressure to conform to a wheel structure. Rental of channels involves a monetary charge and a cost associated with the violation of a student norm not to spend the money of other students. Compared with the much greater sanctions employed by some organizations, these costs

are trivial. These results may indicate that a wheel structure, chosen
by its members, is not an unsatisfactory structure. This line of inquiry
is continued in Chapter 14.

There is also the possibility that the channel renting does not reflect
the actual structure. The average centrality across all four problems is
.502 at 1¢, .923 at 5¢, .987 at 10¢, 1.015 at 25¢, and 1.01 for the forced
wheel. These data suggest additionally that the wheel is the primary structure
at as low as 5¢ channel charge.

The questionnaire administered at the end of the fourth problem asked
each member to rate on a 1-9 scale the extent to which more channels are
needed. There is no linear relationship between the number of channels
used and the extent to which more are needed. The correlation between the
percent of available channels rented and the extent to which more channels
are needed is nonpositive and insignificantly different from zero at $p < .50$.
A similar result holds for the correlations between participation and the
percent of available channels rented and liking of problems and the percent
of available channels rented. These results are not inconsistent with the
concept that structures represent need-satisfying interaction patterns.
Apparently, the group satisfaction with structure is not determined by
the type of structure, at least for the wheel and the all-channel.

THE CARNEGIE-MELLON CHANNEL RENTING EXPERIMENTS

The right hand branch of the strong inference tree of Figure 13.1
involves the successive manipulation of benefits that should cause a shift

in the channel renting curve of the type shown in Figure 13.2. The first step introduces a benefit B_2 that is like B_1 except that the channel rental cost is in minutes of psychology credit hours. All subjects are students who are required to spend five hours as experimental subjects in order to pass an introductory psychology course. They are paid three hours of psychology credit for completing the four B problems. The channel rental cost is in minutes of psychology credits. The purposes of this experiment are (1) to see whether the channel renting curve obtains for other than money costs, and (2) to create a baseline for making comparisons with further steps in Figure 13.1.

Psychology credit time is a form of payment which is not transferable among subjects. We have the problem that equity considerations might compound the effects of monetary inducements if some subjects receive money and others do not. If, to counteract this effect, subjects receiving more money were to divide the extra money among the others by purchasing food and beverages after the experiment, we have the problem that the motivational aspects of the inducements might be altered.

The first step introduces the benefit B_2 that is channel cost in minutes of psychology credit time. I assume that time is also a commodity and that r_{2ij} is negative. <u>Ceteris paribus</u>, the larger the channel cost in minutes, the smaller U_{2ij} and the lesser the likelihood that a channel is rented. The type of predictions made for the Berkeley channel renting experiments will also be made for this channel renting experiment.

A second experiment adds a benefit, B_3, to that of B_2. B_3 is a thirty-

minute psychology credit bonus added to the credit of the first group
member to send in a correct answer to the experimenter. If a person solves
all four problems first, he could earn up to five hours of psychology
credit time. This feat would satisfy the five-hour course requirement.
The bonus is expected to increase the need for speed in obtaining the data
in order to have a chance to claim the bonus. If no channels are rented,
the hub could control the flow of information and reduce a spoke member's
capacity for solving the problem. The need for direct access to the others
should be strengthened by the bonus. Thus, I expect that $r_{3ij} > 0$ and the
effect of the bonus, B_3, would be to increase U_{iij} and thereby increase
the likelihood for channel renting. The added term of $r_{3ij}B_3$ partially
offsets the effects of a channel charge for B_2. The generic equation is now

$$U_{iij} = a_{oij} + r_{2ij}B_2 + r_{3ij}B_3 \qquad (13.2)$$

where $r_{2ij} < 0$ and $r_{3ij} > 0$. The value of B_3 is a constant. The value of
B_2 varies from group to group. The lower B_2, the greater the relative
impact of B_3. For low values of B_2, the effect of the bonus may be significant.
At very high values of B_2, the effect should be negligible.

One effect of the bonus should be a tendency to shift the channel
renting curve upwards and to the right for the intermediate values of B_2.
There will be no effect at very low or very high channel costs (B_2). The
presence of the bonus, B_3, will also affect the task process of a group.
Because the bonus goes to the person with the first correct answers, members
will be more likely to turn in answers before attempting to coordinate the

answers. This should result in a greater number of errors per problem, more answers sent in prior to coordination (F+ milestone), and a tendency to agree on submitting an answer prior to agreeing about the answer (reaching the G+ before the F+ milestone). Once a person has submitted his answer and thereby laid claim on the B_3 bonus, he should cooperate with the others in order to speed up the problem solving. More errors will also result in a greater number of reached milestones.

Another experiment in this sequence is to increase the value of opening more channels. Keeping B_2 and B_3, a new benefit, B_4, can be added by employing a confederate as the hub, Pink. By programming the confederate to be uncooperative except for exchanging data (without relaying it to the others), he will be the only person who has all of the data. The confederate can also perform acts that confirm the group's dependence. These include statements of intention to get all of the bonuses and of intention to remain uncooperative. The presence of an "obnoxious" confederate as the hub should increase the likelihood that at a given channel cost and bonus, more channels will be rented. Thus, for B_4, $r_{4ij} > 0$. The new equation is

$$U_{iij} = a_{oij} + r_{2ij}B_2 + r_{3ij}B_3 + r_{4ij}B_4 \qquad (13.3)$$

where $r_{2ij} < 0$, $r_{3ij} > 0$, and $r_{4ij} > 0$.

The presence of the obnoxious confederate ought to shift the channel renting curve further to the right. While there should be no change at zero channel cost, the effect at very high costs may be different. The fewer channels rented, the more obnoxious the confederate appears. The more channels rented, the less the group has to rely upon the hub for relays. With all channels, no relay is necessary, as the members can get the information directly. At very high costs, no channels are rented on problem one. However, the obnoxious behavior on problem one may increase B_4 and r_{4ij} enough to encourage channel renting on problem two. The use of extra channels on problem two makes the behavior of the confederate less obnoxious on problem two. This may reduce r_{4ij} and B_4 for problem two. The result may be that no channels are rented on problem three. The lack of channels on problem three makes the confederate appear more obnoxious, which leads to channel renting on problem four. Thus, I expect that, on the average, more channels will be rented at higher prices than under the other conditions. However, the problem by problem number of channel rentals may vary considerably, especially at higher prices. The avoidance of obnoxious behavior can be an inducement to change structure by renting channels. The obnoxiousness increases as the number of channels decreases if the source of the obnoxiousness is the exploitation of structural position.

Method

Thirty-eight groups of five undergraduates complete a series of four B problems, presented in the same order as in the Faucheux-Mackenzie experiment. Each group is presented with the usual instructions for solving B problems. The channel renting procedure used here is the same as those used in the Berkeley channel renting experiments except the channel charges are in psychology credit minutes. The charges are 5 minutes, 3 minutes, 2 minutes, 1 minute, 0 minutes.

Two experiments involve a bonus of 30 minutes of psychology credit time. Each of these groups is told that the winner of the bonus for a problem will be announced at the end of the problem. The experimenter does this by means of an intercom system with a speaker in each cubicle. Subjects are not allowed to communicate with each other except by written messages.

The confederate in our experiment was a female undergraduate who was the experimenter's assistant. The confederate was expert in the B problems. She had coded the earlier Faucheux-Mackenzie experimental data and the Berkeley channel renting data. She had also assisted in conducting similar experiments. She was instructed to exchange data with any subject but not to relay the information of one member to the another. When pressed by subjects for more data, she replied "I am not going to give this to you. I want the bonus for myself." Later exchanges showed a tendency towards increasing hostility, sometimes resulting in threats of bodily harm (being isolated, the subjects usually did not know the confederate was a woman) and withholding of data (cf. Chapter 16 for an analysis of hostility). The renting of channels made the "exchange but no relay" instructions less obnoxious, as there was no longer a reason for asking her. Subjects could get the information directly from the other subjects.

The number of groups in each condition is given in Table 13.2.

Refer To Table 13.2 (Page 331)

TABLE 13.2 NUMBER OF EXPERIMENTAL GROUPS BY CONDITION FOR THE CARNEGIE-MELLON CHANNEL RENTING EXPERIMENTS

Condition	Channel Cost (in minutes)					Total
	0	1	2	3	5	
No bonus	1^a	3	4	4	1^a	13^b
Bonus, no Confederate	1^a	4	4	4	1^a	14^b
Bonus with Confederate	1^a	1^a	3	3	3	11^b

[a] These groups were used to check on the end points of the channel renting curve.

[b] The small sample size reflected the limited population of potential subjects and a worry about subject contamination in a small university. The 190 experimental subjects plus the many pilot groups approached 10% of the total student population. These small samples were felt to be large enough to spot trends but too small to be sure of the details of a trend.

Results

The channel renting curves for the three experiments are shown in Figure 13.3. The data for these curves are given in Table 13.3.

Refer To Figure 13.3 (Page 333)

Refer To Table 13.3 (Page 334)

These data do not yet reject the conclusions that (1) the time channel-renting curve (no bonus groups) is downward sloping, (2) the effect of the bonus is to shift the channel renting curve upwards (bonus, no confederate groups), and (3) the effect of an obnoxious confederate is to shift the channel renting curve upwards and to the right.

We have yet to determine whether or not the bonus and the confederate had an effect on altering task processes. The average number of errors per problem was 0.83, 1.72, and .98 for the no bonus, bonus without confederate, and bonus with confederate conditions respectively. Clearly, there are more errors for the bonus without confederate groups than for the groups with no bonus and those with a bonus and a confederate. A t-statistic for the difference in the two means was calculated. Comparing the bonus with no confederate to the no bonus condition, $t=4.01$ ($p < .001$ with 102 d.f.). Comparing the bonus without confederate to the bonus with confederate mean number of errors per problem, $t=3.30$ ($p < .001$ with 104 d.f.). The difference in means between the confederate groups and the no bonus groups

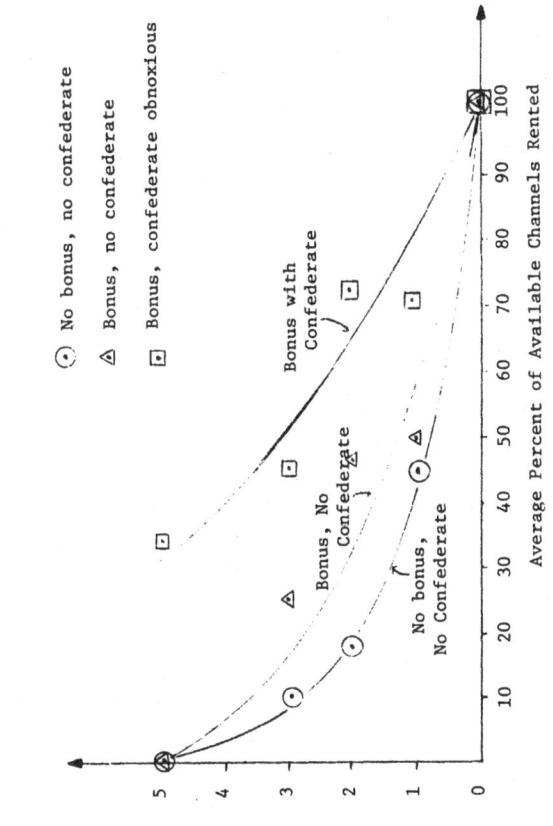

Figure 13.3 Channel-Renting Curves from the Channel-Renting Experiments at Carnegie-Mellon University

TABLE 13.3 AVERAGE PERCENT OF AVAILABLE CHANNELS RENTED

IN C.-M. EXPERIMENT GROUPS BY CONDITION

Condition	Channel Cost (in minutes)				
	0	1	2	3	5
No Bonus	$\frac{24}{24}$ [a]	$\frac{32}{72}$	$\frac{17}{96}$	$\frac{10}{96}$	$\frac{0}{96}$
Bonus, No Confederate	$\frac{24}{24}$	$\frac{40}{90}$ [b]	$\frac{45}{96}$	$\frac{24}{96}$	$\frac{0}{96}$
Bonus, Confederate	$\frac{24}{24}$	$\frac{17}{24}$ [c]	$\frac{52}{72}$	$\frac{33}{72}$	$\frac{25}{72}$

[a] The denominator is the number of channels that could have been rented in this condition. The numerator is the actual number rented.

[b] Data for one problem was misplaced.

[c] Group did not rent any on problem one and 17/18 or 94% on the remaining three problems.

has a t of only 0.78 (p > .20 with 94 d.f.). The average of almost one error per problem (.98) for the confederate groups is surprising given the presence of an expert confederate who knew the answers. The fraction of problems with one or more errors is .54 for the no bonus groups $\left(\frac{28}{52}\right)$, .75 for the bonus groups $\left(\frac{39}{52}\right)$, and .59 for the confederate groups $\left(\frac{26}{44}\right)$.

One of the supposed effects of the bonus is to encourage submittal of answers before the coordination of a correct solution and the coordination of the submittal of a solution. The average number of problems where one or more subjects submitted an incorrect answer to the experimenter before attempting to coordinate the answers was 0.33 for the no bonus groups, .67 for the bonus groups, and .52 for the confederate groups. A t-statistic for the difference in the two means was calculated. Comparing no bonus to bonus without confederate, t=3.73 (p < .001, 102 d.f.). Comparing bonus without confederate to bonus with confederate, t=1.95 (p < .03, 89 d.f.). Comparing no bonus to bonus with confederate, t=1.49 (p < .10, 89 d.f.). Another effect, once an answer is in, is to attempt to get the group to submit an answer. The average number of problems in which a group sent in an answer without first coordinating the answer or the procedure for submitting it was .67 for the no bonus groups, 1.04 for the bonus groups, and 0.84 for the confederate groups. The t-statistic for the differences in means is t=2.01 (p < .03, 100 d.f.) for no bonus and bonus without confederate, t=.89 (p > .10, 87 d.f.) for bonus with and without confederate, and t=.99 (p > .10, 92 d.f.) for no bonus and bonus with confederate.

The number of untimely behaviors for reaching the F+ and G+ milestones is an indicator of relative confusion in the portion of the task process for coordinating the answer. These values for the three conditions are given in Table 13.4.

Refer To Table 13.4 (Page 337)

Using a t-test for the difference in means, for the total number of untimely F+ behaviors, the t-statistics are: 2.21 ($p < .02$, 102 d.f.) for no bonus-bonus without confederate groups, 1.64 ($p < .05$, 92 d.f.) for bonus with and without confederate groups, and 0.43 ($p > .50$, 90 d.f.) for no bonus and bonus with confederate groups. Using a t-test for the difference in means, for the total number of untimely G+ behaviors, the t-statistics are: 1.92 ($p < .05$, 102 d.f.) for no bonus-bonus without confederate groups, 3.13 ($p < .002$, 94 d.f.) for bonus with and without confederate groups, and 1.19 ($p > .10$, 94 d.f.) for no bonus-bonus with confederate groups.

These data do not reject the hypothesis that one effect of the bonus is the alternation of task processes. The effect of the confederate is more subtle because results depend upon the obnoxiousness of the confederate, a condition varying with the number of rented channels. The average number of intermediate milestones per problem (not including the beginning and the end milestones) is significantly less for the confederate groups than for the groups without a confederate. The means are 5.77 for no bonus groups, 6.04 for bonus groups, and 4.45 for confederate groups. The t-statistics for the differences in means are .97 ($p > .10$, 102 d.f.) for no bonus-

TABLE 13.4 TOTAL NUMBER OF UNTIMELY F+ AND G+ MILESTONE BEHAVIORS

Condition	Total Number of Untimely F+ Behaviors	Total Number of Untimely G+ Behaviors	No. of Problems
No Bonus	9.7	13.5	52
Bonus, No Confederate	14.9	19.6	52
Bonus with Confederate	10.7	10.2	44

without confederate groups, 4.61 (p < .001, 92 d.f.) for no bonus-bonus with confederate groups, and 5.50 (p < .001, 92 d.f.) for bonus with and without confederate groups. This is what one would expect when the hub hoards the information and disseminates the answers.

The usual trend in the experiments reported in Chapter 12 and the Berkeley channel renting experiments of this chapter is for the degree of hierarchy to be positively correlated with problem number. There is a trend towards the formation of hierarchy. However, if there were decreasing cooperativeness or if the positive benefits of avoiding certain channels were more valued than efficiency itself, one could expect to simultaneously see a negative correlation between hierarchy and problem number and a very large positive correlation between hierarchy and efficiency. These data are given in Table 13.5 for all three conditions.

Refer To Table 13.5 (Page 339)

The four problems vary in complexity. The fourth problem is relatively complex and has three solutions. Errors tend to increase when groups work on problem four. The data in Table 13.6 are the average (by problem number and experimental condition) fraction of error answers without any group coordination. There is evidence of a downward trend for the no bonus groups, an upward trend for the confederate groups, and a mixed effect for the bonus groups. The no bonus groups learn to coordinate to avoid errors. The bonus groups seem also to learn to coordinate, but the system apparently does not

TABLE 13.5 CORRELATION COEFFICIENTS BETWEEN DEGREE OF HIERARCHY AND PERFORMANCE CHARACTERISTICS FOR CARNEGIE-MELLON EXPERIMENTAL GROUPS

Condition	Condition			Degrees of Freedom
	Hierarchy and Efficiency	Hierarchy and Problem No.	Hierarchy and Time per Problem	
No Bonus	$.888^a$	$.175^e$	$-.587$	50
Bonus, No Confederate	$.936^a$	$.230^d$	$-.504^a$	50
Bonus with Confederate	$.964^a$	$-.294^c$	$-.537^a$	42

a $p < .001$

b $p > .01$

c $p < .05$

d $p < .10$

e $p > .10$

work as well on the fourth problem. The confederate groups start with a
very low value, reflecting the control of the confederate which makes
coordination unnecessary. However, in each succeeding trial the fraction
of error answers without any coordination increases. This may reflect
the effect of a growing hostility on the part of the spoke members towards
the hub confederate. They become less willing to accept her arrogance
and obnoxiousness in order to obtain gains in efficiency at the wage rates
prevailing in this experiment.

Refer To Table 13.6 (Page 341)

One group had a most interesting reaction to its confederate. The
channel cost was five minutes. Renting six channels at five minutes per
channel costs 30 minutes, the value of the bonus. Renting six channels
at five minutes only gives a subject a chance to break even. This group
rented no channels on problem 1, six on problem 2, one on problem 3, and
six on problem 4. These alternations must be due to B_4, the benefit associated
with avoiding obnoxiousness. Another group rented no channels on problem 1,
three on problems 2 and 3, and six on problem 4. A third group in this
condition rented no channels on any problem, but the correspondence to
and from the confederate expressed increasing hostility. Language regressed
to profanity, and reasoned arguments regressed to threats. But they would
not purchase any channels. There is evidence that this group had been
contaminated by a previous group and at least one of the subjects knew

TABLE 13.6 FRACTION OF ERROR ANSWERS SUBMITTED WITHOUT ANY COORDINATION FOR THE CARNEGIE-MELLON EXPERIMENTS

Condition	Problem 1	Problem 2	Problem 3	Problem 4
No Bonus	$\frac{6}{17}$ [a]	$\frac{5}{17}$	$\frac{3}{17}$	$\frac{3}{17}$
Bonus, No Confederate	$\frac{12}{35}$	$\frac{5}{35}$	$\frac{6}{35}$	$\frac{12}{35}$
Bonus, Confederate	$\frac{3}{23}$	$\frac{5}{23}$	$\frac{6}{23}$	$\frac{9}{23}$

[a] The numerator is the number of problems with error answers submitted without any coordination in this experimental condition on this problem. The denominator is the number of problems with error answers submitted without any coordination in this experimental condition.

Pink was a confederate. Subjects acted as if they felt that, since the obnoxious confederate wanted them to rent channels, they would "show her a thing or two" and not rent any, despite serious provocation. Here the occurrence of suspicion seemed to reverse the channel renting effect of the obnoxious confederate. The data in Figure 13.3 for the confederate groups includes this group. Excluding this group would strengthen the earlier conclusion about shifting the channel renting curve upwards and to the right.

The summary statistics here give evidence to lead us to not yet reject the hypothesis that the confederate had an effect on task processes. A serious reading of the actual messages sent and received very clearly shows the effects suggested by the summary statistics.

In addition to differences in the mean number of errors in each condition in the Carnegie-Mellon experiments, there are at least four other indicators of the effects of experimental condition on the processes. These data are summarized in Table 13.7.

Refer To Table 13.7 (Page 343)

Bonus-without-confederate groups require more messages and take more time per problem than either the no-bonus or the bonus-with-confederate groups. Bonus-with-confederate groups show more concern for organizing the groups than the other two types. This is probably due to the attempts to get the obnoxious confederate to alter her processes. The bonus-with-confederate groups sent large numbers of messages of a non-task-oriented nature. Most

TABLE 13.7 SOME FURTHER AVERAGE STATISTICS FOR EFFECTS OF EXPERIMENTAL
CONDITIONS ON PROCESSES FOR CARNEGIE-MELLON EXPERIMENTS

Condition	No. of Messages per Problem [a]	Time per Problem [b]	No. of Messages Concerned with Organizing and Coordination [c]	No. of Non-task oriented Messages [d]
(1) No Bonus	68.3	41.1	2.73	6.1
(2) Bonus Without Confederate	93.6	48.1	2.82	10.0
(3) Bonus With Confederate	73.2	39.7	4.43	22.2

[a] The t-statistics for differences in means are 3.78 ($p < .001$, 102 d.f.), .71 ($p > .10$, 92 d.f.), and 2.48 ($p < .01$, 97 d.f.) for conditions (1) and (2), (1) and (3), and (2) and (3) respectively.

[b] The t-statistics for differences in means are 1.55 ($p < .10$, 102 d.f.), 0.39 ($p > .10$, 92 d.f.), and 1.92 ($p < .05$, 97 d.f.) for conditions (1) and (2), (1) and (3), and (2) and (3) respectively.

[c] The t-statistics for differences in means are .09 ($p > .10$, 91 d.f.), 2.38 ($p < .02$, 93 d.f.), and 1.72 ($p < .05$, 90 d.f.) for conditions (1) and (2), (1) and (3), and (2) and (3) respectively.

[d] The t-statistics for differences in means are 1.53 ($p < .10$, 63 d.f.), 5.07 ($p < .001$, 48 d.f.), and 3.08 ($p < .002$, 87 d.f.) for conditions (1) and (2), (1) and (3), and (2) and (3) respectively.

of these express disapproval of the behavior of the confederate.

While these data of Table 13.7 are not inconsistent with the arguments used to generate the right hand side branch of the strong inference tree of Figure 13.1, they must be viewed with caution. These data are merely the mean values across all channel costs for each condition. A preferable form of analysis is contained in the detailed calculations of task processes for each group separately. These data are not inconsistent with the trial by trial, group by group, condition by condition analyses based upon milestones and milestone structures. Each group, however, is a separate entity and it is rare for two groups or even the same group to behave the same way on every problem. Nevertheless, these summary statistics appear to me to be reasonable surrogates for the more detailed behavior patterns of these groups.

CHAPTER 14

GROUP PREFERENCES FOR TYPE OF STRUCTURE

The preference function for opening a channel that was presented in Chapter 10 has a "constant" term and terms involving evaluations of different types and levels of benefits. That is, for the ij^{th} channel and person x_i,

$$U_{iij} = a_{oij} + \sum_{k=1}^{m} r_{kij} B_k \qquad (14.1)$$

where a_{oij} is the "constant" term. The value of a_{oij} depends upon both the ij^{th} channel and the overall structure. The analysis of the Berkeley and Carnegie-Mellon channel-renting experiments of Chapter 13 investigated various types and values of B_k. This chapter will investigate group preferences for type of structure. I shall demonstrate, ceteris paribus, that for the conditions of my experiments, groups prefer the wheel structure to the chain and the chain to the circle. With experience, furthermore, groups prefer the wheel slightly over the all-channel.

There are three experiments reported in this chapter. The first, called the Waterloo Circle Experiment, is a channel-renting experiment (cf. Chapter 13) using a circle for the free channels. The second, called the Waterloo Lutheran Chain Experiment, is a channel-renting experiment using a chain for the free channels. The third, called the Waterloo Lutheran Discussion Experiment, gives any four channels free and makes the groups reach unanimity about structure before beginning a problem. Unanimity is reached by discussion using written messages. The Waterloo Circle Experiment was run at the University of Waterloo and the other two were run at Waterloo Lutheran University by my student, Professor H. Wedderburn (1972), as a part of a thesis.

The greater the cost of a channel, <u>ceteris</u> <u>paribus</u>, the less likely it is used. There is a cost associated with choosing a set structure and task process. At a bare minimum, these choices involve voting and consultation with other group members. The very raising of the issues can trigger old antagonisms remaining from the past. This cost of organizing or choosing structures and task processes, <u>ceteris</u> <u>paribus</u>, is greater the more complex a problem. With increased complexity comes a combination of more milestones and/or more difficulty in reaching them. This increases the number of combinations of methods for solving the problem and the uncertainty associated with the relative advantage of any given combination. The greater uncertainties and the larger number of combinations create risks for any person insisting upon a particular approach. Even if he is proven ultimately to have been correct in his approach, faulty execution, mistakes, etc. can make him appear foolish, impetuous, "unsound," "hairbrained," "pushy," etc. <u>Ceteris</u> <u>paribus</u>, structures that either (1) reduce the number of combinations by restricting flows of information while permitting easy access to other members, or (2) place no restrictions at all on the flows, which reduces the need for considering the large number of different communication patterns, are preferred structures because they reduce the costs of organizing. These preferred structures are the wheel and the all-channel. A more detailed analysis of the advantages and disadvantages of each is given in Chapter 10.

Ceteris paribus, wheel structures require fewer decisions to organize than circles or chains. In the wheel there is no confusion about where the messages should go: all go to and from the hub person. In the circle and chain, however, two factors make the communication problems potentially very complex: (1) selecting the person to coordinate message flows, and (2) establishing message routing and relay rules. The number of relays to move a message from one member to another can be as high as n-1 in an n-person circle or chain. Errors occur during the task process and because of simple miscopying or failure to copy when relaying. Elaborate standard operating procedures have to get established and enforced for correcting task process errors and eliminating message-relaying errors. Once organized there is no reason why a circle or a chain need be inefficient. It just requires more care to work at the many details to organize one of these structures. Hence, ceteris paribus, groups prefer wheel structures to circles and chains.

The chain requires fewer decisions to organize than the circle because several people can obviously be eliminated as possible coordinators. These are the "end men." It would take n-1 messages for a member at one end of a chain to communicate with a member at the other. The expected number of messages to exchange data among all members is greatest for the end persons and becomes smaller as one approaches the middle of the chain. Once a middle position is selected, the problem of the direction of message flow is reduced. Positions intermediate from the "end men" and the coordinator

can function as coordinators of subgroups. For example, in the chain of
Figure 14.1, if x_3 is the coordinator, x_2 and x_4 can function as message
relay coordinators from x_3 to x_1 and x_5 respectively.

Refer To Figure 14.1 (Page 349)

Members x_1 and x_5 in a circle group, however, are as likely to be coordinators
as any other members. This increases the number of combinations of ways
of organizing which, ceteris paribus, increases the costs of organizing.
Hence, groups prefer the chain to the circle.

The predictions that (1) groups prefer the wheel to the circle, (2)
groups prefer the wheel to the chain, and (3) groups prefer the chain to
the circle are contained in the right hand side branch of the strong
inference tree of Figure 14.2. The method for establishing these preferences
depends upon Equation (14.1) and the channel renting experiments. Recalling
that B_1 is the magnitude of the benefit of money costs of channel renting,
if $B_2=B_3=B_4=0$ and all other conditions are held constant, a preference
of one structure over another can be inferred from the channel-renting
curve location. If structure A is preferred to structure B, the channel-
renting curve for A should be to the left and below that of B. The channel-
renting curve represents the amounts of B_1, or money, subjects are willing
to pay to rent channels in order to not be in a given structure. If a
group is more willing to pay for additional channels, ceteris paribus,
in structure B than in structure A, structure A is the preferred structure.

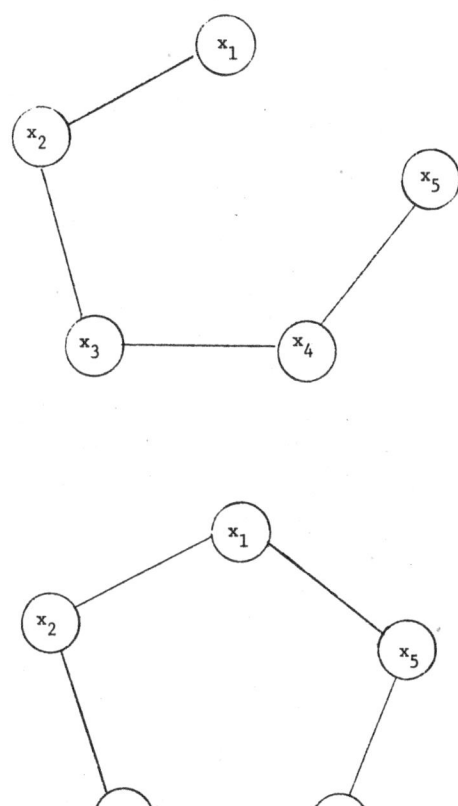

Figure 14.1 Chain and Circle Structures of Five Members

The channel-renting curve for B will be to the right and above that of A. In terms of Equation (14.1), the value of a_{oij} is greater for B than it is for A. Hence, if my reasoning is substantially not incorrect, I expect that the channel-renting curve for the chain will be above and to the right of that for the wheel and the channel-renting curve for the circle will be to the right and above that for the chain. These predictions are investigated using the Waterloo Circle and the Waterloo Lutheran Chain Experiments in comparison with the Berkeley Channel-Renting Experiment of Chapter 13.

Refer To Figure 14.2 (Page 351)

The left hand branch of the strong inference tree of Figure 14.2 guides our investigation of the group's relative preference of the wheel and the all-channel. The data of Chapter 13 show that groups will pay some money to not be in a wheel. These amounts are relatively trivial, however. The data of Chapter 12 show that, at least for a few trials, some groups centralize for B problems. The data for the Berkeley Eight-hour Experiment shows a significant trend towards the formation of hierarchy in solving B problems. The data from Chapters 12 and 13 also show that there is no clear performance advantage for either the wheel or the all-channel. However, there are advantages for forming hierarchies.[1] The

---

[1] The reader is reminded that a wheel group can have a low degree of hierarchy and an all-channel can have a high degree of hierarchy. Centrality measures do not examine processes as does the measure of hierarchy.

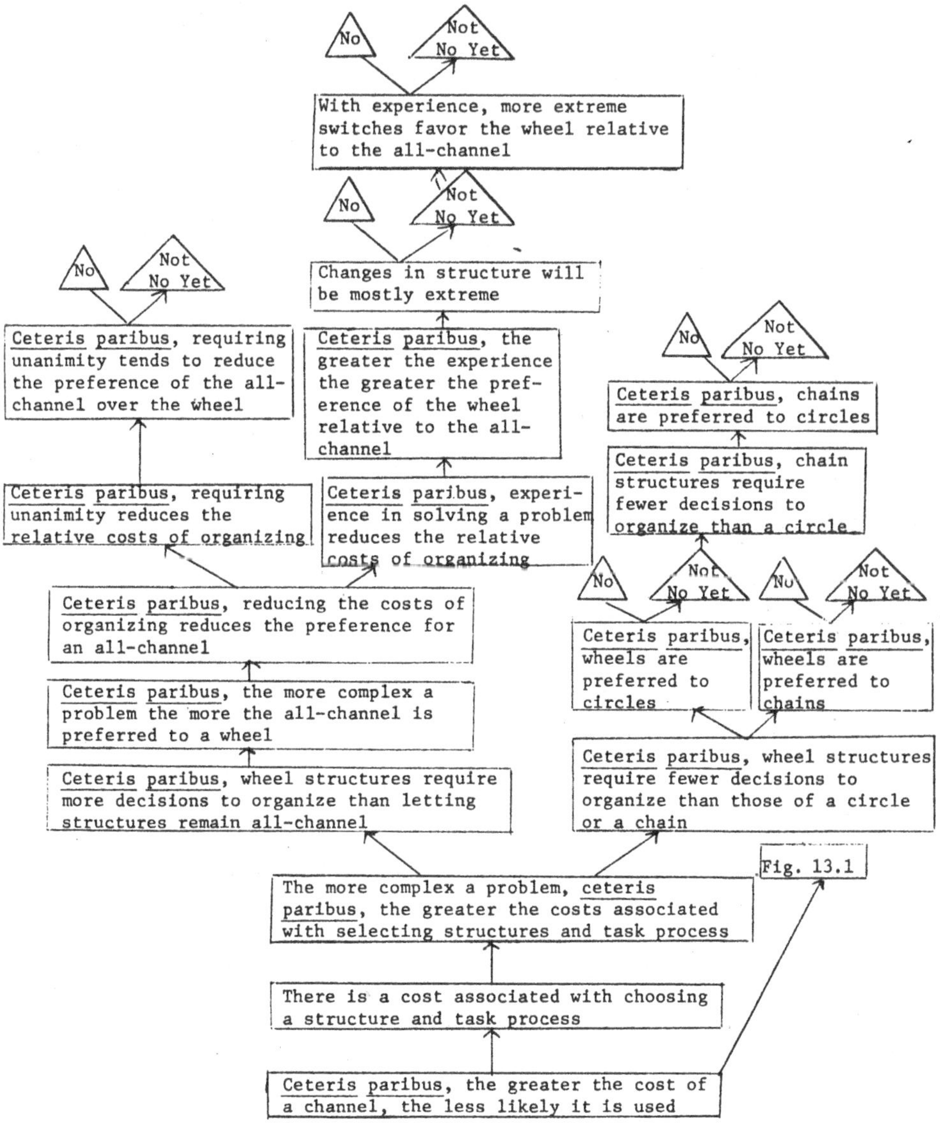

-351-

```
    △No  △Not No Yet
  ┌─────────────────────────┐
  │ With experience, more extreme
  │ switches favor the wheel relative
  │ to the all-channel
  └─────────────────────────┘
           ▲
      △No  △Not No Yet
  ┌─────────────────────────┐
  │ Changes in structure will
  │ be mostly extreme
  └─────────────────────────┘
```

△No △Not No Yet

| Ceteris paribus, requiring unanimity tends to reduce the preference of the all-channel over the wheel | Ceteris paribus, the greater the experience the greater the preference of the wheel relative to the all-channel |

△No △Not No Yet — Ceteris paribus, chains are preferred to circles

| Ceteris paribus, requiring unanimity reduces the relative costs of organizing | Ceteris paribus, experience in solving a problem reduces the relative costs of organizing |

Ceteris paribus, chain structures require fewer decisions to organize than a circle.

△No △Not No Yet   △No △Not No Yet

| Ceteris paribus, wheels are preferred to circles | Ceteris paribus, wheels are preferred to chains |

Ceteris paribus, reducing the costs of organizing reduces the preference for an all-channel

Ceteris paribus, the more complex a problem the more the all-channel is preferred to a wheel

Ceteris paribus, wheel structures require more decisions to organize than letting structures remain all-channel

Ceteris paribus, wheel structures require fewer decisions to organize than those of a circle or a chain

Fig. 13.1

The more complex a problem, ceteris paribus, the greater the costs associated with selecting structures and task process

There is a cost associated with choosing a structure and task process

Ceteris paribus, the greater the cost of a channel, the less likely it is used

Figure 14.2   Strong Inference Tree for Chapter 14

question mark on the left hand branch of Figure 12.6 and these data suggest that one should investigate the possible preferences of wheel and all-channel structures.

If a group selects an all-channel structure, it does not have to make specific decisions about how to organize; it preserves the options for organizing any way it chooses. The selection of a wheel, on the other hand, involves a decision of structure that seriously constrains options to change it if it is not satisfactory. <u>Ceteris paribus</u>, wheel structures require more decisions to organize than all-channels. The more complex the type of problem, the greater the number of decisions. Hence, <u>ceteris paribus</u>, the more complex a problem, the more the group prefers the all-channel to the wheel. <u>Ceteris paribus</u>, reducing the costs of organizing reduces the relative preference for the all-channel. <u>Ceteris paribus</u>, experience in solving a problem reduces the relative costs of organizing. Experience provides information about how to solve the problems and which members are better at solving which phase. This knowledge cuts down the number of issues and uncertainty associated with organizing a group. Hence, holding all other variables constant, the greater the experience, the greater the relative preference of the wheel to the all-channel.

The individual channel-renting decisions in the previous experiments do not necessarily reflect unanimity about structure. For example, an all-channel could occur if several wanted to be hubs of wheels and a wheel could occur if someone forgot to rent the channels he was expected to rent. In the Waterloo Lutheran unanimity experiments, the channel-renting procedure was altered. Subjects could freely communicate about the choice of a structure before the experimenter began each problem. In fact, until the group reached unanimity about structure the experimenter withheld the information necessary to allow the group to begin solving the problem. The requirement of unanimity reduces the costs of organizing. The requirement of unanimity reduces the risks to a member because the agreement reduces the uncertainties about how to behave and can also reduce the number of perceived combinations. The number of combinations is reduced primarily by ignoring the contingencies that arise during the task process. That is, the group acts as if the number of intermediate milestones is just one. The result is that the requirement of prior unanimity reduces the preference of the all-channel relative to the wheel. Further, since wheels and all-channels are the preferred structures, most structural changes will be extreme (changing hub of a wheel, changing from a wheel to an all-channel, and changing from an all-channel to a wheel). Finally, with experience and under the prior unanimity constraint, the extreme switches will be more towards a wheel than towards an all-channel.

THE WATERLOO CIRCLE EXPERIMENT

Method

Eight groups of five fourth-year engineering students at the University of Waterloo solved four B problems in a communications network paradigm. The four problems were presented in the same order as in the Faucheux-Mackenzie experiment. The experiment was a channel-renting experiment similar to those described in Chapter 13 except the free channels formed a circle structure instead of the usual wheel. Subjects were charged a rental fee for the five optional channels. The rental charges were 0¢, 5¢, 10¢, 25¢, and 50¢. Subjects were given an initial amount of money to cover maximum channel costs. A maximum of twenty channels could be rented on the four problems. Accordingly, each member received an initial sum of 20 times the channel charge for his group. Thus, the 50¢ group members each received $10.00, the 25¢ group members $5.00, the 10¢ group members $2.00, the 5¢ group members $1.00, and the 0¢ group members $0.00. The groups were encouraged to work as rapidly as possible.

Results

The basic results of interest are contained in Table 14.1 and illustrated in Figure 14.3. Table 14.1 is the tabulation of the percent of available channels rented by channel-renting price.

Refer To Table 14.1 (Page 355)

Refer To Figure 14.3 (Page 356)

The channel-renting curve for the Waterloo Circle groups is downward sloping and clearly above and to the right of the Berkeley channel-renting curve. Thus, we cannot yet reject the hypothesis that groups prefer the

TABLE 14.1 PERCENT OF AVAILABLE CHANNELS RENTED BY PROBLEM AND CHANNEL COST FOR THE WATERLOO CIRCLE EXPERIMENT

Channel Rent (in cents)	Problem 1	Problem 2	Problem 3	Problem 4	All Four Problems	Number of Groups in Condition
0	100	100	100	100	100	1
5	100	90	100	100	97	2
10	90	70	70	70	75	2
25	60	60	40	40	50	1
50	20	40	0	0	15	1

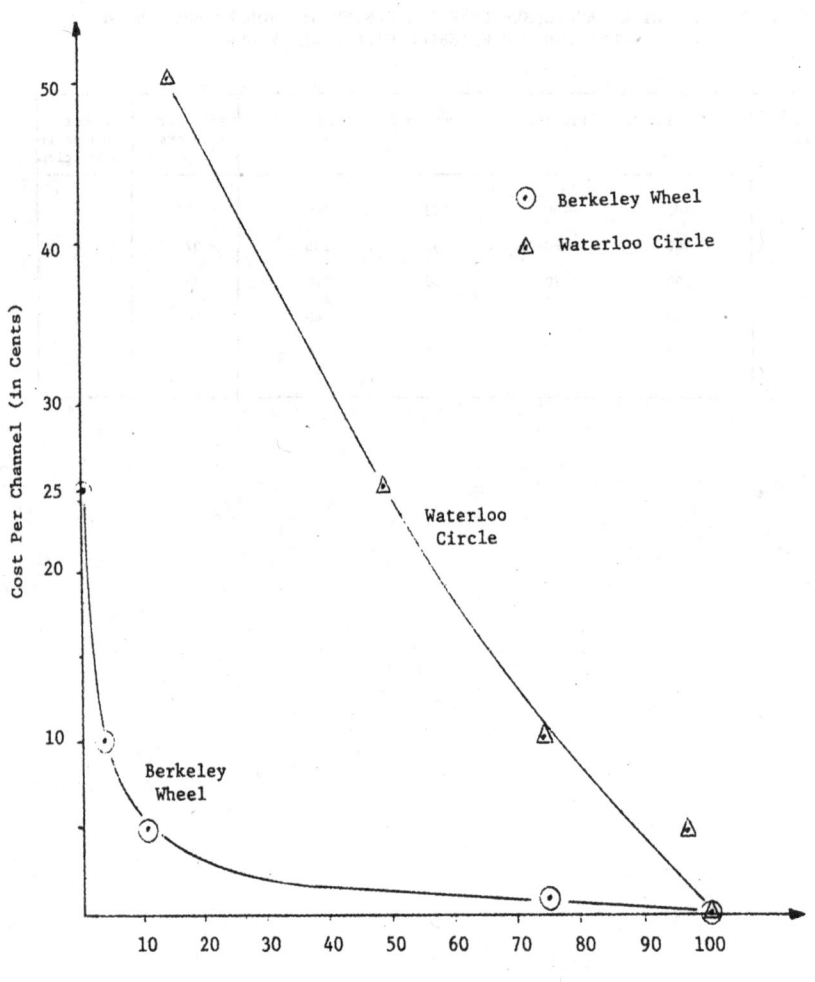

Figure 14.3 Waterloo Circle Channel-Renting Curve Compared to the Berkeley Channel-Renting Curve

wheel structure to the circle.

The circle group conditions were about as fast as the wheel groups (31.5 minutes/problem) and made about the same number of errors (.80 errors per problem) but sent more messages (108.8 per problem). This indicates the problem of making relays in the more restricted network. At the greater channel-renting prices, most of the purchases were for channels that enabled one person to be a hub of a wheel.

The relationship between degree of hierarchy and performance measures is also about the same. The correlation coefficients between the degree of hierarchy and efficiency is 0.927 ($p < .001$), hierarchy and problem number .294 ($p > .10$), hierarchy and time per problem $-.705$ ($p < .001$ and hierarchy and number of messages $-.746$ ($p < .001$). Interestingly enough, the correlation coefficient between the degree of hierarchy and the index of centrality is only .145 ($p > .10$). All these correlation coefficients are for 32 observations.

THE WATERLOO LUTHERAN CHAIN EXPERIMENT

Eighty undergraduates at Waterloo Lutheran University were used to form sixteen groups of five for a communications network experiment of the type described previously. The subjects were volunteers and were given an initial stake to pay for the channels rented. Unspent money, as in the Waterloo Circle Experiments, was the property of the subject. Each group was encouraged to work as fast as possible. The main difference in the Waterloo Lutheran Chain Experiment is that the free channels formed a chain structure. Thus, there were six channels available for rent. Procedures, except for the free channels, were the same in the Waterloo Lutheran Chain as in the Waterloo Circle experiments.

Results

The main results are contained in Table 14.2. Figure 14.4 is a comparison of the Berkeley, the Waterloo Circle, and the Waterloo Lutheran Chain experiments. The data in Table 14.2 yield a downward sloping channel-renting curve for the Waterloo Lutheran Chain experiment. As seen in Figure 14.4, this channel-renting curve is to the right and above that of the Berkeley wheel experiment and to the left and below that of the Waterloo Circle experiment. These data do not yet allow one to reject the two hypotheses that (1) groups prefer the wheel to the chain, and (2) groups prefer the chain to the circle.

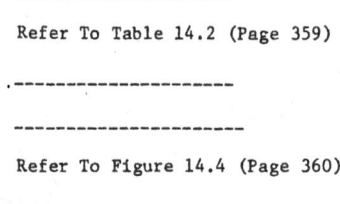

Refer To Table 14.2 (Page 359)

Refer To Figure 14.4 (Page 360)

The Waterloo Lutheran Chain Groups had great difficulty in solving the B problems. The average time per problem was 49.1 minutes, the average number of messages per problem was 139.4, the average number of errors per problem was 1.04, the average efficiency was only 0.26, and the average

TABLE 14.2 PERCENT OF AVAILABLE CHANNELS RENTED BY PROBLEM AND CHANNEL
           COST FOR THE WATERLOO LUTHERAN CHAIN EXPERIMENT

Channel Rent (in cents)	Problem 1	Problem 2	Problem 3	Problem 4	All Four Problems	Number of Groups in Condition
1	100	100	83.3	100[a]	95.2	2
5[b]	86.1	83.3	77.8	100	85.6	6
10	58.3	58.3	58.3	58.3	58.3	4
25	38.9	38.9	62.5	62.5	33.3	3
50	16.7	16.7	0	0	8.4	1

[a] One group did only 3 problems.

[b] Two groups finished only one problem, another finished only two, one finished three, and two finished all four problems.

-360-

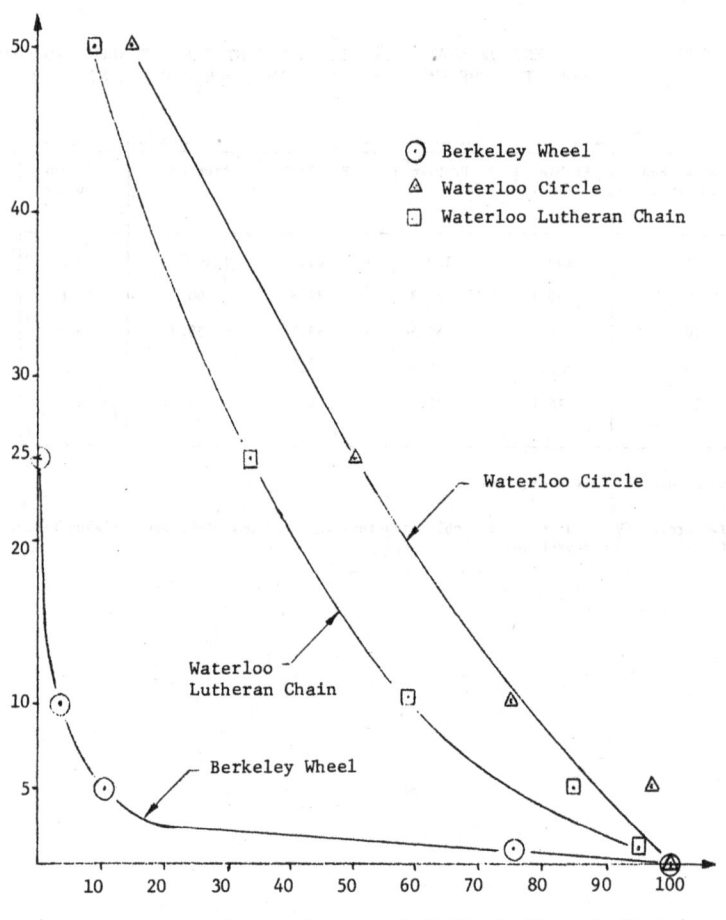

Figure 14.4 Comparison of Channel-Renting Curves from Berkeley Wheel, Waterloo Circle and Waterloo Lutheran Chain Experiments.

degree of hierarchy only 0.15. These numbers are probably low because five groups did not finish a problem they were working on. These groups were terminated because total length of time violated the amount of time all subjects could spend in the experiment. An attempt to verify consistency of procedures was made by having both the author and Mr. Wedderburn give the instructions. The performance did not change, no matter which of us presented the instructions. While we expected that the Waterloo Circle and Waterloo Lutheran groups would experience more difficulty than the Berkeley wheel groups, I cannot but speculate that the subjects in the Waterloo Circle groups were brighter. They were fourth-year engineering students, an honors program. The Waterloo Lutheran subjects were undergraduates from liberal arts programs.

Two subsidiary experiments were performed by Professor Wedderburn that bear on the speculation that the relatively poor performance of the Waterloo Lutheran groups may have been the result of a different population than the Berkeley and the Waterloo Circle groups. Wedderburn ran four groups in the all-channel condition following the Faucheux-Mackenzie procedures. The average time per problem was 49.3 minutes, the average number of messages 140.3. These are significantly greater than the comparable data for both the Faucheux-Mackenzie groups and the Berkeley wheel. A second extra check was made to determine the effect of the chain itself. He had groups solve the four B problems in a chain structure that was enforced. The average time per problem rose to 60.4 minutes and the average number of messages was 128.2. The average time per problem was significantly greater in the enforced chain. The average number of messages is about the same for the all-channel and the enforced chain conditions. These results are given in Table 14.3.

Refer To Table 14.3 (Page 363)

The correlation coefficients between the degree of hierarchy and various performance measures were similar to those of other channel-renting experiments. The correlation coefficient between hierarchy and efficiency was 0.938 ($p < .001$), between hierarchy and problem number 0.173 ($p < .15$), between hierarchy and time per problem $-.677$ ($p < .001$), between hierarchy and number of messages per problem $-.795$ ($p < .001$). The correlation between hierarchy and centrality was significant at $p < .10$, the value being $-.173$. The number of observations is 49.

THE WATERLOO LUTHERAN CHANNEL-RENTING GROUPS WITH PRIOR CONSENSUS ON STRUCTURE REQUIRED

The previous experiments of this chapter have been used to examine the right hand side branch of the strong inference tree in Figure 14.2. The following experiment examines the left hand side branch in Figure 14.2. The main departure of this experiment is the procedure for selecting structure. Unanimity among the subjects for the structure to be used was obtained before each problem began. This unanimity was reached by having groups discuss (via written messages) the choice of structure. It is expected

TABLE 14.3 COMPARATIVE PERFORMANCE DATA FOR THREE
EXPERIMENTAL CONDITIONS

Condition	Average Time per Problem	Average No. of Messages per Problem	No. of Problems
Faucheux-Mackenzie	31.3 (15.9)[a]	108.4 (58.7)	56
Waterloo Lutheran All-channel	49.3 (23.4)	140.3 (52.9)	20
Waterloo Lutheran Enforced Chain	60.4 (28.7)	128.2 (74.9)	28

[a] Standard deviation about the means are indicated by the numbers in parentheses.

that the requirement of unanimity will reduce the preference of the all-channel relative to the wheel, that changes in structure will be extreme, and that experience will further reduce the preference of the all-channel relative to the wheel.

Method

Seventy-five undergraduates from Waterloo Lutheran University were placed in fifteen five-member groups. Each was to solve the four B problems presented in the same order as in the Faucheux-Mackenzie experiment. Any four channels were free. The others could be rented. There was a channel-rental cost of 0¢, 1¢, 5¢, 10¢, and 25¢. They were given the usual instructions for solving the problems. The procedure for determining the structure was different, however. Each group, before the start of each problem, had to reach consensus about the structure they wanted to use on the upcoming problem. The discussion was conducted using written messages. Only after all agreed on a specific structure did the experimenter distribute the information that began the problem solving. No time limits were placed on the discussion phase.

Results

The average number of channels rented at 1¢, 5¢, 10¢, and 25¢ cost are given for each problem in Table 14.4.

Refer To Table 14.4 (Page 365)

TABLE 14.4 PERCENT OF AVAILABLE CHANNELS RENTED BY PROBLEM AND CONDITION
FOR THE WATERLOO LUTHERAN DISCUSSION GROUPS

Channel Cost	Problem 1	Problem 2	Problem 3	Problem 4	All Problems	No. of Groups
0¢ [a]	37	50	33	0	35	4
1¢ [b]	50	25	25	33	33	4
5¢	50	50	50	50	50	4
10¢	0	0	0	0	0	2
25¢	0	0	0	0	0	1

[a] One group completed only two, one group completed three, and two groups completed all four B problems.

[b] One group completed only three problems. The other three completed all four.

These data yield a channel-renting curve that is below and to the left of those of all experiments reported to date except for the 5¢ channel costs. Only four out of the thirteen problems solved at 0¢ cost were solved using all-channels. Eight were solved using a wheel. One rented three channels. Only five out of the fifteen problems at 1¢ cost were solved in an all-channel. The other ten used a wheel. At 5¢ cost eight problems were solved in the all-channel and eight were solved in the wheel. All problems with 10¢ and 25¢ charge used the wheel. These compare with the 100% use of all-channels at zero cost and the almost 100% use at 1¢ cost for the other channel-renting experiments at Berkeley and Carnegie-Mellon. The 50% use of the all-channel at 5¢ cost is the only anomaly. Thus, by strong inference we reject the hypothesis that the requirement of unanimity reduces the preference of the all-channel relative to the wheel. We do not yet reject the hypothesis that there is a tendency for reduced preference of the all-channel relative to the wheel when prior unanimity about structure is required.

The decision about the choice of structure can change from problem to problem. Previous problem channels that were open and become closed on the next problem or that were closed and become open on the next problem are called <u>switches</u>. The number of switches is the number of previously closed channels that are opened and vice versa. If six channels are switched, we call it an <u>extreme switch</u>. For this experiment all extreme switches are of three types: (1) a switch from a wheel to an all-channel, (2) a switch from an all-channel to a wheel, and (3) a switch of the hub in a wheel. When the number of switches is one to five, we say there has been an <u>intermediate</u> <u>switch</u>. When no channels are switched, we say there is a <u>zero</u> <u>switch</u>. The tabulation of the types of switches is given in Table 14.5.

Refer To Table 14.5 (Page 368)

Of the 22 switches, 21 of them are extreme and one is intermediate. The only intermediate switch occurs for a 0¢ cost group that began with three rented channels and stayed an all-channel on the second and third problems. This group did not complete the fourth B problem. Thus, we cannot yet reject the hypothesis that, under the conditions of this experiment, changes in structure will be mostly extreme. An analysis of types of extreme switches is presented in Table 14.6.

Refer To Table 14.6 (Page 369)

The one switch from a wheel to an all-channel occurred for a 0¢ cost group moving into problem two. This group made three errors on problem one and used 122 minutes. It did not complete problem two. The two switches from an all-channel to a wheel occurred in 0¢ and 1¢ cost groups moving into problem two. All switches following problem two were those of changing hubs in a wheel structure. The stability of the choice for a wheel group on later problems is striking. These data do not yet allow us to reject the hypothesis that, with experience, extreme switches favor the wheel to the all-channel whenever unanimity of choice is required.

TABLE 14.5 FRACTION OF DIFFERENT TYPES OF SWITCHES IN CHOICE OF STRUCTURE
FOR THE WATERLOO LUTHERAN DISCUSSION GROUPS

Channel Cost	Zero Switches	Intermediate Switches	Extreme Switches
5¢ and under	$14/32$	$1/32$	$17/32$
10¢ and over	$5/9$	$0/9$	$4/9$
Total	$19/41$	$1/41$	$21/41$

TABLE 14.6 NUMBER OF EACH TYPE OF EXTREME SWITCHES IN THE
WATERLOO LUTHERAN DISCUSSION GROUPS

Condition	Wheel to All-channel	All-channel to Wheel	Wheel to Wheel	Total Number of Extreme Switches
5 cents and under	1	2	14	17
10 cents and over	0	0	4	4

An analysis of the types of switches occurring in the Waterloo Lutheran Chain Channel-renting Experiment throws some light on the effects of the requirement of unanimity about structure. There are two more types of extreme switches for these chain groups: (1) a switch from a chain to an all-channel, and (2) a switch from an all-channel to a chain. Switches from chains to wheels and vice versa are intermediate switches. These data are presented in Table 14.7.

Refer To Table 14.7 (Page 371)

The absence of extreme switches where there is no discussion leading to a unanimous choice of structure in these chain groups compared with 53.7% for the discussion groups indicates that the requirement for consensus had a marked effect on the choice of structure. The fractions of zero switches and intermediate switches are approximately equal for the two experiments.

Examination of the type of channel-renting decisions in the chain experiment also indicates the reasons for renting channels. As mentioned earlier in this chapter, the renting of all-channels does not necessarily imply a preference for the all-channel structure. For example, if several persons request different wheel structures, the result may be an all-channel. Whenever a subject rents sufficient channels to communicate with all others directly, I assume it implies a desire for a wheel structure with himself as the hub. Whenever a subject rents all of the available channels, I assume it implies a preference for the all-channel. If he rents no channels, on the other

TABLE 14.7 FRACTION OF DIFFERENT TYPES OF SWITCHES IN CHOICE OF STRUCTURE FOR WATERLOO LUTHERAN CHAIN CHANNEL-RENTING GROUPS

Channel Cost	Zero Switches	Intermediate Switches	Extreme Switches
5¢ and under	$12/14$	$2/14$	$0/14$
10¢ and over	$9/24$	$15/24$	$0/24$
Total	$21/38$	$17/38$	$0/38$

hand, the implication is ambiguous. The fractions of these four types of decisions for the Waterloo Chain Channel-renting Experiments are presented in Table 14.8.

Refer To Table 14.8 (Page 373)

Despite the fact that 1¢ and 5¢ groups were usually all-channel (88.5% of all available channels were rented), only 21.8% of the choices were explicitly for the all-channel. Of those renting channels, 76.7% made decisions that I have interpreted as favoring a wheel and only 23.3% made decisions clearly favoring an all-channel. For 10¢ and above groups, a similar calculation shows that 85.2% rented for a wheel and 13.8% rented for an all-channel.

There are also further indications of difficulty with the B problems in the Waterloo Lutheran Groups. The average performance measures for the Chain Channel Renting and the Discussion groups are given in Table 14.9. Compared to other experiments, these are relatively poor performances. These data also indicate that the choice of structure beforehand did not enhance performance. The view of this work is that structures are multivariate and relationships among group members include type, direction, and content. These determine process. The choice of structure without solving the problems of task process does very little good (and probably can do harm) in enhancing performance. Even the choice of a wheel without a prior solution to the many process problems does not seem to offer improvements in performance for the B problems.

TABLE 14.8 SUMMARY OF TYPE OF INDIVIDUAL CHANNEL-RENTAL DECISIONS FOR THE WATERLOO LUTHERAN CHAIN CHANNEL-RENTING EXPERIMENT BY PERCENT

Channel Rental Cost	Wheel on Self	Wheel on Another	Non-Rented	All-channel
5¢ and under	38.2	21.8	21.8	18.2
10¢ and over[a]	8.2	30.0	55.7	6.3

[a] The total is 100.2. This is due to round-off error.

TABLE 14.9   SUMMARY AVERAGE PERFORMANCE MEASURES FOR
              THE TWO MAIN WATERLOO LUTHERAN EXPERIMENTS

Condition	Time per Problem	Number of Messages	Number of Errors	Hierarchy	Efficiency	Number of Observations
Chain Channel-renting	52.9 (27.0)[a]	150.0 (70.1)	1.12 (1.4)	.17 (.08)	.22 (.11)	49
Discussion Groups	61.9 (33.4)	154.9 (79.5)	1.44 (1.4)	.29 (.18)	.28 (.17)	55

[a] Number in parenthesis under the mean value is the standard deviation.

The correlation coefficients between hierarchy and several performance measures for the discussion groups are, on the whole, greater for the discussion than for the chain channel-renting experiments. The correlation between degree of hierarchy and problem number is $-.282$ ($p < .05$), between degree of hierarchy and time per problem $-.727$ ($p < .001$), between degree of hierarchy and number of messages $-.766$ ($p < .001$), and between degree of hierarchy and efficiency $.983$ ($p < .001$). The correlation coefficient between degree of hierarchy and centrality is significant at $p < .001$ (.472).

CHAPTER 15

EX ANTE TEST IMPLICATIONS OF THE THEORY

The application of the mapping function of Chapter 9 and the model for the rate of adoption of structure of Chapter 8 was made to perform an _ex post_ analysis of data from the Faucheux-Mackenzie experiment reported in Chapter 12. Because only 122 out of the 128 predictions based upon the mapping function were correct, a question mark was placed on the "not no, yet" outcome for the hypothesis that the mapping function explains structural change events in Figure 12.8. More evidence is needed about the mapping function in order to clear up the status of that hypothesis.

This chapter presents the discussion of several new strong inference steps to (1) reject the mapping function hypothesis, (2) subject the behavioral constitution to possible rejection, and (3) endanger the status of the model for structural adoption. This is accomplished by experiments performed with my student, A. C. Silcox (Silcox, 1972). In this experiment we state a sequence of _ex ante_ predictions of adoption and structural change that follow directly from the theory. We also attempt to manipulate rates of adoption by varying the relative status of certain group members. This manipulation provides a test of implications arising from the fact that the adoption model of Equation (8.29) can be derived from the diffusion of innovation literature.

I have not yet rejected the hypothesis that structures can be different for different milestones. Thus, it is possible for the data phase to have different structure than the answer phase for the minimum list of symbols or A problems. However, for the A problems, if the data phase is centralized the answer phase will also be centralized. We also "know" from the behavioral constitution of Chapter 7 that a structure is adopted when there is unanimity and there are no contrary preemptions. We learned in Chapter 12 that groups tend to centralize for the A problems. Hence, ceteris paribus, one should be able to obtain the adoption of wheel structures for the A problem. Furthermore, a wheel structure for the data sharing phase insures that the group will have a wheel structure for the answer phase.

If there are two experimenter-controlled confederates in a five-member group solving A problems, they can easily cause preemption of a wheel structure about a non-confederate hub of a wheel structure for data sharing. In addition, these two cooperating confederates can prevent consensus for any other as hub. Thus, by withholding data from the others and by casting contrary votes, the two cooperating confederates can control the elections and thereby control structural adoption. The experimenter, then, without direct intervention, can always get a designated confederate to become the hub of a wheel structure for A problems, ceteris paribus. For instance, suppose the confederates are designated by the colors Blue and Orange. It should be possible to have Blue selected as the hub, even though the two confederates account for only 40% of the members.

Following the adoption of a wheel around confederate Blue, by the argument for the maximum span of control model in Chapter 6, Blue's performance establishes a norm for solving A problems. Variable seven of the mapping function of Chapter 9 is the capacity for change. By causing the confederate Blue to violate the time norm, we can create a capacity for change that, by the mapping function, will result in the wheel structure becoming non-centralized. The mapping function predicts that the group structures will become non-centralized following the delays. It also predicts that when there is no capacity for change, the structure, <u>ceteris paribus</u>, will remain centralized. To examine this latter hypothesis, a control condition is established whereby confederate Orange attempts to recall the structure about Blue when Blue does not violate the norm. According to the mapping function, as long as Blue does not violate the norm, and Orange sends Blue the data, Blue will remain the hub.

Following decentralization of the wheel about Blue, by the same arguments, our confederates can cause Orange to become the hub of a new wheel. After Orange establishes the norm, delays will create a capacity for change and more decentralization. Cooperation by Blue and Orange can cause the reelection of Blue as hub. The sequence of structural manipulations is given in Figure 15.1.

Refer To Figure 15.1 (Page 378)

The results of Chapter 12 indicated that the model for the rate of adoption of structure

$$k_1 = \alpha + \beta V_F - \gamma V_U + \varepsilon \qquad (15.1)$$

provided reasonable fits for the data for the data and answer phases of the Faucheux-Mackenzie experiment. Variables V_F and V_U are the number of

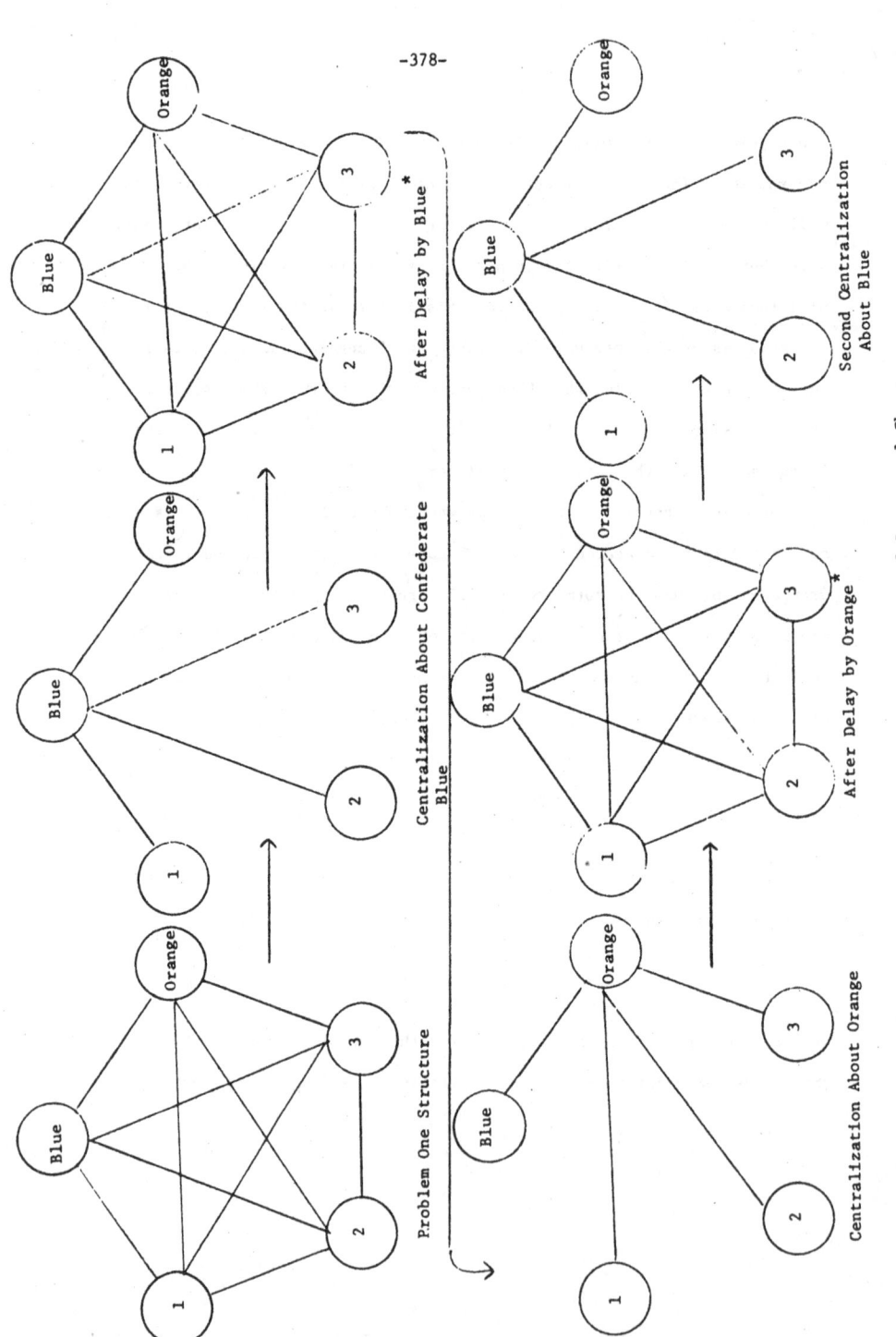

Figure 15.1 Ex Ante Predictions of the Mackenzie-Silcox Experiment of Structural Change

*This is shown as an all-channel as in the usual case. Actually, this all-channel merely represents that the structure

favorable and unfavorable votes per unit adoption period time respectively. Subsequent analysis has demonstrated that a model of the form

$$k_1 = \alpha + \beta''(V_F - V_U) + \epsilon \qquad (15.2)$$

also provides good fits for these data. This model has to be modified somewhat because of confederate interventions. Let $h(E)$ denote the number of unfavorable elections (cf. Chapter 7). A model of the form

$$k_1 = \frac{\alpha + \beta'(V_F - V_U) + \epsilon}{h(E)} \qquad (15.3)$$

effectively alters β'' by replacing it with $\beta'/h(E)$. The variable $k_1 - \alpha$ is called the __gross adoption rate__. The gross adoption rate is given by Equation (15.4):

$$k_1 - \alpha = \frac{\beta'(V_F - V_U) + \epsilon}{h(E)} \qquad (15.4)$$

Arguments by Rogers (1962), Bernhardt and Mackenzie (1972), and others claim that, _ceteris paribus_, the greater the perceived net advantages for adoption, the greater the gross adoption rate. If one of the confederates is introduced as having more expertise and more status than others in the group, he should have greater idiosyncrasy credits or status (cf. Hollander, 1964). Hence, _ceteris paribus_, the greater the relative status of the confederate to be elected, the greater we expect the gross adoption rate to be.

The strong inference tree for this chapter is presented in Figure 15.2. The main experiment is the left hand side branch. The subexperiment on status is indicated by the right hand side branch of Figure 15.2. Figure 15.2 is a new branch for Figure 15.5.

Refer To Figure 15.2 (Page 381)

WATERLOO STRUCTURAL ADOPTION EXPERIMENT

Method

Fifty-seven subjects and two confederates were used in nineteen experimental groups. Subjects were drawn from the list of subjects in the Psychology Department pool at the University of Waterloo and from advertisements. Subjects were paid $1.00 for time spent during instructions and for completing a questionnaire at the end of the experiment. In addition, each subject received $.20 for every problem worked. They were to solve as many problems as possible in a two-hour period. Thus, the more problems solved the greater the take home pay. One confederate was the wife of one of my students and was a freshman at the University of Waterloo. The other confederate was Mr. A. C. Silcox.

After receiving instructions for solving A-type problems, the subjects and confederates were seated in booths in a communications network in the same manner as in the Faucheux-Mackenzie experiment described in Chapter 12. The eight A problems used in the Faucheux-Mackenzie experiment were repeated in the same order. After problem nine, I repeated the eight problems in

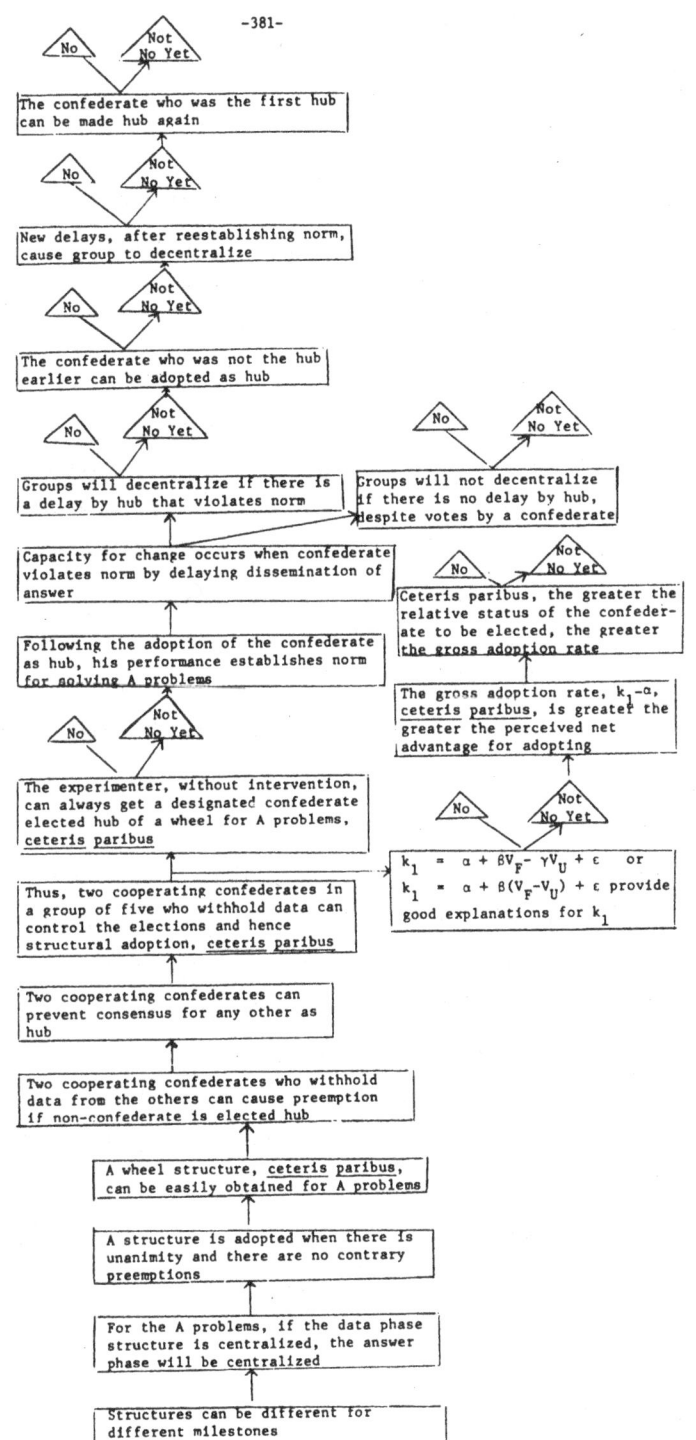

Figure 15.2 Strong Inference Tree for Chapter 15

the same order. On these later problems, different subjects received different information and the confederate presented the minimum list of answers in different order. Out of the 57 subjects only three indicated any suspicion that the problems were being repeated.

Mr. Silcox was the high status confederate. He was older and dressed in a business suit. I introduced him to the group as a Ph.D. student in organizational behavior who was expert in "bureaucratic inefficiencies." In addition, he was introduced as having had many advanced courses and having conducted research. It was explained that he was in the experiment because he had no direct experience in this type of experimentation and because I wanted him to have some experience as a subject as an asset to his later work. Mr. Silcox had agreed to be a subject under the same conditions as the other subjects. In this scenario the "experiment" was really a demonstration in which the subjects were helping Mr. Silcox out. Mr. Silcox was subject Blue. The lower status confederate was Aggie Beynon, the cute young wife of Mr. Beynon.[1] She introduced herself in the same manner as the other subjects. She was careful to dress in the manner of other college women at the University of Waterloo. She was subject Orange. Orange is the lower status confederate, denoted LSC. Blue is the higher status confederate, designated HSC.

Subjects were allowed to form their structure on problem one without intervention by the confederates. The structure on problem one was always

---

[1] Mr. W. D. Beynon is the student with whom I worked in the experiment described in Chapter 16.

an all-channel. On problem two, attempts were made by both confederates to become the hub of a wheel. The HSC announced the answer on problem two and during the adoption period. After the group centralized on Blue, he maintained his position for at least three problems.[2] Following the delay, Orange attempted to form a wheel with herself as the hub. She announced the answer on the problems during this adoption period. She maintained the wheel (with herself as hub) for at least three problems and then delayed. Following the delay, Blue attempted to become hub again. Blue maintained his position as hub until the two hours were over.

The period between the sending of the answer from the hub and the receipt of data from the other four was standardized. These times were carefully controlled and were adjusted for task complexity. The standard times were used to insure that the confederate conformed to a performance norm based upon the Faucheux-Mackenzie A problem times. The delay times were approximately three times the standardized times. The standard times varied from 1/2 minute to 3 minutes. The delay times varied from 3 minutes to 9 or 12 minutes.

Standard persuasion messages were used during the adoption process and had three purposes: (1) to insure one confederate did not present a more logical argument than the other, (2) to control the agenda and proposed state of each ballot, and (3) to indicate whether the reason for change

---

[2] The answers, the standard times, and the delay times are tabulated for each problem in Appendix 15.1.

was due to the general situation or due to the inadequacy of a particular member. Each confederate used two lists of standard messages. List A was used when attempting to get Blue selected as hub for the first time. List B was used by Orange, after Blue's first delay, in her effort to become hub. Blue used a version of list B for the switch from Orange to Blue following Orange's delay. There was no competition between confederates in the last two attempts to switch hubs.

The problems, normal times, delay times, and lists A and B of persuasion messages are contained in Appendices 15.1 and 15.2 of this chapter.

There were essentially six experimentally distinct time periods for this experiment: (1) pre-intervention by confederates, (2) first adoption of Blue as hub, (3) first stable period with Blue as hub, (4) first adoption of Orange as hub, (5) stable period with Orange as hub, and (6) second adoption of Blue as hub. The author acted as the "mailman" who date-time-number stamped all messages before sending them. He could read these messages. Consequently, he could provide voting information to the confederates to help them control their voting. All subject messages were sent and none altered in any way.

The preintervention period was problem one. During this problem the confederates broadcasted their information to the subjects and included their names to help the subjects know the color identification of each. A typical message is: "Hi, I'm Aggie. Here is my information. What's yours?" Confederates let the subjects solve problem one. More details about the other five periods are contained in Silcox (1972). The descriptions here are reasonably complete, however.

There were two related experiments or controls. The first used no imposed delays and followed the procedure of the main experiment up to the first adoption of the HSC or Blue as the hub of a wheel. The LSC or Orange attempted to recall the structure to become hub following the third post-centralization problem. Because there were as many as thirty problems solved, the LSC ran out of persuasion messages (List B in Appendix B), in which case she improvised new ones. This control experiment is called the No-delay Experiment in this Chapter. A second control experiment, called the Low Status Differential with Delay Experiment, attempted to make Blue appear as an ordinary subject. For this experiment Mr. Silcox was not introduced as an expert. He introduced himself as an engineering undergraduate and was careful to dress in the manner of a typical engineering undergraduate and did not wear either a suit or a tie.

There were eight groups in the main experiment (designated the High Status Differential with Delay Experiment), four in the No-delay Experiment, and seven in the Low Status Differential with Delay Experiment. The predicted structural results for each of the three experiments for the six periods are presented in Table 15.1.

Refer To Table 15.1 (Page 386)

TABLE 15.1 PREDICTED STRUCTURAL RESULTS BY PERIOD AND EXPERIMENTAL CONDITIONS

Period	Experimental Condition		
	HSD Delay	HSD No Delay	LSD Delay
1. Pre-intervention	all-channel	all-channel	all-channel
2. First HSC Adoption	wheel about HSC	wheel about HSC	wheel about HSC
3. First Stable Delay by HSC	wheel about HSC Decentralization	wheel about HSC Remains a wheel about HSC	wheel about HSC Decentralization
4. First LSC Adoption	wheel about LSC		wheel about LSC
5. Second Stable Delay by LSC	wheel about LSC Decentralization		wheel about LSC Decentralization
6. Second HSC Adoption	wheel about HSC		wheel about HSC
No. of Groups	8	4	7

Results

For the eighteen groups, all but four predictions were correct. From Table 15.1 there are 8 x 8 + 4 x 4 + 7 x 8 = 136 predictions. The four incorrect predictions were as follows: one group each in period 6 (second HSC adoption) in the HSD Delay and HSD No-delay conditions had serious conflicts that manifested themselves in overtly hostile remarks (when a subject had been elected and the confederates caused a preemption), there were two incorrect predictions in period 4 (first LSC adoption) in the No-delay condition. One was caused deliberately by the experimenter when the HSC "retired." The second one occurred when the HSC made an error. The error caused an inadvertent delay. These incorrect predictions are all due to changed conditions from those intended for problem solving. The hostility occurring in the two cases in period 6 is the source of the experiment in Chapter 16. Using the mapping function there are approximately 450 predictions, all of which are correct.

The model for the rate of adoption of structure of Equation (15.4) was applied in six cases: there were three adoptions of structure in both the HSC delay and LSC delay experiments. The values of the coefficient of multiple determination, R^2, ranged from 0.92 to 0.99, with t-statistics ranging from 5.1 to 19.7. The presence of only four groups for the HSC No-delay and the fact that one of these had to be discarded because of a miscue from the experimenter means that there were only three values of k_1, an insufficient number on which to base a reliable regression analysis. The data for the three Mackenzie-Silcox experiments are presented in Table 15.2.

Refer To Table 15.2 (Page 389)

The regression equation from (15.4) is

$$\hat{k}_1 = \alpha + \beta' A_b \qquad (15.5)$$

where A_b is the adoption bias and we interpret β' as the propensity to adopt a structure and $\hat{k}_1$ is the predicted value. The gross adoption rate, $k_1 - \alpha$, is given by

$$\hat{k}_1 - \alpha = \beta' A_b \qquad (15.6)$$

The good fits provided by Equation (15.5) to the actual values of k_1 suggest that Equation (15.6) provides a good estimate for each group for each adoption period for the HSC Delay and LSC No-delay experiments. These calculations are performed and the results are listed in Table 15.3.

Refer To Table 15.3 (Page 390)

An analysis of the differences in gross adoption rates in Table 15.3 shows very weak effects of status upon difference in gross adoption rates. A randomization test for matched pairs (Siegel, 1956) was performed. At $p < .05$, for a one-tailed test, the only significant difference was between the first and second adoption of HSC in the High Status Differential Delay Experiment. A Kolmogorov-Smirnov two-sample test (Siegel, 1956) was applied

TABLE 15.2 STRUCTURAL ADOPTION PROCESS DATA FOR THE MACKENZIE-SILCOX EXPERIMENTS

Group	First Adoption of HSC				First Adoption of LSC					Second Adoption of HSC				
	V_F	V_U	$h(E)$	$A_b{}^a$	k_1	V_F	V_U	$h(E)$	A_b	k_1	V_F	V_U	$h(E)$	A_B	k_1
High Status Differential Groups															
2	12.0	5.8	19	.4	.9	4.8	1.5	19	.2	.2	3.1	.9	14	.2	.2
4	27.0	9.0	15	1.1	4.7	2.0	.4	9	.2	.4	3.4	.6	9	.3	.5
5	4.2	1.6	25	.1	.2	2.0	.5	15	.1	.1	2.1	.7	16	.1	.2
6	2.9	1.9	27	.1	.1	1.0	.4	15	.1	.1	2.0	.5	10	.1	.2
7	6.6	2.1	24	.2	.5	3.8	1.0	17	.2	.2	3.0	2.2	23	.0	.1
8	2.0	.9	26	.0	.1	1.3	.3	11	.1	.1	3.1	.5	11	.2	.3
9	2.5	1.0	23	.1	.2	2.2	.2	12	.1	.2	.9	.3	9	.1	.1
17	9.0	4.2	21	.2	.7	9.0	1.5	9	.8	1.4	...	N/A[b]			
Low Status Differential Groups															
1	3.9	1.6	30	.1	.2	...	N/A[b]				2.9	1.5	35	0.0	.1
3	3.3	2.0	36	.0	.1	1.6	.4	11	.1	.1	10.0	1.5	9	.9	1.5
13	3.0	1.5	38	.0	.1	2.2	.6	9	.2	.3	2.5	1.3	14	.1	.4
14	4.6	2.0	43	.1	.2	8.2	3.2	34	.1	.2	...	N/A[b]			
15	6.1	2.8	21	.2	.4	4.2	1.1	16	.2	.4	2.8	.8	11	.2	.2
16	4.1	2.0	44	.0	.1	1.4	.4	11	.1	.1	4.6	1.2	10	.3	.6
18	12.4	4.2	20	.4	1.2	3.2	.7	10	.2	.5	4.9	1.6	25	.1	.2
High Status No-delay Groups															
10	4.5	1.8	32	.1	.2										
11	3.4	1.8	39	.0	.1										
12	3.6	1.7	27	.1	.2										
19	...	N/A[b]													

$$A_b = \varepsilon \cdot \frac{V_F - V_U}{h(E)}$$

[a]

[b] Experimental conditions changed when confederate voted just after subjects had elected a subject as center. Conflict and hostility towards confederate occurred.

TABLE 15.3 GROSS ADOPTION RATE BY GROUP, ADOPTION PERIOD, AND EXPERIMENTAL CONDITION

	Group	Experimental Condition		
		First HSC Adoption	First LSC Adoption	Second HSC Adoption
High Status Differential Delay Groups	2	1.6	.4	.2
	4	4.6	.3	.4
	5	.4	.2	.1
	6	.2	.1	.2
	7	.6	.3	.0
	8	.2	.2	.3
	9	.2	.3	.1
	17	.8	1.4	N/A[a]
Low Status Differential Delay Groups	1	.2	N/A[a]	.1
	3	.1	.4	1.4
	13	.1	.7	.1
	14	.2	.6	N/A[a]
	15	.5	.6	.3
	16	.1	.4	.5
	18	1.2	.8	.2
HSD No Delay Groups	10	.3		
	11	.2		
	12	.3		
	19	N/A[a]		

[a] Cf. footnote b of Table

to test the difference between the adoption rate of the first HSC and first LSC in the High Status Differential Experiment. At $p < .05$ the difference was significant and the HSC first adoption occurred more quickly.

These results suggest that either the status differential has little effect or that the experimenter's manipulation of the status differential was inadequate. Because the gross adoption rate for the first HSC adoption in the High Status Differential Delay condition is higher than in the Low Status Differential Delay condition, and because, within the High Status Differential Delay Condition, the HSC is not adopted more quickly than the LSC, there may be an inconsistency that is due to an inadequate experimentally manipulated status differential. To examine this possibility Mr. Silcox examined the relationship between differences in gross adoption rate between the HSC and LSC confederates and the average status difference reported on the questionnaire administered at the end of each group's problem solving. The three subjects rated the relative status of each group member on a 1-9 point scale with 5 being the value for the rater. The average status difference between the HSC and LSC is the difference in the two scores averaged over the three subjects. The results is illustrated in Figure 15.3.

Refer To Figure 15.3 (Page 392)

Figure 15.3 provides evidence that (1) the manipulation of status by the experimenter was faulty and (2) one should not yet reject the hypothesis

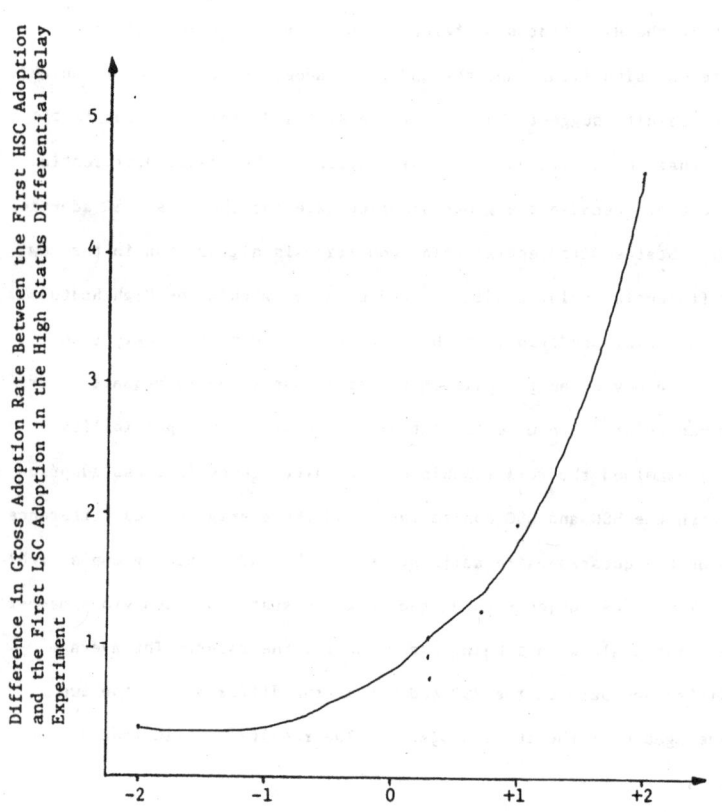

Figure 15.3 Relation Between Average Status Difference and Gross Adoption Rate Difference For the High Status Differential Delay Experiment

to test the difference between the adoption rate of the first HSC and first LSC in the High Status Differential Experiment. At $p < .05$ the difference was significant and the HSC first adoption occurred more quickly.

These results suggest that either the status differential has little effect or that the experimenter's manipulation of the status differential was inadequate. Because the gross adoption rate for the first HSC adoption in the High Status Differential Delay condition is higher than in the Low Status Differential Delay condition, and because, within the High Status Differential Delay Condition, the HSC is not adopted more quickly than the LSC, there may be an inconsistency that is due to an inadequate experimentally manipulated status differential. To examine this possibility Mr. Silcox examined the relationship between differences in gross adoption rate between the HSC and LSC confederates and the average status difference reported on the questionnaire administered at the end of each group's problem solving. The three subjects rated the relative status of each group member on a 1-9 point scale with 5 being the value for the rater. The average status difference between the HSC and LSC is the difference in the two scores averaged over the three subjects. The results is illustrated in Figure 15.3.

Refer To Figure 15.3 (Page 392)

Figure 15.3 provides evidence that (1) the manipulation of status by the experimenter was faulty and (2) one should not yet reject the hypothesis

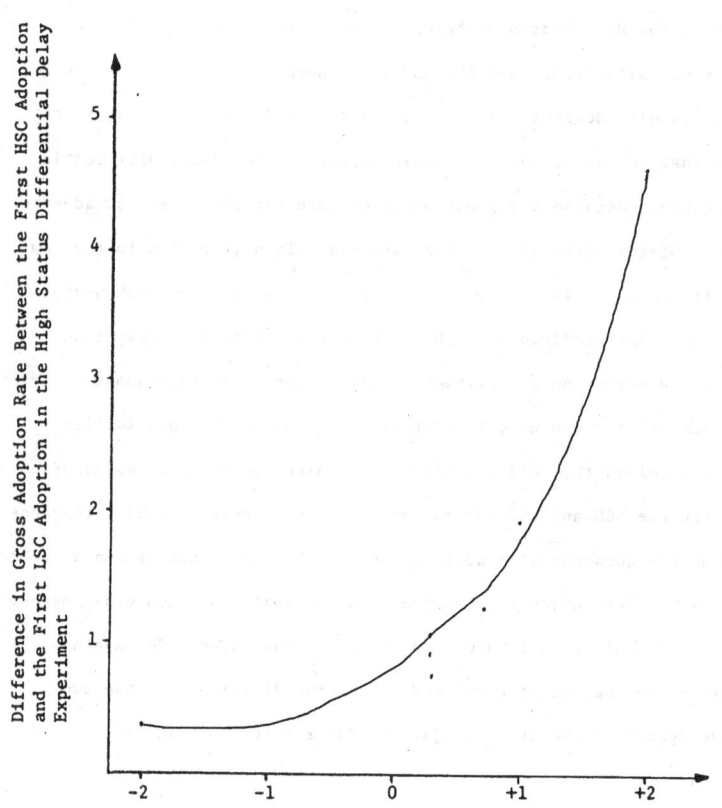

Figure 15.3 Relation Between Average Status Difference and Gross Adoption Rate Difference For the High Status Differential Delay Experiment

that, _ceteris paribus_, the greater the relative status of the confederate to be elected, the greater the gross adoption rate. These conclusions, however, are merely suggestive because of differences in experimental conditions and because, if Hollander is correct, relative status may be a dependent variable based partly on performance in the group. For example, both the HSC and LSC competed during the first HSC adoption but the HSC did not compete with the LSC during the first LSC adoption. The lack of competition tends to reduce V_U and hence raise A_b and thence the gross adoption rate. Consequently, the reported differences (though small) in gross adoption rate may be partially accounted for by the manipulation. However, the reported insignificant difference between the first LSC gross adoption rates and the second HSC gross adoption rates are interesting because both conditions do not involve other confederate competition. On the other hand, the relative status of the HSC may have declined from what it was during the first HSC adoption period because of the delays that caused the group to seek a new structure. There are other anomalies that suggest that the experimenter's manipulation of status differences was not altogether effective.

DISCUSSION

These experiments established that, for these conditions, the hypotheses indicated in the strong inference tree of Figure 15.2 cannot yet be rejected. We found that the experimenter could, without intervention, obtain a wheel group with a designated confederate as its hub. We found that the prediction that a capacity for change would cause a centralized group to decentralize was correct. We determined that if there is not a capacity for change, conditions remaining the same, a centralized group will remain centralized despite recalls by another confederate. These predictions are based upon the mapping function of Chapter 9. We also found that under these conditions we could cause changes in the hub of a wheel group. We found that a modified adoption process rate model provides a reasonably close fit for the data. There are indications that the greater the relative status of a confederate, the greater the gross adoption rate for his adoption.

There were two cases where the confederates created hostility by preempting the election of a subject to cause the election of a confederate. This hostility may be due to a violation of the axiom of consummation (C2 of Chapter 7). This possibility is investigated in Chapter 16.

Although theories of leadership are not the main concern of this book, the effects of status on the gross adoption rate has implications for this literature (cf. Hollander and Julian, 1969). The results are not inconsistent with a view that leadership and influence are closely related (cf. Mackenzie, 1970, for one analysis using risky shift paradigm), that leadership is minimally a dynamic process that is almost continuously contingent upon many factors lying outside the characteristics of the leader. These results, while marginal, do suggest that a Fiedler-type of static contingency model may need modification. The demonstrated and repeated capability for changing leaders in a small group could suggest less static "independent" contingencies. It would seem not inappropriate to consider the possibility of more process-oriented models for understanding leadership.

APPENDIX 15.1 CONFEDERATE'S ANSWER SHEET, NORMAL AND DELAY TIMES

Confederate's Answer and Time Sheet

Problem	Answer
1,9,17,25,33	2,3,0,5,9
2,10,18,26,34	B,F,S,Y,J
3,11,19,27,35	L, △, ▯, ▽, ○, □, ⊙, ⌂, ⴺ, ⴿ
4,12,20,28,36	0,1,2,3,4,5,6,7,8,9
5,13,21,29,37	A,M,L,Q,H,J,Y,S,F,B
6,14,22,30,38	WHITE, GRAY, BLUE, VIOLET, YELLOW, GREEN, BLACK, BROWN, ORANGE, RED
7,15,23,31,39	B,A,F,M,S,L,Y,Q,J,H
8,16,24,32,40	ⴺ, L, ⴺ, △, ⌂, ▯, □, ○

Answer Phase Length by Trial
(Time in Minutes)

Problem	Normal Time	Delay Time
1,9,17,25,33	As Soon As Possible	3
2,10,18,26,34	1/2	4 1/2
3,11,19,27,35	3	12 or 9
4,12,20,28,36	1/2	4 1/2
5,13,21,29,37	2	9
6,14,22,30,38	3	12 or 9
7,15,23,31,39	1	6
8,16,24,32,40	1 1/2	7 1/2

APPENDIX 15.2 PERSUASION MESSAGES USED BY CONFEDERATES

List A for the First HSC Adoption Period

The High Status Confederate's Persuasion Messages Were:

1. "We need to work faster. To do this, send your data to me. I will find the solution and send it out to all of you. It should save time."
2. "Send only me your data. Sending it to others as well only causes confusion."
3. "Too many people are receiving data. That's why we're disorganized. Send your data to me only."

The Low Status Confederate's Persuasion Messages Were:

1. "I have an idea to speed things up. Why don't you all send your messages to me--then I will work out the answer and submit the same answer to everyone.
2. "Unless everyone sends just me their messages we will get confused. Please send only me your messages. OK?"
3. "Things are getting very disorganized because too many messages are being sent. Send messages to me only."

List B for the First LSC Adoption Period

The Low Status Confederate's Persuasion Messages Were:

1. "Blue must have had a late/good night because he's slowing down. Why don't you send me your messages and I will speed the process up."
2. "Please, please, please, give Blue a rest--I think he needs one. Let me speed this experiment up or we'll die of boredom."

3. "We'll never make money with Blue. Give me a chance and I'll make you rich (and keep you from getting bored)."

The High Status Confederate did not compete for the hub position in this period.

List B for the Second HSC Adoption Period

The High Status Confederate's Persuasion Messages Were:
1. "Orange is getting slow. She must be tired. Why not send your data to me again. I am ready to go."
2. "The pace is slowing. Let me speed it up again. I am rested now. I think Orange needs a break."
3. "With Orange as centre our earning rate is getting lower. Why don't you let me be centre (again). We'll make more money. It's less boring that way."

The Low Status Confederate did not compete for the hub position in this period.

CHAPTER 16

A TEST FOR THE VALIDITY OF THE AXIOM OF CONSUMMATION
AND A MODEL FOR INTERPERSONAL HOSTILITY

The experiment reported in Chapter 15 indicated two cases where the confederates intervened after the three subjects had already adopted another subject as the hub of a wheel for solving A problems. In both cases, there was evidence of hostility towards the confederates when they preempted the adoption. Axiom C2 of the behavioral constitution (cf. Chapter 7) states that an adopted structure will be consummated (or implemented). Therefore, the actions of the confederates that prevented consummation violated the behavioral constitution. Violating an axiom of the behavioral constitution breaks a norm if the axiom is indeed valid. The breaking of this norm could have inadvertently created a conflict that resulted in the hostility towards the confederates.

The subject of this chapter is the empirical investigation of the validity of the Axiom of Consummation. The experiment attempts to reproduce the conditions leading to the formation of hostility from the Mackenzie-Silcox experiment. By deliberately preventing the consummation of an adopted structure and controlling the types of messages from two confederates, we seek to validate the Axiom of Consummation by creating interpersonal hostility that is directed initially towards the person causing the direct violation. A control experiment where the Axiom of Consummation has not been violated uses exactly the same message sequences. The result should be interpersonal hostility directed initially towards the other confederate.

This experiment, which I shall call the Mackenzie-Beynon experiment, was conducted with Mr. Beynon at the University of Waterloo. The design of the experiment and the measure of interpersonal hostility was jointly planned. This experiment served as the basis for Mr. Beynon's MASc thesis in the Department of Management Sciences.

Because this experiment grew out of the few anomalies in the Mackenzie-Silcox experiment, the strong inference tree grows outward and upward from one of the higher branches of Figure 15.2. The strong inference tree for this experiment is given in Figure 16.1. After presenting the strong inference tree, I shall discuss the measure of interpersonal hostility as a dependent variable. The development of the measure of interpersonal hostility and the use of the Mackenzie-Beynon experiment to validate it has led to the start of an entirely different strong inference tree, as shown later in Figure 16.3.

Recall that the Mackenzie-Silcox experiments made a series of ex ante predictions regarding changes in structure based upon the behavioral constitution and the mapping function when the groups solved sequences of A-type problems. It was demonstrated that, by having the hub delay emission of the answer, we could get one of the confederates adopted as the hub of a wheel and then cause the group to decentralize. This delay created a capacity for change and the result was the temporary decentralization of the group. It was also shown that, following the delay by Confederate #1 (Blue), it was always possible to get Confederate #2 (Orange) adopted as the new hub, replacing #1. Given that #2 was adopted without preemption, then, by Axiom C2 a wheel structure will be consummated with #2 as its hub. This branch is indicated by the extreme left hand side branch of

Figure 16.1. Our main interest is the middle branch of Figure 16.1.

Suppose Confederate #2 is adopted as hub <u>and</u> Confederate #1 preempts the adopted structure about #2. Then the wheel about #2, while adopted, is not consummated. This action by #1 violates the Axiom of Consummation. If the behavioral constitution, which is merely a "they act as if" type of explanation, is "real," it probably represents a norm. The preemption action by #1 would then violate this norm. One would expect efforts to remove the violation. Normally, one might expect Confederate #1 to plead a version of <u>mea culpa</u>, apologize, amend his ways by conforming overtly, and see the restoration of #2. If #1 did not conform even after attempts by the others, one would not be surprised if, <u>ceteris paribus</u>, the group began to treat #1 as a deviant and eventually ostracized him. However, this group cannot get along without #1's data and cooperation and it cannot get rid of him. In these circumstances, if both confederates remain adamant and each refuses to yield to the other (or to any other subject), the group cannot proceed. The wasted time is costing money.

One would expect that efforts to resolve the dilemma would be initially directed to the norm violator, Confederate #1. His unyielding stubbornness could cause message exchanges that result in an impasse between himself and at least one other subject. Later, the subjects would be likely to form impasses with the non-violator, Confederate #2. I expect that the time to the first impasse of a subject with #1 will be less than the time to the first impasse with Confederate #2.

These manipulations raise the question of whether the resulting pattern of impasses and hostility is due to the violation of the Axiom of Consummation or to the truculence of the Confederates. A control experiment, whose strong inference branch is the right hand side branch of Figure 16.1, attempts to answer this question. It proceeds as in the main experiment, except that Confederate #2 is not fully adopted as the hub when we release Confederate #1. #1 preempts the election of #2. Since #2 was never adopted, #1 has not violated the Axiom of Consummation. Both confederates then engage in behavior that is choreographed precisely the same as in the main experiment. They each send the same messages at exactly the same intervals as in the main experiment. Their adamant behavior frustrates the group because the structure remains unresolved. Impasses begin to occur between the subjects and the confederates. This time, however, the "usurper" (#2) is seen as the cause of the group's difficulties. The time to the first impasse between #2 and any subject should be less than the time to the first impasse between #1 and a subject.

Because the main experiment resulted in a deliberate violation of the Axiom of Consummation and both experiments used stubborn confederates and the same message sequences, the difference between the two experiments is the norm violation. One would expect, then, that the time to the first impasse between a subject and #1 in the main experiment will be less than the time to the first impasse between a subject and #2 in the control experiment. This prediction is shown at the top of the middle branch in Figure 16.1.

Refer To Figure 16.1 (Page 402)

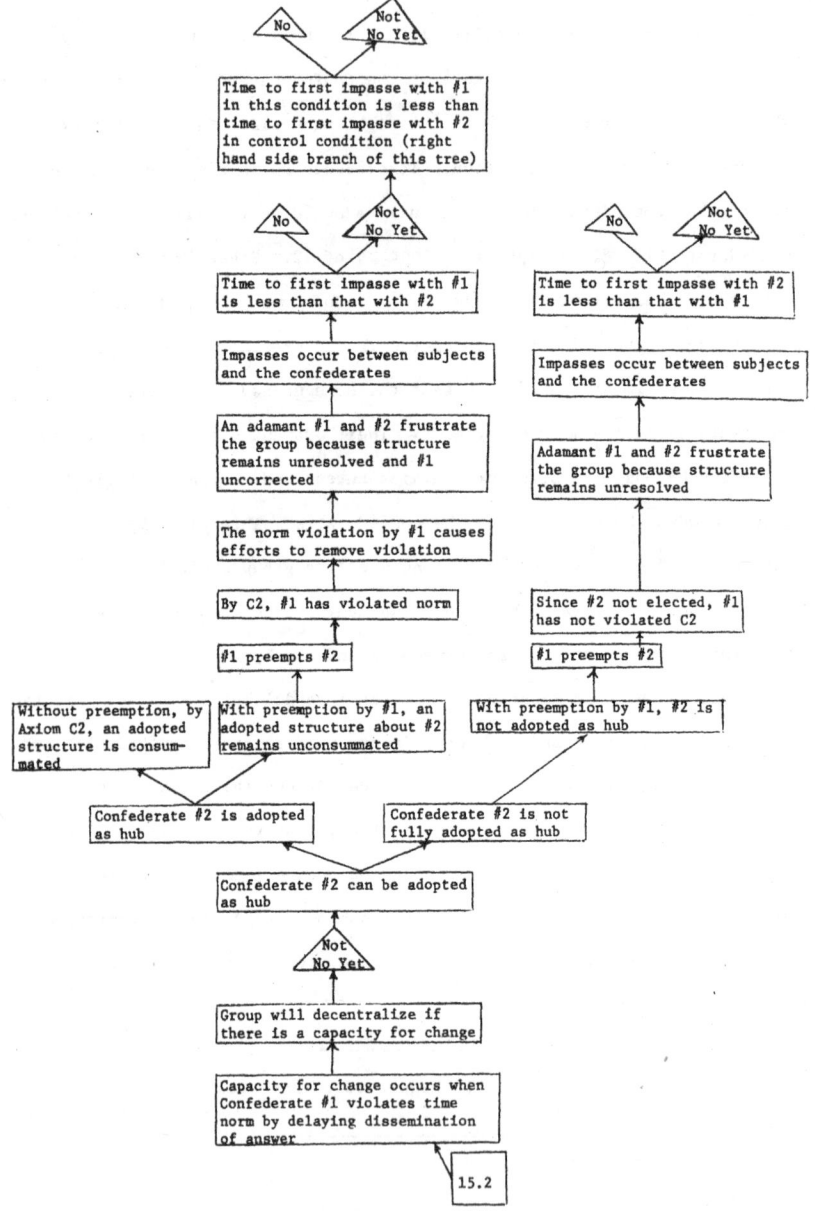

Figure 16.1 Strong Inference Tree for Validity of Behavioral Constitution

HOSTILITY

Conflict, frustration, fear, hostility, anger, instrumental and noninstrumental aggression, and violence are interrelated concepts that have been subjects for numerous scientific, philosophical, and rhetorical discussions. The early work by Dollard, Doob, Miller, Mowrer, and Sears (1939) followed by the series of efforts by Berkowitz (1960a, 1960b, 1962, 1969), the work by Pepitone (1964) and many other social psychologists have examined evidence for behavior related to these topics. The works by Boulding (1962), McNeil (1965), Singer (1971), and Fawcett (1972) provide alternative approaches and reviews of extant research.

One of these concepts, hostility, is usually viewed as a special type of attitude mediating between stimuli and overt behavior. Conceptualizations of hostility tend to be imprecise. One useful summary and source of ideas about hostility is the work of Pepitone (1964). His discussion of the changes in levels of hostility are based upon instrumentality notions. Unfortunately, in the context of the type of experiment proposed in this chapter, I need a concept that allows greater specificity in terms of the actual life history of each experimental group. Because the main experiments concern structure, hostility is an experimental by-product. In order to keep earlier commitments to rely on the actual behaviors contained in the life history and because I am not studying hostility directly, I have had to deviate somewhat in both conceptualization of hostility and method of validation. I admit the inherent weakness of a procedure in which one uses the results of an experiment on structure to validate a measure for interpersonal hostility. Clearly a more direct test is preferred. Consequently, even though I venture to offer a new strong inference tree for formation of interpersonal hostility, it is a very tender growth and is not to be taken too seriously. On the other hand, the reported data are interesting. The following paragraphs describe hostility with respect to groups solving A-type problems in a communications network experiment where there is a confederate-caused conflict.

A MODEL FOR CHANGES IN LEVELS OF INTERPERSONAL HOSTILITY

Two persons are said to be in overt conflict if (1) each has a position on an issue which is incompatible with the other; (2) each desires his position; (3) each is aware of (1) and (2); and (4) one can only win if the other loses. The event at which there is first overt conflict is called the _trigger_ _event_. When the overt conflict is resolved there is a second event called the _resolution_ _event_. In between the trigger event and the resolution event there are many interactions and varying degrees of hostility are generated. After the resolution event, the degree of hostility may fail to return to pre-trigger event levels but will remain latent. Evidence of this latent hostility occurs when seemingly mild messages evoke strong responses which seem disproportionate to the nature of the stimulus.

The trigger must be identified and we must provide a method for calculating degrees of hostility between members, for each member, and for the entire group. The trigger event in this experiment is created by intervening after adoption to prevent consummation. This may set off a leadership struggle. The resolution event occurs when one of the two contending leaders yields to the other.

Since we are dealing with data derived from messages, we need a measure for hostility stated in terms of messages. Tentatively, we think that there is a regular pattern to message sequences between group members. Consider a pair of persons, say x_i and x_j, who have reached the trigger event. They may exchange many messages. There are three readily identifiable sequences of four messages called here 4-message sequences that are very important in determining the level and direction of change of hostility. These three types of 4-message sequences are composed of 10 basic types of messages. Table 16.1 contains the description of these 10 messages. Each message is designated z_{mk} where m is the message number in a 4-message sequence with m = 1 designating the first, m = 2 the second, m = 3 the third, m = 4 the last, and k the content descriptor with k = 1 designating messages either stating or acknowledging an issue, k = 2 designating a non-issue task-oriented message, and k = 3 designating a message that ignores an issue.

Refer To Table 16.1 (Page 406)

There may be many 4-message sequences between a pair, x_i and x_j. Let t = 1, 2, ..., T be the message sequence number. On the tth 4-message sequence, there are three main sequences:

As we shall see, a four message sequence permits a "double checking" of a message that indicates a person is ignoring or resolving ones position. It also allows one to differentiate between an impasse 4-message sequence and a holding 4-message sequence.

TABLE 16.1 Ten Basic Types of Messages[1] in Hostility 4-Sequences

Notation	Individual Sending Message x_i	x_j	Message Number in 4-Sequence	Issue Stated?	Task-Oriented Message (non-issue)	Issue Acknowledged?	Issue Ignored?
z_{11}	Yes	--	1	Yes	No	--	--
z_{12}	Yes	--	1	No	Yes	--	--
z_{21}	--	Yes	2	--	--	Yes	--
z_{22}	--	Yes	2	--	Yes	--	--
z_{23}	--	Yes	2	--	--	--	Yes
z_{31}	Yes	--	3	Yes	No	--	--
z_{32}	Yes	--	3	No	Yes	--	--
z_{41}	--	Yes	4	--	--	Yes	--
z_{42}	--	Yes	4	--	Yes	--	--
z_{43}	--	Yes	4	--	--	--	Yes

[1]There are other types of possible messages. However, with respect to the proposed hostility calculus, these 10 are the more relevant.

(a) Resolution 4-Message Sequence

$$Z_1(t) = [z_{11}(t), z_{21}(t), z_{31}(t), z_{41}(t)]$$

In a resolution 4-message sequence, x_i states his position on an issue $[z_{11}(t)]$; then x_j replies by acknowledging x_i's position $[z_{21}(t)]$; x_i repeats it $[z_{31}(t)]$; and finally x_j acknowledges it again $[z_{41}(t)]$. It is not necessary for x_j to agree with x_i. He may disagree and even though he expresses his disagreement, manage to also acknowledge x_i's position. Resolution 4-message sequences are assumed to reduce hostility.

(b) Holding 4-Message Sequence

$$Z_2(t) = [z_{11}(t), z_{22}(t), z_{32}(t), z_{42}(t)]$$

In a holding 4-message sequence, x_i begins by stating his position on an issue $[z_{11}(t)]$; then x_j replies by attempting to bring the discussion down to the level of completing the task $[z_{22}(t)]$; whereupon x_i also sends a task-oriented non-issue message to x_j $[z_{32}(t)]$; and finally x_j again sends a task-oriented non-issue message to x_i $[z_{42}(t)]$. Holding 4-message sequences are assumed to neither increase nor decrease hostility.

(c) Impasse 4-Message Sequence

$$Z_3(t) = [z_{11}(t), z_{23}(t), z_{31}(t), z_{43}(t)]$$

In an impasse 4-message sequence, x_i begins by stating his position on an issue $[z_{11}(t)]$; then x_j replies by ignoring x_i's position (usually stating a counter-position or changing the subject) $[z_{23}(t)]$; whereupon x_i again insists on his position [$z_{31}(t)$]; and finally x_j ignores him <u>again</u> [$z_{43}(t)$]. This seems to be a most exasperating 4-message sequence which is assumed to increase hostility.[2]

The difference between a message that ignores a position and one that begins a holding sequence by subordinating the interaction to completing a problem is often subtle. Sometimes the decision of whether one is looking at an impasse or a holding sequence depends upon the response of x_i on the third message. If he restates his position, it is an impasse and x_j's message was perceived by x_i as one that was ignoring his position. Sometimes an impasse may occur inadvertently because x_j incorrectly perceived what x_i was attempting to say.

The remaining possible 4-message sequences are undefined with respect to hostility and it is assumed that they do not affect hostility. It is possible to have overlapping 4-message sequences if more than one issue is raised during a 4-message sequence. These are handled by allowing special messages to do double duty. The pair may impasse more than once on an issue. Each successive impasse increases hostility. Impasses are numbered

---

[2]This model is based solely upon the type and number of 4-message sequences. It is conceivable and probably likely that impasses can be resolved without direct resolutions. For example, x_i can "make allowances" or "forgive" x_j and thereby not react in the same manner as one might expect from only examining the interactions. I shall maintain, however, that during the discussion the hostility felt is determined by the net number of outstanding impasses. The making allowances or "forgiving" processes are assumed to occur during a break in the interactions. It is also conceivable that this post-discussion resolution of impasses can act to increase hostility. This can occur whenever a person "thinks about the problem" and begins to interpret the messages as "ignores" rather than "acknowledges." I suspect that attribution of intent is a major determinant of these probable post-discussion adjustments for levels of hostility.

consecutively regardless of issue. Let $l_{ij}(t)$ be the __impasse level__ as felt by x_i towards x_j at the end of the tth 4-message sequence. A new impasse increases the impasse level by one and a resolution decreases it by one.

From x_i's view of x_j, let t_1, t_2, and t_3 be the number of resolution sequences, the number of holding sequences, and the number of impasse sequences respectively.

$$t = t_1 + t_2 + t_3 \qquad (16.1)$$

The impasse level, $l_{ij}(t)$, felt by x_i towards x_j at the tth 4-message sequence is given by

$$l_{ij}(t) = t_3 - t_1 \qquad (16.2)$$

That is, the impasse level is the number of impasse 4-message sequences minus the number of resolution 4-message sequences. The value of l_{ij} is defined as zero if x_i and x_j have not interacted. Note that the number of holding sequences is assumed to have no effect on $l_{ij}(t)$.

The __hostility__ felt by x_i towards x_j, designated $C_{ij}(t)$, is assumed to be cumulative with[3]

---

[3] If the level of $l_{ij}(t)$ is already high from a previous conversation, one can expect very sharp and perhaps angry responses to what is an apparently innocuous remark. For a very low level of $l_{ij}(t)$, on the other hand, the response may be surprisingly mild. Furthermore, impasses developed toward an x_j may be transferred to another person, x_k, if x_i sees x_k as a member of the same population set as x_j. The hostility will not always be expressed at a level appropriate to $C_{ij}(t)$ because of fear of adverse reinforcements or because x_j is using strong language in order to provoke x_i. These types of reactions were observed during the campus confrontations in the U.S. during the late 1960's when a spokesman for the administration met with a group of "radicals." He would attempt to not express his true anger and they would use deliberately strong language in order to provoke him. If he became angry, he would give the "radicals" a new issue.

$$C_{ij}(t) = \sum_{v=0}^{v=1_{ij}(t)} v \qquad (16.3)$$

Example 16.1 If $1_{ij}(t) = 1$, $C_{ij}(t) = 1$. If $1_{ij}(t) = 2$, $C_{ij}(t) = 1 + 2 = 3$. If $1_{ij}(t) = 3$, $C_{ij}(t) = 1 + 2 + 3 = 6$. In general, if $1_{ij}(t) = P$, $C_{ij}(t) = P(P + 1)/2$.

The change in the impasse level from the tth to the $t + 1^{st}$ 4-message sequence is

$$\Delta 1_{ij}(t) = 1_{ij}(t+1) - 1_{ij}(t) \qquad (16.4)$$

where: $\Delta 1_{ij}(t) = \begin{cases} -1 & \text{if at t+1, there is a resolution 4-message sequence} \\ 0 & \text{if at t+1, there is a holding 4-message sequence} \\ +1 & \text{if at t+1, there is an impasse 4-message sequence} \end{cases}$

The change in the level of hostility due to $1_{ij}(t)$, designated $\Delta C_{ij}(t)$, is

$$\Delta C_{ij}(t) = C_{ij}(t+1) - C_{ij}(t) \qquad (16.5)$$

where: $\Delta C_{ij}(t) = \begin{cases} -1_{ij}(t) & \text{if at t+1, there is a resolution 4-message sequence} \\ 0 & \text{if at t+1, there is a holding 4-message sequence} \\ 1_{ij}(t+1) & \text{if at t+1, there is an impasse 4-message sequence} \end{cases}$

It should be noted that Equation (16.5) assumes hostility increases faster than it decreases.

Example 16.2 If $C_{ij}(t) = 6$, and there is an impasse sequence during t+1 $C_{ij}(t+1) = 10$ for an increase of 4. If $C_{ij}(t) = 6$, and there is a resolution

-411-

sequence during t+1, $C_{ij}(t+1) = 3$ for a decrease of 3.

The formulae for hostility and changes in hostility can be used to evaluate the hostility felt by x_i towards x_j at any point in time after the conflict trigger has been pulled. It is quite possible for there to be no hostility following the pulling of the conflict trigger. For example, either x_j or x_i can yield to the other. They can ignore the issue by going into a holding sequence. The impasse can begin at any point. The number of net impasses can increase or decrease depending upon the 4-message sequences. The initial conditions resulting from the pulling of the conflict trigger can result in all levels of hostility, depending upon the 4-message sequences that result. Hence, attempts to correlate initial conditions with values obtained from a questionnaire administered at the end of an experiment may result in low correlations because such a procedure implicitly ignores the active process of hostility formation. Figure 16.2 is a schematic diagram of the hostility formation process based upon the type and number of 4-message sequences. The diagram ends at the fourth 4-message sequence because of space limitations. It actually can go on much longer. Additionally, even though a resolution event has occurred that terminates one conflict, there is no reason why another cannot occur and start up this process all over again. I assume that the hostilities from different conflicts are additive. The numbers to the right of the fourth 4-message sequence are the values of $C_{ij}(4)$ of Equation (16.3). Clearly, hostility formation, as described here here, is an active process.

Refer To Figure 16.2 (Page 412)

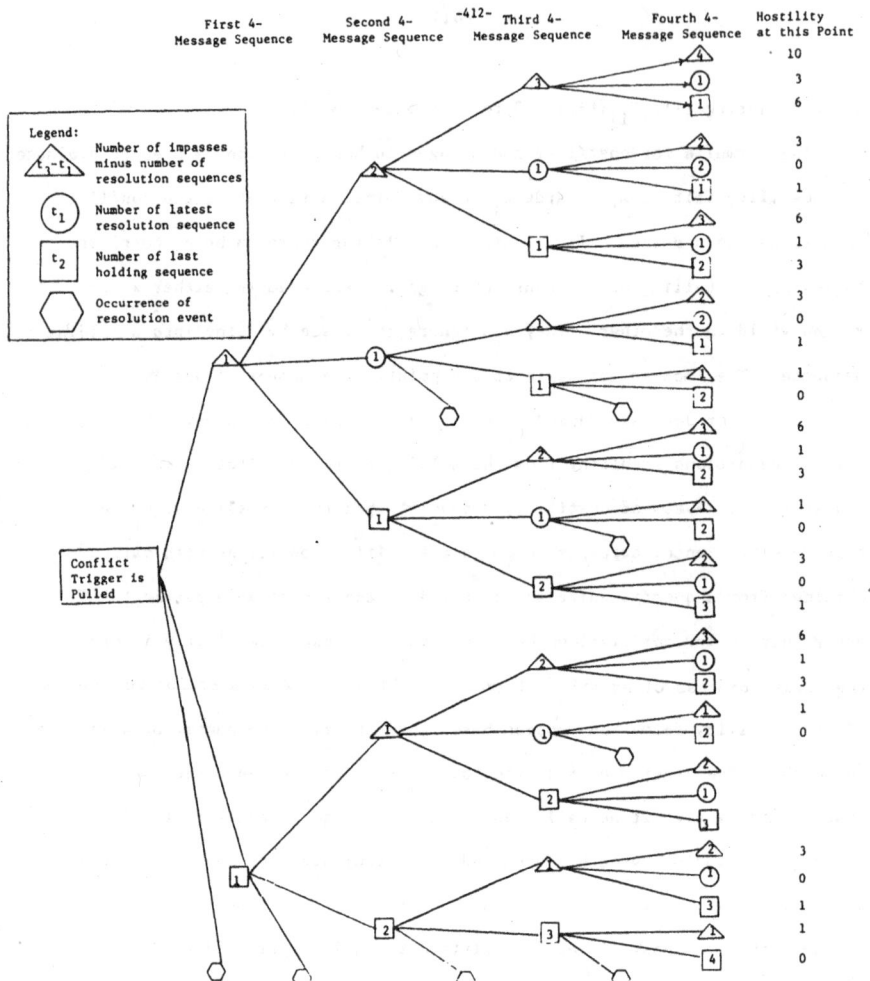

Figure 16.2 Hostility Formation Process Based Upon Type And Number of 4-Message Sequences

Properties of C:

(1) The hostility felt by x_i towards x_j is the same as that felt by x_j towards x_i if and only if the impasse level felt by x_i towards x_j is the same as that felt by x_j towards x_i:

$$C_{ij}(t) = C_{ji}(t) \text{ iff } l_{ij}(t) = l_{ji}(t)$$

In many cases $l_{ij}(t) \neq l_{ji}(t)$ and so $C_{ij}(t) \neq C_{ji}(t)$.

(2) The hostility felt by x_i towards the group $[C_i(t)]$ is the sum of the hostilities felt by x_i towards each of its members:

$$C_i(t) = \sum_{j=1}^{n} C_{ij}(t) \qquad (16.6)$$

(3) The hostility felt by the group towards itself $[C(t)]$ is the sum of the individual hostilities $C_i(t)$:

$$C(t) = \sum_{i=1}^{n} C_i(t) = \sum_{i,j=1}^{n} C_{ij}(t) \qquad (16.7)$$

(4) The hostility felt by x_i towards himself is undefined in terms of interaction pattern and is assumed to be zero:

$$C_{ii}(t) = 0 \qquad (16.8)$$

(5) The hostility felt by x_i towards x_j is determined by the number of

impasse sequences minus the number of resolution sequences:

$$C_{ij}(t) = \sum_{v=1}^{t_3-t} v \qquad (16.9)$$

(6) The hostility felt by x_i towards x_j is constant over time as long as a defined 4-message sequence does not occur over that time period.

(7) The hostility felt by x_i towards x_j is always non-negative.

The elementary nature of the expression for $C_{ij}(t)$ and its discrete values of 0, 1, 3, 6, 10, 15, 21, 28, ..., $\frac{(1_{ij}(t))(1_{ij}(t)+1)}{2}$ would seem too mechanical and too free of content to properly represent a measure of hostility. Although I have already indicated why one should not rely solely upon a code of the "severity" of remarks to estimate hostility, this type of evidence was employed to construct the hostility measure. Using data from the Mackenzie-Silcox experiment of Chapter 15 and other pilot groups, we seemed to find ascending levels of impasse-provoking issues for the A problems. We were struck by the simultaneous shift in issue and the change in use of English. The original issue of who should be leader became transformed into other issues and these in turn into others until the original task process-type issues were replaced by interpersonal disagreements expressed in an often offensive and threatening manner. While not every group took the same route up this ladder, its description is interesting because it is evidence of the active process nature of hostility formation. These levels are presented in Table 16.2. As the levels become more removed

from the original issue, hostility seems to increase. The apparent regularity
suggested that a simple measure whose values accumulated and progressively
worsened (such as Equation (16.3)) would be a useful surrogate for a code
for rank ordering severity of comment.

Refer To Table 16.2 (Page 416)

The progression from issue A to issue J in Table 16.2 is not inconsistent
with the behavioral constitution. Assuming that x_i and x_j are in conflict,
that both have to agree, and that either can preempt the other, it is reasonable
that the first issue should be "Who should be the leader" because that was
the initial source of the conflict trigger. Impasse on this level means
that neither can gain consensus except by giving in. The next thing to
attempt is the amending of issue A to issue B for the data phase or B_1 for
the answer phase. Impasses on both of these milestone structures could
lead to an attempt to create a tradeoff that bargained future structure
for current structure (C). Failing this, that issue could be amended to
one of attempted preemption that would prevent a solution from being formed (D).
This bargaining ploy could result in accusations of the intent of such a
threat, especially if another impasse occurred (E). Another impasse would
mean that the threat was accepted and probably countered. Being blocked
by another may lead to a search for a coalition that could bring pressure
to bear by expressing commitment against x_j's position (F). Impasse here
could lead to expressed suspicions about x_j's intention (G) to direct

TABLE 16.2 ASCENDING LEVELS OF IMPASSE-PROVOKING ISSUES

Issue	Description
A	Who should be leader
B	How should data be shared
B_1	Who should circulate answer
C	Bargaining future leadership change for present leadership by sender
D	Announcing use of sender's control (i.e., data) by sender
E	Accusation of receiver's intentions
F	Commitment against receiver's position[1]
G	Negative validation of receiver's intentions
H	Denouncement of receiver's arguments[2]
I	External controls affecting group
J	Negative validation of receiver's integrity

[1] At this level and beyond the language usually becomes regressive

[2] At about this level sender may offer to resolve impasses in the medieval manner of trial by combat.

denouncements of the arguments (H). Ascending further, one may reach issue I, where further noncooperation would result in threats. The final impasse level we observed is the denigration of the integrity of the other subject in most explicit language (J). Impasses that blocked attainment of consensus led to amendments. These led to more and more amendments of issue that eventually were not directly task related. Impasses occurring at the level of denouncement were usually accompanied by profanity (In one group, the quiet wife of a Baptist minister cursed the confederate).

The preceding discussion of one possible process for the formation of hostility suggests a new line of research with a wholly new strong inference tree. As one can see from Figure 16.3, this tree is almost all root and has only two puny leaves--one of which is dead. This sapling will be examined using the Mackenzie-Beynon data to compare the value of C_{ij} from Equation (16.3) with a subjective evaluation of hostility by the subjects. Because of the experimental design, the resolution event will occur early in the two-hour problem-solving period. The questionnaire is administered 1-1 1/2 hours later. The hypothesis is that there is a strong correlation between the two measures of conflict. This, of course, is a very weak validity measure that, while indicative of a relationship, should not be taken too seriously. Much more work and many upward and outward growths from the sapling of (16.3) are required.

Refer To Figure 16.3 (Page 418)

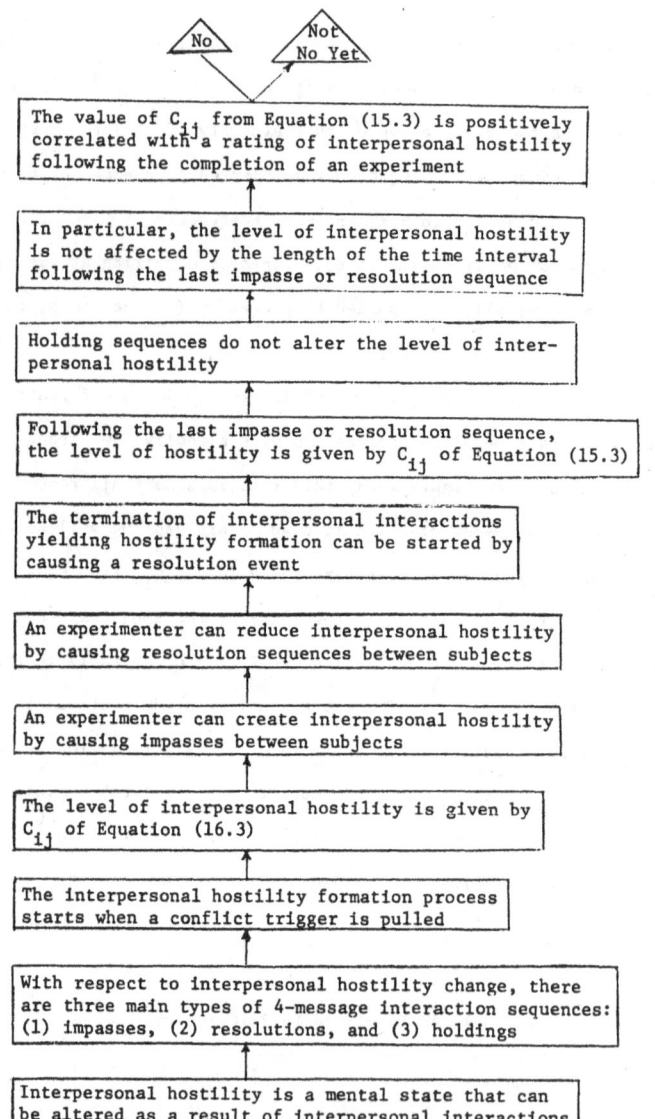

Figure 16.3 A Strong Inference Sapling for the Formation of Interpersonal Hostility

AXIOM OF CONSUMMATION EXPERIMENT

Method

Thirty-nine subjects were recruited from the undergraduate population of the University of Waterloo. Mr. Beynon and a graduate student in sociology (J. Hornick) were the two confederates in the thirteen groups of five members. Mr. Owen Ricker acted as the experimenter who gave out the instructions, data, passed messages, administered the questionnaire, and debriefed the subjects after the experiment.

The procedures for payment, the use of the A problems, the type of instructions, and the procedures leading to the adoption of Confederate #1 (Blue) as the hub of a wheel were identical to those of the Mackenzie-Silcox experiment reported in Chapter 15. Following the adoption of Confederate #1 as the hub, however, the procedures of this experiment differed from the earlier experiment.[4]

Once Confederate #1 was adopted as the leader, he completed every problem in the standard times established previously until he came to problem 10. On that problem he delayed 1 1/2 minutes longer than the standard of 1/2 minute. On problem 11 he increased the delay to nine minutes for a problem whose standard is three minutes. (The normal and delay times for these problems are listed in Appendix A of Chapter 15.) These delays caused the group to decentralize. We arranged for the adoption of Confederate #2 (Orange) to occur in problem 11. This began at three minutes after the beginning of problem 11 when Confederate #2 suggested that he become the "leader" for problem 12. The long delay in problem 11 allowed sufficient time for voting. On the fourth minute into problem 11,

---

[4]Extra messages were undertaken to insure that conflicts did not get out of hand. We ran 14 pilot groups to establish procedures and to train personnel. We were very cautious and were prepared to abort any group where, in our opinion, events were becoming too serious. We carefully debriefed each group and attempted to cause resolution sequences by explaining in detail, the role of the confederates. This extensive debriefing caused us to discard two groups who indicated that they knew about the experiment.

Confederate #1 solicited votes concerning the selection of Confederate #2 as the new hub. He did not compete with Confederate #2. Exactly seven minutes from the start of problem 11, Confederate #2 asked for confirmation of his being hub for problem 12. Both confederates kept a tally of the votes and confirmations. When each confederate had unanimity for the change, he notified the experimenter by submitting a pink adoption sheet. This way we knew that every subject had agreed to the change and that at this point Confederate #1 had been voted out and Confederate #2 had been voted in. To make sure, after both pink sheets were received by the experimenter, he notified both confederates that Confederate #2 had been adopted. At this time we were absolutely sure that Confederate #2 had been adopted as the hub for problem 12. By the axiom of consummation, Confederate #2 was the hub for problem 12.

At one minute into problem 12, Confederate #1 deliberately violated this axiom by broadcasting "I will not send my data to Orange. I am still the coordinator. Send data to me." This violation also pulled the conflict trigger because there were two persons with inconsistent positions and both appeared to want to win. The confederates then followed precisely the impasse-producing sequence of messages listed in Table 16.3 up to broadcast #6. After broadcast #6 the remaining ten of Table 16.3 could be sent with additional comments in order to facilitate interaction with the subjects. These last ten were to be cut short if sufficient interactions had occurred and/or if either of the confederates believed the overt hostility expressed in the messages received from the subjects was getting too high. The resolution event occurred at the end of problem 12 when Confederate #2 yielded to Confederate #1 by announcing this to the subjects. Confederate #1 was adopted for problem 12. Confederate #1 remained the hub until the two hours were up.

Refer To Table 16.3 (Page 422)

The control experiment was identical to the main experiment just described except for problems 11 and 12. Confederate #2 made no attempt to change the structure on problem 11 (the one with the nine minute delay). No voting occurred on problem 11. However, at the beginning of problem 12, Confederate #2 sent out a broadcast that he become the "leader," the same one used in the main experiment on problem 11. One minute after problem 12 began, Confederate #1 sent out broadcast #1 of Table 16.3 wherein he stated his intention to remain as leader. This message by Confederate #1 pulled the conflict trigger. Confederate #2 yielded to Confederate #1 at the end of problem 12 and Confederate #1 was adopted. The procedures following problem 12 were the same in both experiments.

Both experiments were ended at two hours of problem solving time, followed by a questionnaire given in Appendix A, and a debriefing after receiving payment. An effort to resolve hostility and to explain the experiment was made during the debriefing.

A comparison of the main experiment and the control is given in Table 16.4.

Refer To Table 16.4 (Page 423)

TABLE 16.3 THE IMPASSE-PRODUCING SEQUENCE USED BY BOTH CONFEDERATES

Message Broadcast Number	Time from the Conflict Trigger Event (min.)	Sender*	Message Content
1	0†	Blue	I will not send my data to Orange. I am still the coordinator. Send data to me.
2	2	Orange	If Blue won't send his data, I'm not sending him mine! He is too slow.
3	4	Orange	Blue refuses to send data. Ask him to cooperate so we can get going again.
4	6	Blue	Tell Orange to smarten up. Support me and I can get his data.
5	8	Orange	Blue is wasting our money. Straighten him out--data to Orange.
6	10	Blue	Please ask Orange to send to me. He is screwing us up.
7	11	Blue	Orange is power hungry! Get him to cooperate.
8	12	Orange	Please tell Blue to send data to me (Emphatically).
9	13	Blue	Send Orange a Fuddle Duddle message! He is fouling us up.
10	14	Orange	Blue is holding us up. Let him know he's through.
11	15	Blue	I still am coordinator. Tell Orange that please.
12	16	Orange	I hope Blue knows how to crawl! He has held us up for 15 minutes.
13	17	Blue	Orange has completely disrupted the group! Hang him.
14	18	Orange	Will you please get Blue's data for me. He's not going to leave here alive.
15	19	Blue	Orange is a Maniac! Get his data for me.
16	20	Orange	KILL BLUE!! I need his data.

*Each message was sent to every member. Blue is Confederate #1 and Orange is #2.
†The conflict trigger event.

TABLE 16.4 MANIPULATIONS ATTEMPTED UNDER EXPERIMENTAL AND CONTROL CONDITIONS

Manipulation Attempted	Main Experiment	Control	Comments
Confederate #1 Adopted as Original Leader of the Group	Yes	Yes	
Confederate #1 Controls Trial Time,			
(a) establishing a performance norm	Yes	Yes	
(b) maintaining the performance norm	Yes	Yes	
(c) achieving Task Competent Status	Yes	Yes	
(d) Establishing a Capacity for Change	Yes	Yes	
Confederate #2 Adopted as Leader to Replace Confederate #1	Yes[†]	No	[†]Difference Between Two Experiments
Confederate #1 Triggers Leadership Conflict with Confederate #2			[†]Resulting from difference between experiments
(a) Blocking Goal-directed Activity	Yes	Yes	
(b) Preventing Consummation of Adopted Structure	Yes[†]	No	
Confederate #1 Maintains Conflict with Confederate #2	Yes	Yes	
Impasse-generating Message Sequences used by Confederate #1 and Confederate #2,			
(a) Attempting to escalate the level of hostility in the group	Yes	Yes	
Confederate #2 Yields to Confederate #1 at end of Problem 12	Yes	Yes	
Confederate #1 Remains Hub of Wheel until End of Two-Hour Period	Yes	Yes	

There were five main experimental groups and five control experimental groups.

Results

Of the original thirteen groups, we use only ten to report results. Two groups were thrown out because some subjects indicated during the debriefing session following the experiment that they had had prior knowledge of the manipulations before they entered the experiment. A third group was eliminated because of a change in experimental conditions when unplanned errors occurred.

The major hypothesis contained in the strong inference tree of Figure 16.1 can be summarized as in Table 16.5.

Refer To Table 16.5 (Psge 425)

The data contained in Table 16.6 indicate that we are not yet able to reject these four hypotheses at this time. All four hypotheses are not incorrect in every case.

Refer To Table 16.6 (Page 426)

This experiment also provides additional confirmation that we should not yet reject the mapping function and voting process results of Figure

TABLE 16.5 MAJOR HYPOTHESES CONTAINED IN FIGURE 16.1 AS TIME TO FIRST IMPASSE

Experiment	Confederate Role	
	Blue (#1)	Orange (#2)
Main	t_1[a]	t_2
Control	t_3	t_4

[a]Using this notation for the different times to first impasse, the hypotheses are: (1) $t_3 > t_1$, (2) $t_2 > t_1$, (3) $t_3 > t_4$, and by direct deduction we also conclude that (4) $t_2 - t_1 > 0 > t_4 - t_3$.

TABLE 16.6 TIME TO FIRST IMPASSE FOR MACKENZIE-BEYNON EXPERIMENTS

Main Experiment			Control Experiment			Differences Relevant to the Hypotheses[a]			
	Time to First Impasse from the Conflict Trigger Event			Time to First Impasse from the Conflict Trigger Event		(1)[c]	(2)	(3)	(4)
Subject Number	Toward Blue (t_1)	Toward Orange (t_2)	Subject Number	Toward Blue (t_3)	Toward Orange (t_4)	t_3-t_1	t_2-t_1	t_4-t_3	$t_2-t_1 > 0 > t_4-t_3$
1	6	—[b]	16	15	4	>0	>0	<0	Yes
2	6	20	17	15	4				→
3	6	—	18	15	14				
4	6	12	19	10	4				
5	6	8	20	—	4				
6	6	12	21	—	12				
7	6	18	22	12	4				
8	6	14	23	—	4				
9	6	18	24	—	4				
10	6	16	25	—	14				
11	6	16	26	—	8				
12	6	18	27	—	4				
13	6	—	28	15	4				
14	6	—	29	10	4				
15	6	12	30	—	4				

[a] cf. Table 16.5, footnote a.
[b] no impasse occurred
[c] this difference applies to all possible combinations of the 15 observations for the experimental condition with the 15 observations for control condition

-427-

Of a total of 55 attempted manipulations, all 55 were achieved. These data are presented in Table 16.7.

Refer To Table 16.7 (Page 428)

The only empirical hypothesis in the strong inference "sapling" of Figure 16.3 for interpersonal hostility formation is the positive correlation between the measure of hostility of Equation (16.3) and the subjective evaluations from a questionnaire administered after the end of the two-hour problem-solving period. The questionnaire is reproduced in full as Appendix 16.1. Because the hostility measure of Equation (16.3) is new (and hence, probably incorrect) and because the subjective evaluation is highly dependent upon the manner in which these evaluations are made, the data bearing upon this hypothesis are presented in complete detail. The subject identification by experiment is tabulated in Table 16.8.

Refer To Table 16.8 (Page 429)

The ratings by each subject for both confederates for cooperation, contribution, hostility, and attraction are tabulated in Table 16.9.

Refer To Table 16.9 (Page 430)

These data are rearranged in Table 16.10 in which the means and

TABLE 16.7 NUMBER OF MANIPULATIONS ATTEMPTED AND ACHIEVED IN
MAIN AND CONTROL MACKENZIE-BEYNON EXPERIMENTS

Manipulation Attempted	Main Experiment		Control Experiment		Total No. of times	
	No. of times Attempted	Achieved	No. of times Attempted	Achieved	Attempted	Achieved
Blue Adopted as Original Leader of the Group	5	5	5	5	10	10
Blue Controls Trial Times	5	5	5	5	10	10
Orange Adopted as Leader to Replace Blue	5	5	0	0	5	5
Blue Triggers Leadership Conflict with Orange	5	5	5	5	10	10
Blue Maintains Conflict with Orange	5	5	5	5	10	10
Impasse-Generating Message Sequence Used by Blue and Orange	5	5	5	5	10	10
Total	30	30	25	25	55	55

TABLE 16.8   IDENTIFICATION OF SUBJECTS BY GROUP

Subject Number	Subject Color	Group † Number	Experiment Main	Experiment Control
1	green	816	x	
2	black	816	x	
3	red	816	x	
4	red	819		x
5	black	819		x
6	green	819		x
7	red	820	x	
8	black	820	x	
9	green	820	x	
10	black	822	x	
11	red	822	x	
12	green	822	x	
13	black	823		x
14	red	823		x
15	green	823		x
16	black	824	x	
17	red	824	x	
18	green	824	x	
19	green*	825		x
20	red	825		x
21	black	826		x
22	green	826		x
23	red	826		x
24	red	827		x
25	green	827		x
26	black	827		x

†Group Number 815 was run under the experimental condition, but was not administered the questionnaire. There were 14 pilot groups used in developing the experimental procedures and the questionnaire of Appendix 16.1.
*Black did not completely fill in the questionnaire.

TABLE 16.9 RESPONSES TO POST-EXPERIMENT QUESTIONNAIRE

Subject Number	Subjective Evaluation of Question			
	(a) Cooperation	(b) Contribution	(c) Hostility	(d) Attraction
1	0[a]	4	9	0
	1[b]	4	8	1
2	1	7[*]	8	1
	2	–	9	1
3	5	8	9	0
	2	2	9	0
4	3	8	8	1
	2	1	9	0
5	7	8	7	5
	2	4	9	2
6	7	8	6	2
	5	7	8	2
7	2	9	5	1
	0	3	9	1
8	4	6	4	0
	7	6	2	0
9	2	8	9	1
	4	8	8	2
10	5	9	5	5
	4	6	7	5
11	2	6	4	1
	2	1	1	1
12	9	9	4	4
	4	9	4	4
13	5	8	8	2
	1	6	8	1
14	8	9	4	4
	1	1	6	0
15	5	9	2	4
	4	5	3	4
16	0	6	5	0
	4	4	0	1
17	0	0	9	0
	7	7	0	4
18	0	2	9	0
	8	7	3	4
19	6	8	0	6
	1	4	7	1
20	3	5	6	5
	2	2	4	0
21	2	6	1	4
	0	1	7	0
22	9	6	1	4
	0	2	2	0
23	8	8	0	0
	0	0	3	1
24	6	9	3	9
	3	7	9	0
25	2	7	7	0
	1	1	7	1
26	7	8	3	5
	3	5	6	3

[*] Did not answer

[a] The upper number is the evaluation of confederate #1 (Blue).

[b] The lower number is the evaluation of confederate #2 (Orange).

standard deviations about each mean are reported. These data indicate that the confederate for whom the first impasse occurred is perceived to be less cooperative, less attractive, and having made less contribution. In addition, the subjects felt more hostile towards the confederate for whom the first impasse occurred. The average hostility felt towards the confederate to whom the first impasse occurred is the same for each experiment ($t = -.57$ $p > .20$). The average hostility felt towards the other confederate is about the same for both conditions ($t = 1.0$, $p > .15$).

Refer To Table 16.10 (Page 432)

The measured levels of hostility using Equation (16.3) are strongly correlated with the subject's hostility from the questionnaire. The value of the coefficient of multiple determination (R^2) was 0.88. A second regression was run for these two sets of data. The questionnaire only goes up to 9. A subject who is furious cannot rate above 9. Hence, there is a cutoff and the level of hostility from the questionnaire cannot rise above 9 even though the value of $C_{ij}(t)$ can be very large due to many impasses. The second regression averaged the value of $C_{ij}(t)$ for each value on the 10-point questionnaire scale. The relationship between these two values of hostility are shown graphically in Figure 16.4.

Refer To Figure 16.4 (Page 433)

TABLE 16.10 MEANS AND STANDARD DEVIATIONS FOR SUBJECT RATINGS OF BOTH CONFEDERATES ON FOUR TRAITS FOR BOTH MACKENZIE-BEYNON EXPERIMENTS

Experiment	Confederate Number One				Confederate Number Two			
	Cooperation	Contribution	Hostility	Attraction	Cooperation	Contribution	Hostility	Attraction
Main	2.5 (2.8)	6.2 (2.9)	6.7 (2.3)	1.1 (1.7)	3.8 (2.5)	5.4 (2.6)	5.0 (3.7)	2.0 (1.8)
Control	5.6 (2.3)	7.6 (1.2)	3.9 (3.0)	3.9 (2.5)	1.8 (1.5)	3.3 (2.4)	6.4 (2.4)	1.1 (1.3)
t-Statistic for Difference in Means of Both Experiments	-3.02	-1.65	2.60	-3.19	2.35	1.88	-1.03	1.52
Significance of t-statistics	$p < .005$	$p < .10$	$p < .01$	$p < .005$	$p < .025$	$p < .05$	$p > .20$	$p < .10$
Degrees of Freedom	21	14	23	22	17	21	18	19

[a] Standard deviation about the mean

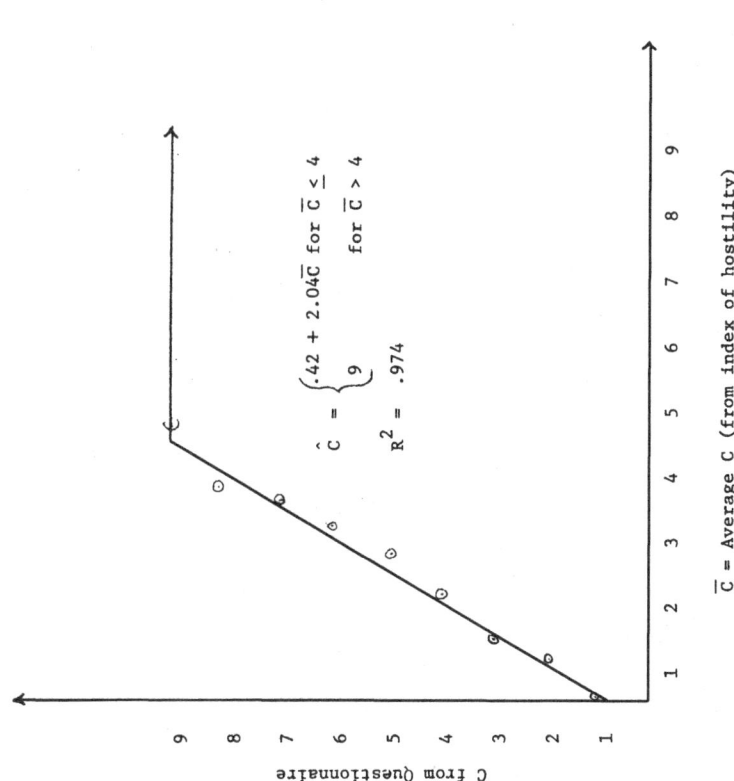

FIGURE 16.4 RELATIONSHIP BETWEEN AVERAGE VALUE OF EQUATION 16.3 FOR EACH VALUE ON THE 10-POINT QUESTIONNAIRE SCALE

The data for Figure 16.4 are tabulated in Table 16.11. The cutoff imposed by the 10-point questionnaire scale results in a regression equation that is linear up to average values of $C_{ij}(t)$, $\bar{C}$, of 4.0 and is a constant value of nine for average values of $C_{ij}(t)$, $\bar{C}$, greater than 4.0. That is,

$$\hat{C} = \begin{cases} .42 + 2.04\bar{C} & \text{for } \bar{C} \leq 4 \\ 9.0 & \text{for } \bar{C} > 4 \end{cases} \qquad (16.10)$$

The t-statistic of the significance of the coefficient of $\bar{C}$ is 40.3. The value of the coefficient of multiple determination is .974 and the correlation between $\bar{C}$ and $\hat{C}$ is .987. Consequently, we cannot yet reject the hypothesis that there is a positive correlation between the values for Equation (16.3) and the values from the questionnaire.

Refer To Table 16.11 (Page 435)

It would appear that the model for the formation of interpersonal hostility is not an altogether poor predictor for the rated level of interpersonal hostility from the questionnaire, at least for the conditions of these experiments. However, the coefficient of 2.04 in Equation (16.10) suggests that the value of interpersonal hostility from Equation (16.3) may be too low by a factor of two. Another possibility is that it is incorrect to use a 10-point scale. Perhaps a 5-point scale would reduce the coefficient of 2.04 closer to unity.

Finally, there is a negative correlation between the measured level of hostility and the subjects' perceived attraction towards the confederate. The value is -.47 (p < .001). This result and the result for hostility is not inconsistent with the findings of Byrne (1969) if one assumes that

TABLE 16.11 DATA FOR THE REGRESSION EQUATION 16.10

Number of Observations	$\bar{C}$	$\hat{C}$	Predicted $\hat{C}$	Residual
2	0.00	0	.42	-.42
5	0.20	1	.83	.17
5	0.80	2	2.05	.05
6	1.17	3	2.66	.34
6	1.83	4	4.09	-.09
3	2.67	5	5.72	-.72
5	3.00	6	6.54	-.54
6	3.33	7	7.15	-.15
7	3.43	8	7.35	+.64
12	4.50	9	9.00	.00

hostility is an attitude and that the violation of norms is evidence of different attitudes.

The failure to produce counterexamples of the theory using the manipulations in this experiment, the 100 percent correct predictions of times to first impasse, and the supporting questionnaire results are consistent with a conclusion that the axiom of consummation may indeed be an accepted norm. Although this is only a partial validation of the behavioral constitution, I don't think that we can yet reject it as a possible calculus of interpersonal influences with respect to structural change. The surprisingly high correlation between the hostility measures of Equation (16.3) and the values for a questionnaire administered approximately 1-1 1/2 hours later should be viewed with caution. This is only one check of its possible validity.

APPENDIX 16.1 THE QUESTIONNAIRE ADMINISTERED AFTER THE END OF THE EXPERIMENT FOR THE MACKENZIE-BEYNON EXPERIMENT

This experiment has been conducted to provide data for analyzing group organizational processes. It is necessary to obtain your personal feelings in order to further the understanding of these processes. In this questionnaire you are asked to relate these feelings as accurately as possible.

The first five (5) questions ask for personality profiles of the members with whom you interacted. (Please ignore profile on your own colour.) You are asked to relate your feelings about each member on the following issues:

a) Did this member co-operate in reaching the decisions made by the group?
b) Did this member make a beneficial contribution toward organizing the group?
c) What degree of hostility do you feel towards this member?
d) What degree of attraction do you feel towards this member?

1. Please complete the personality profile for: BLACK
   (circle one number in each row.)

ISSUE	NOT AT ALL		A LITTLE		A MODERATE AMOUNT		A GREAT AMOUNT		A VERY GREAT AMOUNT	
a) Co-operation	0	1	2	3	4	5	6	7	8	9
b) Contribution	0	1	2	3	4	5	6	7	8	9
c) Hostility	0	1	2	3	4	5	6	7	8	9
d) Attraction	0	1	2	3	4	5	6	7	8	9

2. Please complete the personality profile for: BLUE
   (circle one number in each row.)

ISSUE	NOT AT ALL		A LITTLE		A MODERATE AMOUNT		A GREAT AMOUNT		A VERY GREAT AMOUNT	
a) Co-operation	0	1	2	3	4	5	6	7	8	9
b) Contribution	0	1	2	3	4	5	6	7	8	9
c) Hostility	0	1	2	3	4	5	6	7	8	9
d) Attraction	0	1	2	3	4	5	6	7	8	9

3. Please complete the personality profile for: GREEN
   (circle one number in each row.)

ISSUE	NOT AT ALL		A LITTLE		A MODERATE AMOUNT		A GREAT AMOUNT		A VERY GREAT AMOUNT	
a) Co-operation	0	1	2	3	4	5	6	7	8	9
b) Contribution	0	1	2	3	4	5	6	7	8	9
c) Hostility	0	1	2	3	4	5	6	7	8	9
d) Attraction	0	1	2	3	4	5	6	7	8	9

4. Please complete the personality profile for: ORANGE
(circle one number in each row.)

ISSUE	NOT AT ALL		A LITTLE		A MODERATE AMOUNT		A GREAT AMOUNT		A VERY GREAT AMOUNT	
a) Co-operation	0	1	2	3	4	5	6	7	8	9
b) Contribution	0	1	2	3	4	5	6	7	8	9
c) Hostility	0	1	2	3	4	5	6	7	8	9
d) Attraction	0	1	2	3	4	5	6	7	8	9

5. Please complete the personality profile for: RED
(circle one number in each row.)

ISSUE	NOT AT ALL		A LITTLE		A MODERATE AMOUNT		A GREAT AMOUNT		A VERY GREAT AMOUNT	
a) Co-operation	0	1	2	3	4	5	6	7	8	9
b) Contribution	0	1	2	3	4	5	6	7	8	9
c) Hostility	0	1	2	3	4	5	6	7	8	9
d) Attraction	0	1	2	3	4	5	6	7	8	9

The remaining three (3) questions ask for your personal feelings about the experiment.

6. To what degree did the 20¢ per trial, and the two hour time limit encourage the group to work as quickly as possible? (circle appropriate number).

NOT AT ALL		A LITTLE		A MODERATE AMOUNT		A GREAT AMOUNT		A VERY GREAT AMOUNT	
0	1	2	3	4	5	6	7	8	9

7. Give your feelings about the task. (circle one number in each row)

	NONE		A LITTLE		A MODERATE AMOUNT		A GREAT AMOUNT		A VERY GREAT AMOUNT	
Difficulty	0	1	2	3	4	5	6	7	8	9
Interest	0	1	2	3	4	5	6	7	8	9
Satisfaction	0	1	2	3	4	5	6	7	8	9

8. If you have any additional comments about the experiment, we would appreciate them.

CHAPTER 17

SUMMARIZING THE EMPIRICAL WORK

There are seven separate strong inference trees in Chapters 12-16 that represent the progress of investigation in the theory of group structures presented in Chapters 1-10. In addition, there is a slender sapling for a measurement of interpersonal hostility in Chapter 16. The purpose of this chapter is to make a summary of the empirical work reported in Chapters 12-16 in terms of a strong inference tree for the whole theory.

The strong inference tree for the whole will differ somewhat from a simple tree of trees from each of the different experimental chapters. The strong inference trees in each chapter are heuristic devices that guide the choice of experiment, structure the analysis, and connect the analyses to the experiments in a chapter. In retrospect some of the movements up a tree are not essential to the logic of the whole theory. Some of these are merely checks and some of these are special cases that are redundant when considering the totality. Some branches of one tree may be logically placed in different parts of a summary tree now that we are free of the necessity of temporal placement. The summary strong inference tree facilitates scrutiny of possible errors in logic and provides a framework from which to make further attempts to refute the theory.

The summary strong inference tree covering so many investigations is quite large. Figure 17.1 is a schematic representation of the summary strong inference tree. The horizontal lines represent a step in an argument, a theoretical point, a hypothesis, the statement of an experimental condition, or an assumption that bridges the theory with the type of empirical measurement.

A vertical or slanted line with an arrowhead represents the relationships between the horizontal lines. The triangle at the top of any branch represents the outcome of "not no, yet." Circled portions of the tree of Figure 17.1 beginning with A and ending with H are schematic summaries of the trees in Figures 17.2-17.9 respectively. The entire tree stands upon the base of definitions, conventions, measures, models, and procedures described in Chapters 1-10. Figure 17.1 is a schematic of a strong inference tree that assumes the correctness of the underlying conceptual base. Figure 17.1 is an attempt to summarize the major relationships and empirical results of substantive implications of the theory.

Refer To Figure 17.1 (Page 441)

The base of Figure 17.1 is Part A. Part A represents some basic theoretical laws of the theory. There are no empirical results in Part A. Part B represents a strong inference tree for the channel-renting experiments reported in Chapter 13. Part C represents effects of problem complexity and difficulty of organizing on choice of structure and some voting behavior. Part C represents some results reported in Chapters 12 and 13. Part D, building out of Part C, presents the effects of experience and prior unanimity on the relative preference of the all-channel and the wheel. Part D comes from Chapter 14. Part E extends Part A by representing the dependence of learning upon multiple structures and the stability of hierarchies. Part E is from Chapter 12. The adoption processes and the mapping function

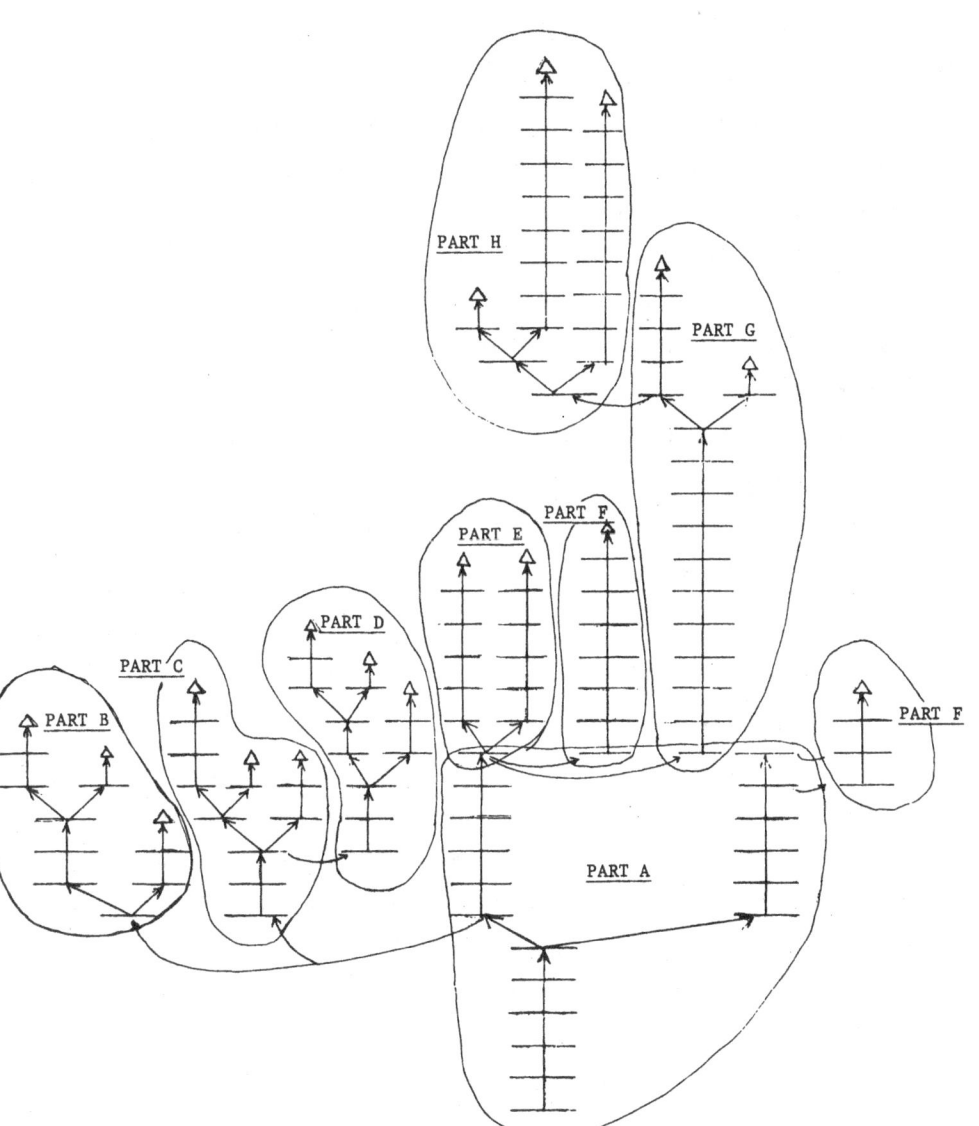

FIGURE 17.1 Schematic Strong Inference Tree Summarizing the Experiments in Chapters 12-16. The Circled Portions of This Tree Represent More Detailed Trees in Figures 17.2-17.9.

were applied to some special problems in structural change. These are summarized in Part F. The left hand branch of Part A is from Chapters 12 and 15 and the right hand branch comes from Chapters 12, 14-16. Part G represents the reasoning for employing confederates in an experimental group to control group structures for A problems. Part G comes from Chapter 15. Finally, Part H represents the experiments used in Chapter 16 to study the validity of one of the axioms of the behavioral constitution of Chapter 7. Part H depends upon the outcomes of Part G, which in turn depend upon Part A.

The position in a strong inference tree is very fragile when it is 32 steps away from the base. The sequences of assumptions, laws, hypotheses, results, etc. required to reach the extremities offer great hope that we can reject the theory.

PART A   BASIC THEORETICAL LAWS

The underlying definitions, conventions, measures, models, and implications are summarized in Chapter 10. We begin Part A by assuming the correctness of these prior decisions. Figure 17.2 focuses upon Part A of Figure 17.1. We begin by assuming that the task processes of a group can be represented by the reaching of a sequence of milestones. Using these concepts from Chapter 4, we can also assume that there is a structure corresponding to each group milestone and that the structures can be different for different milestones. This conjecture is demonstrated repeatedly by the data. If the structures can differ for different milestones, what is the basic idea for determining what structures occur? One answer is that a group structure represents a need-satisfying interaction pattern. This assumption grows out of the observation that each group member has absolute control over the usage rate of the half-channels from himself to others in the group. Absolute control means merely that, if one wants to badly enough, one can always use a half-channel. Absolute control is not a guarantee of satisfaction. In fact, actually using a channel may be very painful or extremely costly. Structures describe the pattern of interaction among these absolute controllers. Structures that are stable represent a form of consensus whereby each member explicitly or implicitly agrees to use or not use his half-channels. Once he decides to use some and not others, his usage will not change until circumstances change. This consensus presumably is due to no one having good reason to alter the structure by exercising his absolute controls. In the sense that there is an opportunity cost associated with not using other available structures, the unanimity implies the existence of a need-satisfying pattern of interaction. It is not assumed that each person is happy with the structure. It is only assumed that, comparing the alternatives and considering the costs associated with change, he is more satisfied with the structure than with its alternatives.

Refer To Figure 17.2 (Page 444)

If, then, a group structure represents a need-satisfying interaction pattern, we need some conceptualiziation of a preference function describing the relative net benefits for using or not using a given half-channel.

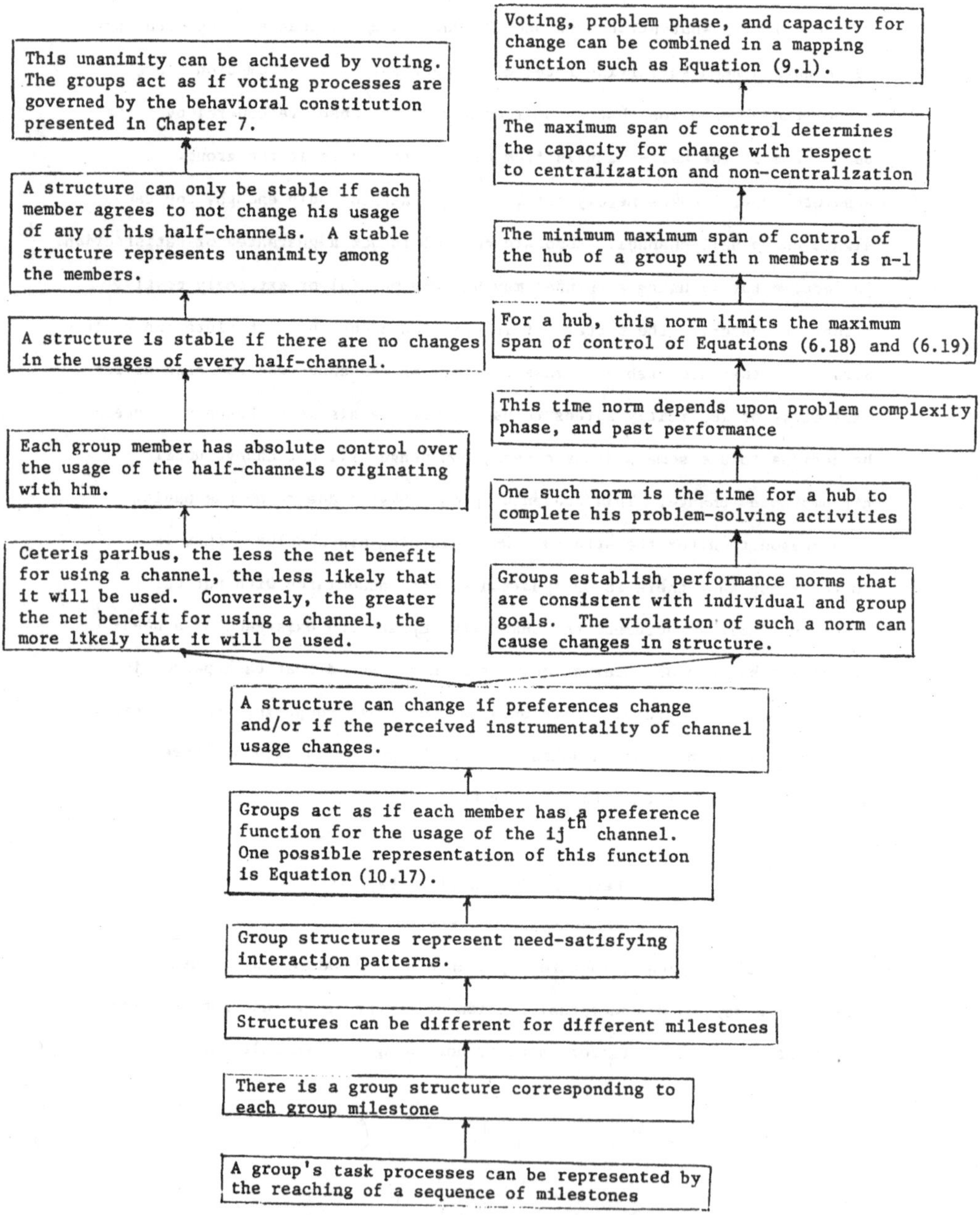

-444-

```
┌─────────────────────────────────────┐         ┌─────────────────────────────────────┐
│ This unanimity can be achieved by   │         │ Voting, problem phase, and capacity │
│ voting. The groups act as if voting │         │ for change can be combined in a     │
│ processes are governed by the       │         │ mapping function such as Equation   │
│ behavioral constitution presented   │         │ (9.1).                              │
│ in Chapter 7.                       │         └─────────────────────────────────────┘
└─────────────────────────────────────┘                          ▲
                 ▲                                               │
┌─────────────────────────────────────┐         ┌─────────────────────────────────────┐
│ A structure can only be stable if   │         │ The maximum span of control         │
│ each member agrees to not change    │         │ determines the capacity for change  │
│ his usage of any of his half-       │         │ with respect to centralization and  │
│ channels. A stable structure        │         │ non-centralization                  │
│ represents unanimity among the      │         └─────────────────────────────────────┘
│ members.                            │                          ▲
└─────────────────────────────────────┘         ┌─────────────────────────────────────┐
                 ▲                              │ The minimum maximum span of control │
┌─────────────────────────────────────┐         │ of the hub of a group with n        │
│ A structure is stable if there are  │         │ members is n-1                      │
│ no changes in the usages of every   │         └─────────────────────────────────────┘
│ half-channel.                       │                          ▲
└─────────────────────────────────────┘         ┌─────────────────────────────────────┐
                 ▲                              │ For a hub, this norm limits the     │
┌─────────────────────────────────────┐         │ maximum span of control of          │
│ Each group member has absolute      │         │ Equations (6.18) and (6.19).        │
│ control over the usage of the       │         └─────────────────────────────────────┘
│ half-channels originating with him. │                          ▲
└─────────────────────────────────────┘         ┌─────────────────────────────────────┐
                 ▲                              │ This time norm depends upon problem │
┌─────────────────────────────────────┐         │ complexity phase, and past          │
│ Ceteris paribus, the less the net   │         │ performance                         │
│ benefit for using a channel, the    │         └─────────────────────────────────────┘
│ less likely that it will be used.   │                          ▲
│ Conversely, the greater the net     │         ┌─────────────────────────────────────┐
│ benefit for using a channel, the    │         │ One such norm is the time for a hub │
│ more likely that it will be used.   │         │ to complete his problem-solving     │
└─────────────────────────────────────┘         │ activities                          │
                                                └─────────────────────────────────────┘
                                                                 ▲
                                                ┌─────────────────────────────────────┐
                                                │ Groups establish performance norms  │
                                                │ that are consistent with individual │
                                                │ and group goals. The violation of   │
                                                │ such a norm can cause changes in    │
                                                │ structure.                          │
                                                └─────────────────────────────────────┘
```

A structure can change if preferences change and/or if the perceived instrumentality of channel usage changes.

Groups act as if each member has a preference function for the usage of the ij^{th} channel. One possible representation of this function is Equation (10.17).

Group structures represent need-satisfying interaction patterns.

Structures can be different for different milestones

There is a group structure corresponding to each group milestone

A group's task processes can be represented by the reaching of a sequence of milestones

FIGURE 17.2   PART A OF THE STRONG INFERENCE TREE OF FIGURE 17.1. PART A REPRESENTS BASIC THEORETICAL LAWS

I assume that the groups _act_ _as_ _if_ each member has a preference function for the usage of the ij^{th} channel. Although I do not know the form of such a function, one possible representation is given by Equation (10.17). Or, for person x_i, there is a function U_{iij} for the usages of the ij^{th} channel, where

$$U_{iij} = a_{oij} + \sum_{k} r_{kij} B_k \qquad (17.1)$$

where all factors affecting U_{iij} are called benefits (benefits are measured by the magnitude of the factor). The benefits are designated by B_k, and the evaluation of the net benefit of B_k by x_i for the ij^{th} channel is r_{kij}. If B_k has net positive benefits, $r_{kij} > 0$. If B_k has net negative benefits, $r_{kij} < 0$. If B_k does not affect U_{iij}, then $r_{kij} = 0$. The parameter a_{oij} is the net benefit to x_i if all of the B_k are zero. The parameter a_{oij} is assumed to depend, in part, upon the overall structure (whether it is a wheel, an all-channel, etc.). A structure can change if preferences change and or if the perceived instrumentality of channel usage changes.

According to the preference function of Equation (17.1), _ceteris paribus_, the less the net benefit for using a channel, the less likely that it will be used. Conversely, the greater the net benefit for using a channel, the more likely that it will be used. Recalling the earlier discussion about absolute control, a structure is said to be stable if there are no changes in the usages of every half-channel. However, a structure can only be stable if each member (an absolute controller) agrees not to change the usage of any of his half-channels. There can be limited changes in the evaluation of U_{iij} that result in no change in usage. A stable structure represents unanimity among the members. It is assumed that this unanimity can be achieved by voting. I assume that groups *act* *as* *if* voting processes are governed by the behavioral constitution presented in Chapter 7.

Following up the right hand side of Figure 17.2, I argue that groups establish performance norms that are consistent with individual and group goals. The violation of such a norm can cause changes in structure because it either alters the preference or changes the instrumentality for usage of a given half-channel. One performance norm is the time the group allows a hub to complete his problem-solving activities. This time norm depends upon problem complexity, problem phase, and past performance. For a hub, this norm limits the maximum span of control of Equations (6.18) and (6.19). In a wheel group the minimum maximum span of control of n members is n-1. The maximum span of control determines the capacity for change with respect to centralization and decentralization. If the group of n members is centralized about a hub whose maximum span of control is less than n-1, or if a non-centralized group contains a member whose maximum span of control is greater than or equal to n-1, there is said to be a capacity for change. Voting, problem phase, and capacity for change can be combined in a mapping function such as Equation (9.1). One such mapping function predicts the state of a group structure as being centralized or non-centralized on problem T+1, given information available during problem T.

PART B CHANNEL RENTING EXPERIMENTS

Part B grows from a lower limb of the left hand side branch of Part A. In Part B I examine implications that follow simply from the preference function of Equation (17.1). Part B represents the channel-renting experiments of Chapter 13. The right hand side refers to the Berkeley channel-renting experiments and the left hand side to the Carnegie-Mellon channel-renting experiments.

Refer To Figure 17.3 (Page 448)

The basic idea behind each of these experiments is to hold a_{oij} constant and vary the magnitude of B_k in Equation (17.1). Then, depending upon both the magnitude of B_k and a presumed sign of the r_{kij}, I should be able to experimentally control increases or decreases in the relative preferences for certain channels. Each group was given four free channels that formed a wheel. There were six additional channels that were available for renting. I used different rental costs for different groups.

In the Berkeley experiment, the channel cost was in money. The amount of money is B_1. Money is considered a commodity. Hence, the larger B_1, the less the value of U_{iij}, if ij refers to one of the channels available for rental. This assumes that $r_{1ij} < 0$. It follows then that it will be rented. Furthermore, the money channel-renting curve is downward sloping. This conclusion was not yet able to be rejected with the data from the Berkeley Experiment.

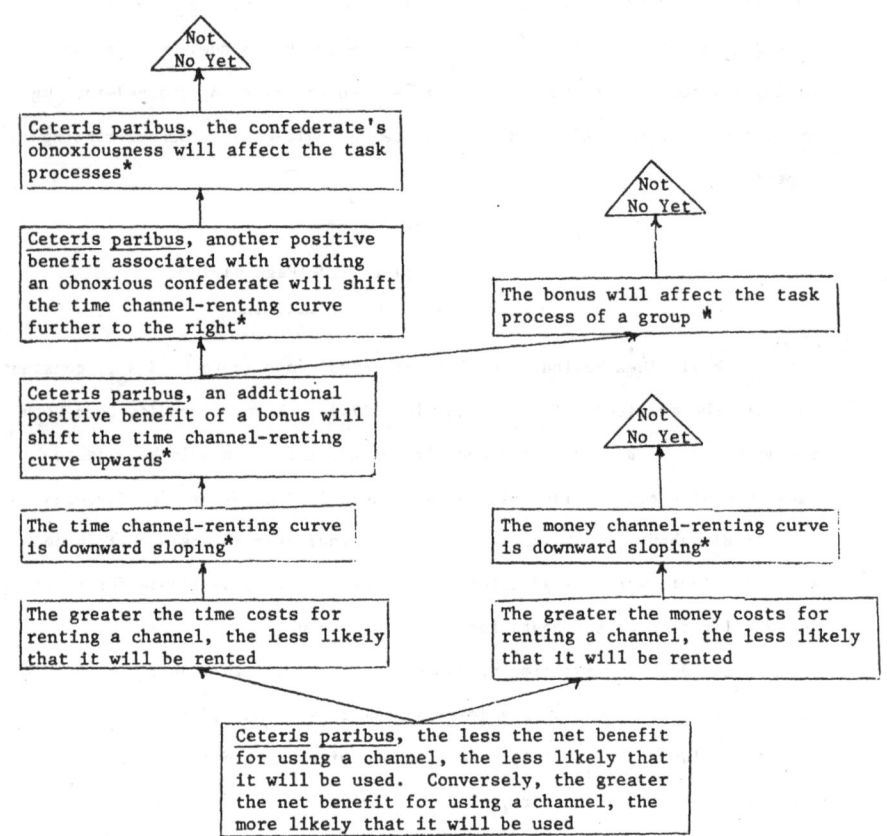

FIGURE 17.3   PART B OF THE STRONG INFERENCE TREE OF FIGURE 17.1.   PART B REPRESENTS THE CHANNEL-RENTING EXPERIMENTS OF CHAPTER 13.

*Items with asterisk have been demonstrated empirically.

The left hand branch of Figure 17.3 goes a few steps further by employing psychology credit time as a form of payment. The Carnegie-Mellon Experiments began by using psychology credit time (Students were required to spend five hours as experimental subjects in order to pass an undergraduate psychology course). Let B_2 be channel-rental cost. Like r_{1ij}, r_{2ij} is also < 0. In this experiment $B_1=0$. Following an argument that is parallel to that for the Berkeley channel-renting experiment, I expected the time channel-renting curve to be downward sloping. It was. The next step was to keep B_2 and add a new benefit, B_3, for which $r_{3ij} > 0$. The new benefit would partially offset B_2 and should cause an upward shift to the time channel-renting curve. The benefit, B_3, was a 30-minute bonus awarded by the experimenter to the first subject to submit a correct answer to a B problem. This bonus was awarded for all four problems. The time channel-renting curve does appear to shift upwards. This means that subjects tended to rent more channels at the same channel-renting price when there was a bonus. Subsequent analyses also showed that the bonus had an effect on the task processes of a group.

The next step was to superimpose yet another benefit, B_4, upon B_2 and B_3 for which $r_{4ij} > 0$. This should shift the time channel-renting curve further to the right. The benefit, B_4, was created by using an "obnoxious" confederate as hub of the wheel formed by the free channels. I argued that group members would be willing to rent channels in order to bypass this confederate. There is no reason to reject the hypothesis that the time channel-renting curve shifted further to the right. In addition, the confederate's obnoxiousness affected the task processes.

PART C   PROBLEM COMPLEXITY, DIFFICULTY OF ORGANIZING, AND SOME VOTING BEHAVIOR

Part C represents some effects due to organizing and problem complexity on the preference for structures and voting. Part C grows out of the same limb of Part A as Part B. Part C begins with the proposition that, <u>ceteris paribus</u>, the less the net benefit for using a channel, the less likely it will be used and vice versa. This proposition is interpreted by assuming that there is a cost associated with choosing structures and task processes. It then follows that, <u>ceteris paribus</u>, the more complex a problem and the more decisions required to organize, the greater the costs associated with selecting structures and task processes. Several consequences flow from this latter proposition, the one referring to voting as the right hand side branch, and the one referring to structural preferences as the left hand side branch of Figure 17.4.

Refer To Figure 17.4 (Page 451)

The greater the complexity of a problem, the greater the costs associated with selecting structures and task processes. One should then expect that, <u>ceteris paribus</u>, the greater the complexity, the less the incidence of explicit voting on structures. Because the A problems are less complex than the B problems, it follows that there should be more voting for A problems than for B problems. This, indeed, proved to be the case.

The left hand branch attempts to examine the relative preference of certain structures to others in terms of the number of decisions required

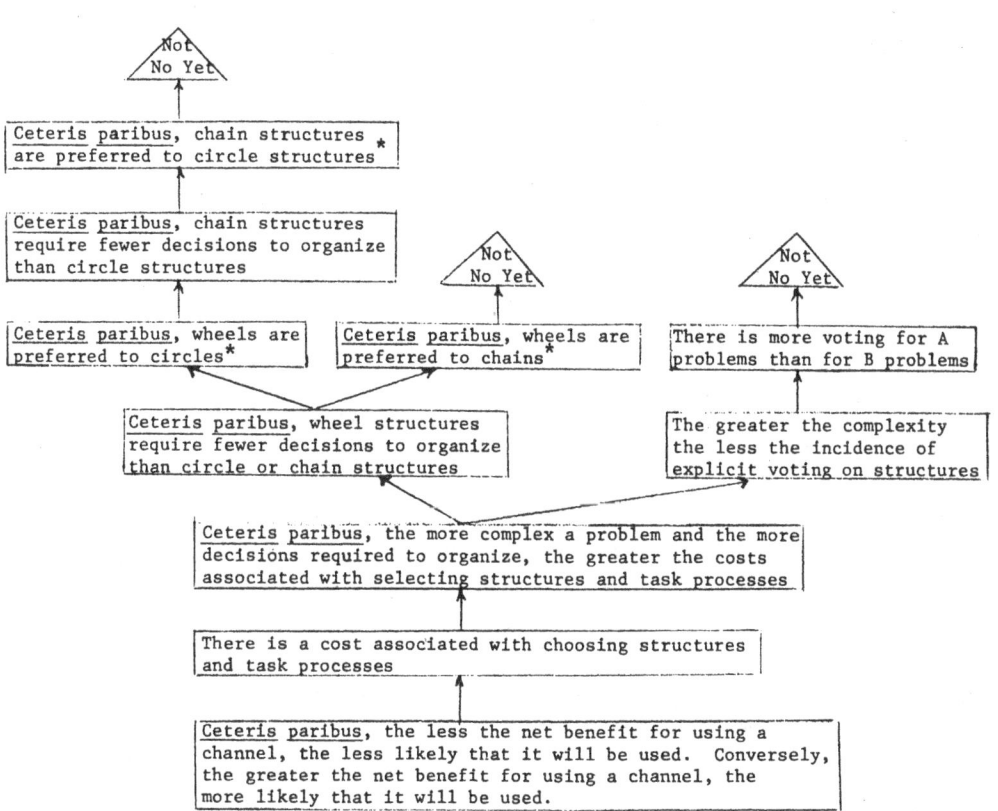

FIGURE 17.4 PART C OF THE STRONG INFERENCE TREE OF FIGURE 17.1. PART C REPRESENTS EFFECTS DUE TO COMPLEXITY OF PROBLEM AND ORGANIZING

to organize. On the average and <u>ceteris paribus</u>, wheel structures require fewer decisions to organize than circle or chain structures. <u>Ceteris paribus</u>, then, wheels are preferred to chains and wheels are preferred to circles. This preference difference, using Equation (17.1), is probably due to greater value of a_{oij} for the channels to be rented in the less preferred structures, the argument being that if the structure is satisfactory as given, the value of extra channels is lower than if the given structure is less satisfying.

In order to compare wheels, chains, and circles, we use some of the experiments reported in Chapter 14. A wheel is preferred to a chain if the money channel-renting curve for the wheel is to the left of that for the chain. A simple argument establishes this proposition: a money channel-renting curve that is to the right of another means that subjects are more willing to rent channels at the same price. The renting of a channel to alter a given structure is one sign that the given structure is not satisfactory. The more channels that subjects rent, the less satisfactory the structure under the given conditions. Hence, if at every channel-renting cost, subjects, on the average, rent more channels for one given structure than for another, the second given structure is preferred to the first. A wheel, then, is preferred to a chain if the money channel-renting curve for the wheel is to the left of that for a chain. The Waterloo Lutheran Chain experiment established that the wheel is preferred to the chain, at least for the B problems.

By the same argument, a wheel is preferred to a circle if the money channel-renting curve for the wheel is to the left of that for the circle. The hypothesis that a wheel is preferred to a circle was not refuted by the data from the Waterloo Circle Groups reported in Chapter 14. Continuing the argument, _ceteris paribus_ and on the average, chain structures require fewer decisions to organize than circle structures. If the aforementioned arguments are correct, one should expect that chain structures are therefore preferred to circle structures, _ceteris paribus_. This means that the money channel-renting curve for the chain is to the left of that for the circle. This was the case in the limited experiments reported in Chapter 14.

PART D   STRUCTURAL PREFERENCE

Part D represents effects of experience and prior unanimity on the preference of the wheel structure to the all-channel. The all-channel is generally considered preferable to the wheel in communications network experiment literature. The experiments reported in Chapter 12 have already demonstrated that this is not the case for A problems, and those reported in Chapter 14 have shown that this is not generally true even for B problems. In Part D we examine some circumstances in which it is true. Part D grows from the top limb of the "trunk" of Part C. Part D summarizes the Waterloo Lutheran Experiments of H. Wedderburn. The strong inference tree for Part D is given in Figure 17.5.

Refer To Figure 17.5 (Page 454)

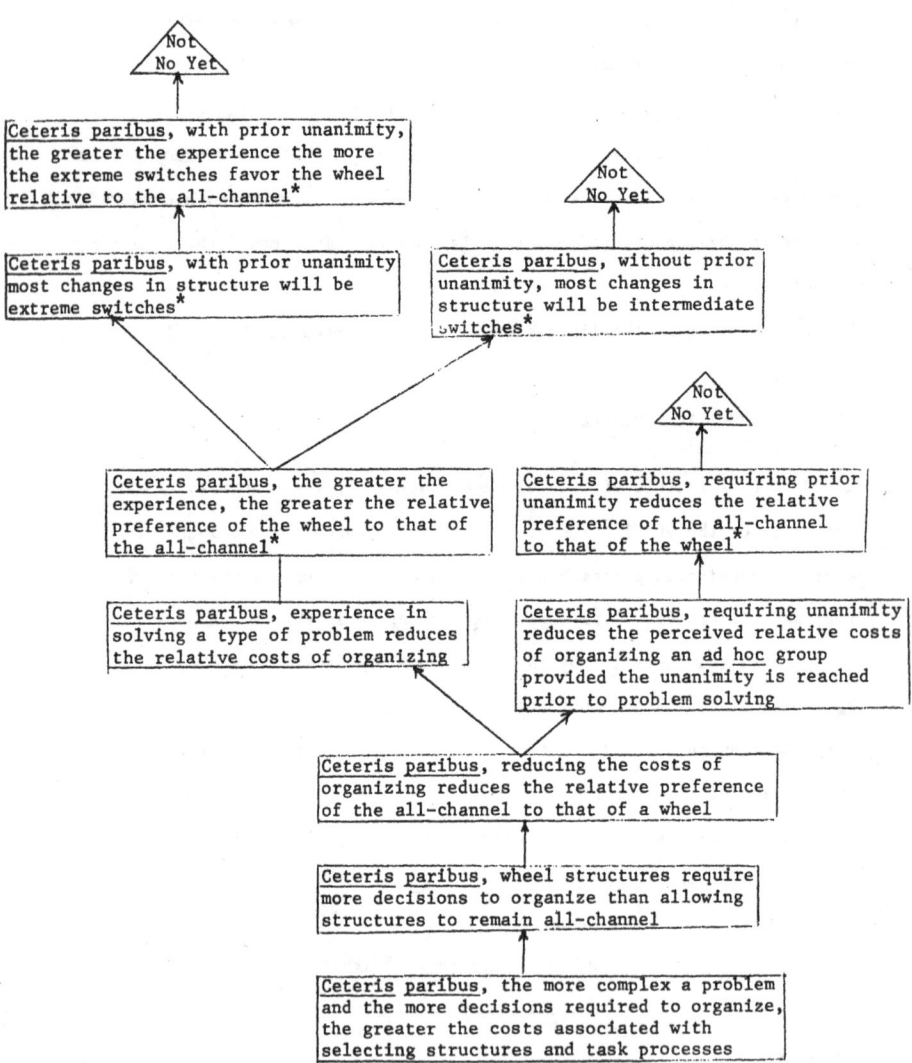

FIGURE 17.5 PART D OF THE STRONG INFERENCE TREE OF FIGURE 17.1. PART D REPRESENTS EFFECTS OF EXPERIENCE AND PRIOR UNANIMITY ON THE PREFERENCE OF THE WHEEL RELATIVE TO THAT OF THE ALL-CHANNEL

The Waterloo Lutheran Experiment was a channel-renting experiment with two new variations: (1) the subjects were given any four out of ten channels and not just those to a pre-selected hub; (2) the subjects were allowed to communicate freely about the choice of structure to be used on the upcoming problem. In fact, the subjects were required to have unanimity before being allowed to even begin the problem. These two variations are believed to result in a reduction in the cost of organizing a group. The first variation does not put any member "on the spot," since the group could form five different wheels or a chain group. If the group wants a wheel, they can choose their own hub without having one pre-assigned by the experimenter. The second variation, that requires unanimity before beginning a problem, is the more important variation. This variation allows us to know that the choice of structure is correct. Previously it took only one member to bind the entire group to an all-channel. There was always doubt that the aggregation of individual choices was the same as the group choice. The second variation allows us to check that possibility.

Logically, the choice was not between the wheel and the all-channel. The wheel required effort to organize. The methods of channel-renting reduced the problems of structures to that of selecting only one to begin with instead of the more or less continuous modifications taking place across the various milestones in the Faucheux-Mackenzie experiment. The method of channel-renting reduced the need to consider choice of structure in terms of an influence calculus such as that of Chapter 7. However, even this reduced problem could be avoided by becoming an all-channel.

The all-channel is an amiable device for avoiding having to make a decision. It limited no one and raised no problems. Consequently, in these experiments the choice between a wheel and an all-channel is probably the choice between a wheel and making no decision.

The requirement of prior unanimity reduces the costs of organizing a wheel because the hub can be picked without having to consider task processes and the many structures for the different group milestones. Once a group decides that a leader is useful, they have only to elect one, a process well engrained in North American students. The alternative of "no leader yet" results in an all-channel. The prior unanimity procedure separates the problems of organizing for solving problems from those of actually solving problems.

The argument on the right hand side branch of Figure 17.5 follows from the proposition that reducing the costs of organizing reduces the relative preference of the all-channel to the wheel, ceteris paribus. The aforegoing argument, that the procedure of attaining prior unanimity reduces the costs of organizing, implies that, ceteris paribus, with this procedure the costs of organizing to form a wheel have been decreased. Hence, ceteris paribus, requiring prior unanimity reduces the relative preference of the all-channel to the wheel. Data in Chapter 14 strongly suggest that we ought not yet reject this hypothesis.

The left hand branch examines implications in this experiment due to the effects of experience with the B problems. Arguing that because, ceteris paribus, experience in solving a type of problem reduces the relative costs of organizing to solve it, the greater the experience, the greater the relative preference of the wheel to the all-channel. Data in Chapter 14 do not reject this yet. The next steps up the left hand side branch concern the nature of changes in the types of structure agreed upon by the procedure of prior unanimity. From the earlier Waterloo Lutheran Chain Experiment one would argue that without prior unanimity most changes in structure will be intermediate switches. They are. However, <u>ceteris paribus</u>, with the prior unanimity most of the switches are extreme switches. Finally, <u>ceteris paribus</u>, with prior unanimity, the greater the experience, the more the extreme switches favor the wheel to the all-channel.

Chapter 14 is a very important chapter because it offers a method for analyzing group preferences for wheels and all-channels. The conclusions are that, with experienced groups and if it is not too difficult to organize, the wheel seems to be preferred to the all-channel, at least for A and B problems. This conclusion may upset many who have been preaching the "obvious" preference of the all-channel. Re-examining the actual data from the earlier communications network studies would, in my opinion, lead a fair-minded person to conclude that these data from earlier studies have been illogically extended from the domain of fact whence they were derived. He might also conclude that these data, based as they are, for the most part, on static concepts of structure, constitute a data bank of information about structure that does not, in fact, have much to do with it.

PART E   LEARNING, MULTIPLE STRUCTURES, AND STABILITY OF HIERARCHIES

Part E examines the dependence of learning upon multiple structures and tendencies to form hierarchies. Chapter 12 provides most of the data for this portion of the overall strong inference tree. The relationships between degree of hierarchy and measures of effectiveness and efficiency were consistent across all of the studies. While this tree does partially validate both the learning curve analysis of Chapter 10 and the index of the degree of hierarchy of Chapter 5, the main point is the implied validation of a concept of group structure that includes the possibility of different substructures. The main point in Part E, then, is the apparent usefulness of a multivariate concept of a group structure, an idea introduced in Chapter 2.

Part E grows directly out of the top limb of the left hand side branch of Part A. Any structure that is stable represents an unanimity and this unanimity can be achieved by voting. In particular, if there is more than one group milestone there can be more than one group structure. And while consistency may be sought after, there is no *a priori* reason why the structure for one milestone is necessarily the same as that for another for any given time period. The main propositions are that (1) the preference for channel usage may vary for different milestones, and (2) structures may differ for different milestones. Because the second one depends upon the first, it is the one used to construct the main branches of the strong inference tree for Part E, as illustrated in Figure 17.6.

Refer To Figure 17.6 (Page 459)

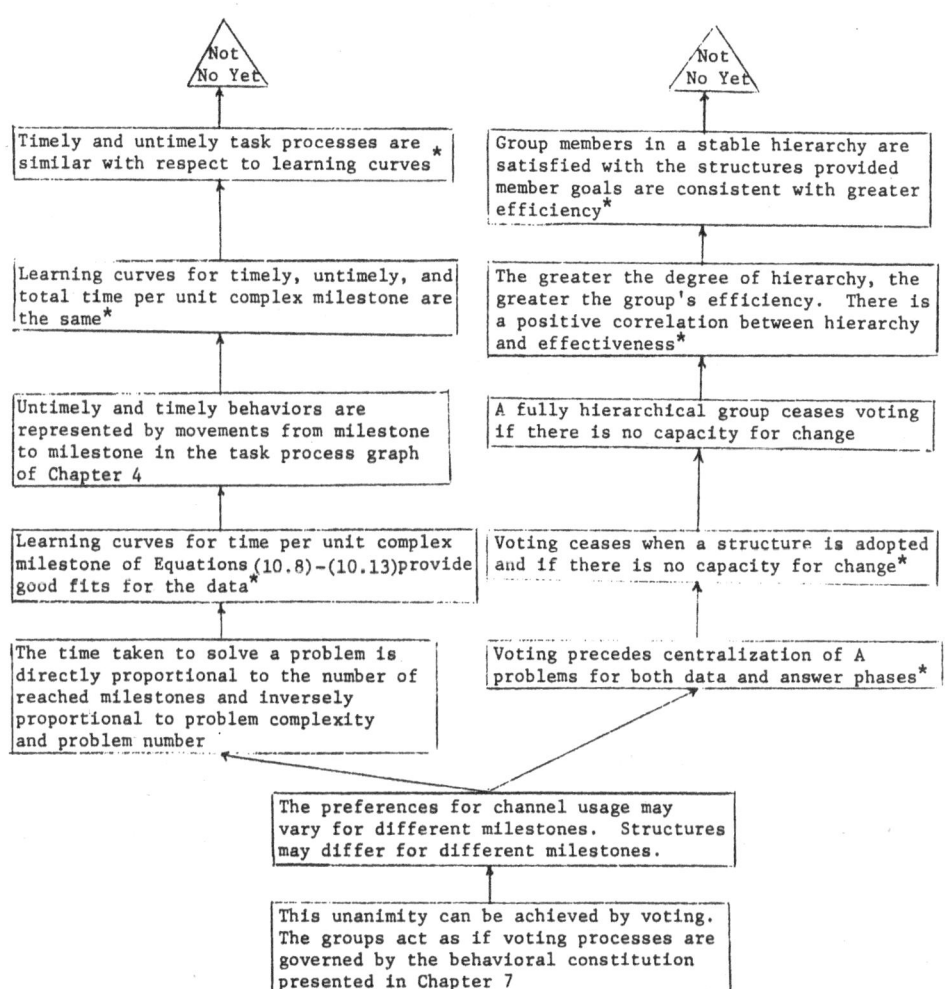

FIGURE 17.6 PART E OF THE STRONG INFERENCE TREE OF FIGURE 17.1. PART E REPRESENTS DEPENDENCE OF LEARNING UPON MULTIPLE STRUCTURE AND THE STABILITY OF HIERARCHIES

The right hand branch of Figure 17.6 begins with the hypothesis that voting precedes centralization for A problems for both the data and the answer phases. Data do not yet reject this conclusion. For both phases voting ceases when a structure is adopted and if there is no capacity for change. This conclusion is not yet rejected by the data from Chapter 12. In the special case that the adopted structure is a wheel, if it is also a full hierarchy, voting ceases if there is no capacity for change. Most groups, however, fail to have 1.0 degree of hierarchy. These groups do act as if they were attempting to become a full hierarchy. For example, the greater the needs of a group to seek efficiency, the stronger this tendency. The data from the many experiments show that (1) the greater the degree of hierarchy, the greater the efficiency of the group; (2) there are negative correlation coefficients between the degree of hierarchy and measures of ineffectiveness such as time per problem, number of errors per problem, and number of messages to solve a problem. The data from the Faucheux-Mackenzie experiment reported in Chapter 12 also suggest that if member goals are consistent with greater efficiency, group members in a stable hierarchy are satisfied with the structures.

The left hand side branch of Figure 17.6 is less a potpourri of results. It represents the attempt to use the possibility of different milestones reached in the solution of a problem to model learning curves for B problems from the 8-hour Berkeley experiments. The major proposition is that the time taken to solve a problem is directly proportional to the number of reached milestones *and* inversely proportional to both problem complexity and problem number. From this proposition we define the quantity in the learning curve as time per unit complex milestone. This variable, say $Z(T)$, is hypothesized to be related to problem number T by Equations (17.2) and (17.3)

$$Z(T) = Ae^{-bT} + B \qquad (17.2)$$

where $b > 0$, and B is given by

$$B = \lim_{T \to \infty} E(Z(T)) \qquad (17.3)$$

Equations like (17.2) were fit to the data for (1) timely time per unit complex milestone, (2) untimely time per unit complex milestone, and (3) total time per unit complex milestone. Data reported in Chapter 12 indicate that the hypothesis that equations like (17.2) for these three types of time provide good fits for the actual data and should not yet be rejected.

The theory of the task process analysis of Chapter 4 argued that group problem-solving can be conceived of as if the groups move sequentially from group milestone to group milestone. The group milestone's identity is determined by the type of problem. All possible transitions from milestone to milestone are represented in a task process graph. There is a logical sequence to the milestones. Milestones reached in logical order are timely milestones. Milestones reached out of timely order are untimely milestones. Because both timely and untimely milestones are defined on the same set, the time taken to reach one should not depend upon whether it was timely or untimely. Hence, learning curves for timely, untimely, and total time per unit complex milestone should be about the same. This is the case for the 8-hour Berkeley

B problem data. It follows that timely and untimely task processes are similar with respect to learning curves. The main effect of errors is the prolongation of problem-solving time by forcing a group to reach more milestones. There does not appear to be a qualitative difference between timely and untimely problem-solving processes, at least with respect to the learning of appropriate problem-solving processes.

PART F   ADOPTION PROCESSES AND MAPPING FUNCTIONS

Part F represents a strong inference tree for the adoption processes of Chapter 8 and the mapping function of Chapter 9. Part F is in two parts. The left hand side branch concerns adoption processes and grows out of the top limb of the left hand side branch of Part A. Data for this part of the total strong inference tree comes from Chapters 12 and 15. The right hand side branch of Part F grows out of the upper limbs of the right hand side branch of Part A. Data for this portion of Part F comes from Chapters 12, 15, and 16. The strong inference tree for Part F is given in Figure 17.7.

Refer To Figure 17.7 (Page 463)

The analysis of change and the derivation of change models in Chapter 8 suggested that the adoption of a structure can be modeled by a diffusion of innovation model of the type:

$$\frac{dn_t}{dt} = k_1 \, n_t (N - n_t) \tag{17.4}$$

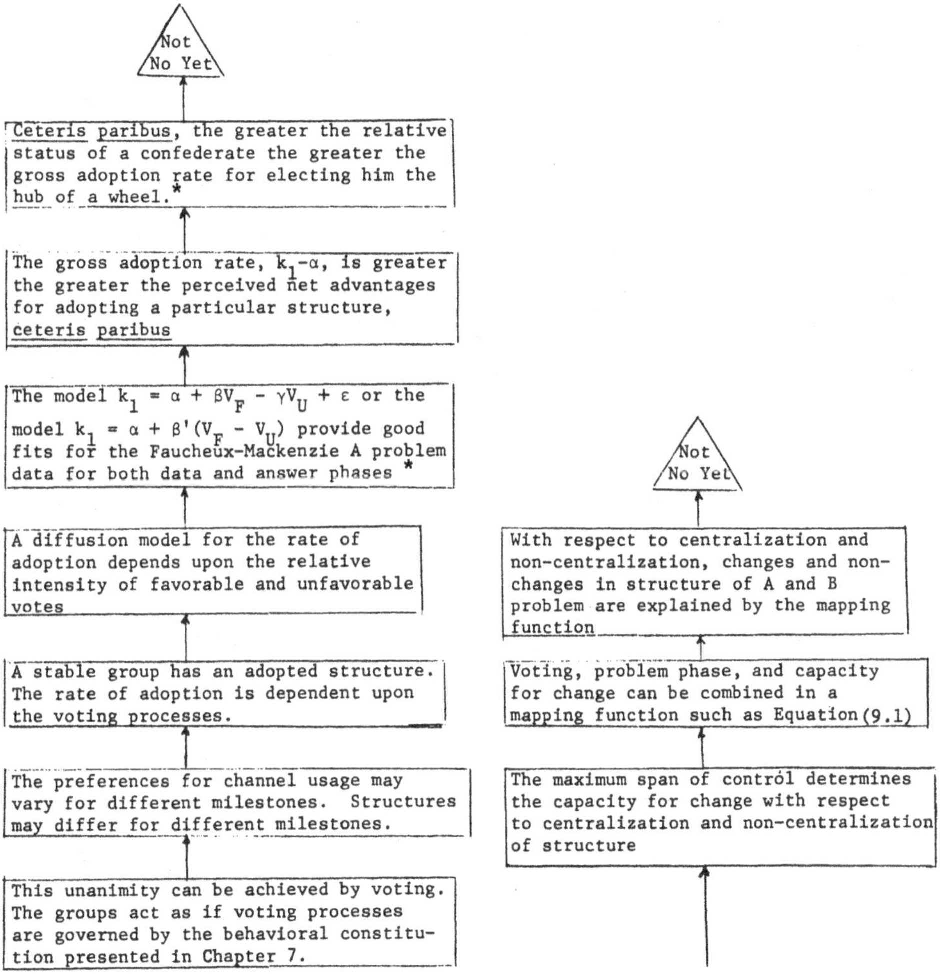

/Not\
/No Yet\

Ceteris paribus, the greater the relative status of a confederate the greater the gross adoption rate for electing him the hub of a wheel.*

The gross adoption rate, $k_1-\alpha$, is greater the greater the perceived net advantages for adopting a particular structure, ceteris paribus

The model $k_1 = \alpha + \beta V_F - \gamma V_U + \varepsilon$ or the model $k_1 = \alpha + \beta'(V_F - V_U)$ provide good fits for the Faucheux-Mackenzie A problem data for both data and answer phases *

/Not\
/No Yet\

A diffusion model for the rate of adoption depends upon the relative intensity of favorable and unfavorable votes

With respect to centralization and non-centralization, changes and non-changes in structure of A and B problem are explained by the mapping function

A stable group has an adopted structure. The rate of adoption is dependent upon the voting processes.

Voting, problem phase, and capacity for change can be combined in a mapping function such as Equation (9.1)

The preferences for channel usage may vary for different milestones. Structures may differ for different milestones.

The maximum span of control determines the capacity for change with respect to centralization and non-centralization of structure

This unanimity can be achieved by voting. The groups act as if voting processes are governed by the behavioral constitution presented in Chapter 7.

FIGURE 17.7 PART F OF THE STRONG INFERENCE TREE OF FIGURE 17.1. PART F REPRESENTS ADOPTION PROCESSES AND THE MAPPING FUNCTION ANALYSIS FOR STRUCTURAL CHANGE.

where $t=0$, $n_t=n_o$, and n_t is the number of half-channels whose state has been adopted (a half-channel may be adopted opened or closed), N is the total number of half-channels, n_o is the number of half-channels already adopted when the structural adoption process begins. The parameter k_1 is related to the effectiveness of influence efforts to obtain more adoptions.

The parameter k_1 is the important parameter needed to explain the rate of adoption. The solution to (17.4) when transformed by calculating the $\log_e \frac{n_t}{N-n_t}$ is linear with time and the slope of the curve is k_1. The arguments for the basic Equation (17.4) are given in Chapters 8, 10, 12, and 15. The arguments for the determinants of k_1 are also made in these earlier chapters. While these arguments need not be repeated here, we can summarize the main conclusions: (1) The rate of adoption is dependent upon the voting processes, (2) the value of k_1 depends upon the relative intensity of favorable and unfavorable votes (cf. Chapter 7), (3) the models

$$k_1 = \alpha + \beta V_F - \gamma V_U + \epsilon \qquad (17.5)$$

and

$$k_1 = \alpha + \beta'(V_F - V_U) + \epsilon \qquad (17.6)$$

both provide good fits for A problem data for both data-sharing and answer phases. The terms V_F and V_U are the intensities of favorable and unfavorable votes respectively for the adopted structure. While an analysis of the Faucheux-Mackenzie data does result in an excellent fit for the answer phase, the fit on the data sharing phase is not as good. Overall, while I would not yet reject this hypothesis, it certainly is high on my list of problems to be investigated.

The constant term α can be subtracted from both sides of Equations (17.5) and (17.6) to form $k_1-\alpha$ on the left hand side of each equation. The term $k_1-\alpha$ is called the gross adoption rate. An experiment in Chapter 15 used the gross adoption model to examine the effects of status differentials on gross adoption rates. Arguing that, *ceteris paribus*, $k_1-\alpha$ is greater the greater perceived net advantages for adopting a particular structure, it is assumed that groups will perceive a net advantage to adopting a high status confederate as the hub of a wheel to solve A problems. Consequently, I conclude that the greater the relative status of a confederate, *ceteris paribus*, the greater the gross adoption rate for electing him the hub of a wheel for solving A problems. Using the data from subject ratings of status rather than the experimenter's attempted manipulation of status, the data from the Mackenzie-Silcox experiment do not yet reject this conclusion.

The right hand side of Part F examines the mapping function of Equation (9.1). The mapping function is a function that predicts the centralization or the non-centralization of groups solving Faucheux-Mackenzie problems on problem T+1, given information available on problem T. The mapping function made 122/128 correct predictions for the Faucheux-Mackenzie experiments and made correct predictions in every case in Chapters 15 and 16. The small number of incorrect predictions were due to an even smaller number of "stray" messages. The predictions came through but the timing was a little off. Strictly speaking, despite many hundreds of correct predictions, there are a few counterexamples and so one must reject the mapping function. It looks promising but it needs more work to make it right. For the time being, I tentatively accept the mapping function as not being rejected yet, at least for the conditions of my experiments.

A reader might say that the evidence to accept it is very strong. One could make the case that these data came from intelligent human beings who are free to write whatever they feel, whenever they feel it, etc. As a result one should expect a few stray messages now and then, especially from "irrepressible" college students. He might even raise arguments that there exists something unarticulated like "randomness" that "explains" these discrepancies. These and other arguments are certainly admissible. There are moments when I tend towards accepting such rationalizations. I am mainly persuaded that there are errors in measurement in recording votes, electoral outcomes, and maximum span of control calculations and that, perhaps, these errors in measurement may account for the discrepancies. The admission of other types of "error" to save a hypothesis is surely clear evidence of a deficiency in the theory. Otherwise "these other factors" should be in the theory. The previous omission of "these other factors" suggests that one should patch up the theory to allow their inclusion. Unless the theory is presented as an approximation with clearly stated restrictions, the employment of ad hoc and post hoc hypotheses to explain away troublesome anomalies seems to be an unsound mode of deductive-nomological explanation.

PART G   CONTROLLING GROUP STRUCTURES

Part G grows out of the top branches of the strong inference tree of Part A. Part G represents the reasoning for employing confederates to control group structures for A problems. There are no new ideas in Part G. Part G represents an attempt to take the known (at this time) theory of

structural change and apply it to _cause_ changes in structure. The making
of _ex ante_ predictions based on the theory and then the actual causing of
the predicted changes is one method for validating the mapping function and
voting process models. The data for Part G comes from the Mackenzie-Silcox
experiment reported in Chapter 15. The strong inference tree for Part G
is given in Figure 17.8.

Refer To Figure 17.8 (Page 468)

Figure 17.8 presents a strong inference tree for Part G whose base
is the possibility of different structures for different milestones. This
possibility must be considered when making _ex ante_ predictions for structural
change. Fortunately, for A problems, if the data phase structure is centralized the structure of the answer phase is dependent and will also be
centralized. The converse is not true. The next step up in Figure 16.8
is recalling that a structure is adopted where there is unanimity _and_
there are no contrary preemptions. This reminds us that one can prevent
adoption by preventing unanimity or casting preemptions that are contrary
to the desires of others in the group.

We know from Chapter 12 that, _ceteris paribus_, groups solving A problems
form wheel groups and hierarchies. If in such a group I placed two confederates, I should be able to cause the preemption of any non-confederate
who was elected as the hub of the wheel. The preemption can be accomplished
merely by instructing the confederate to withhold data from this non-confederate.

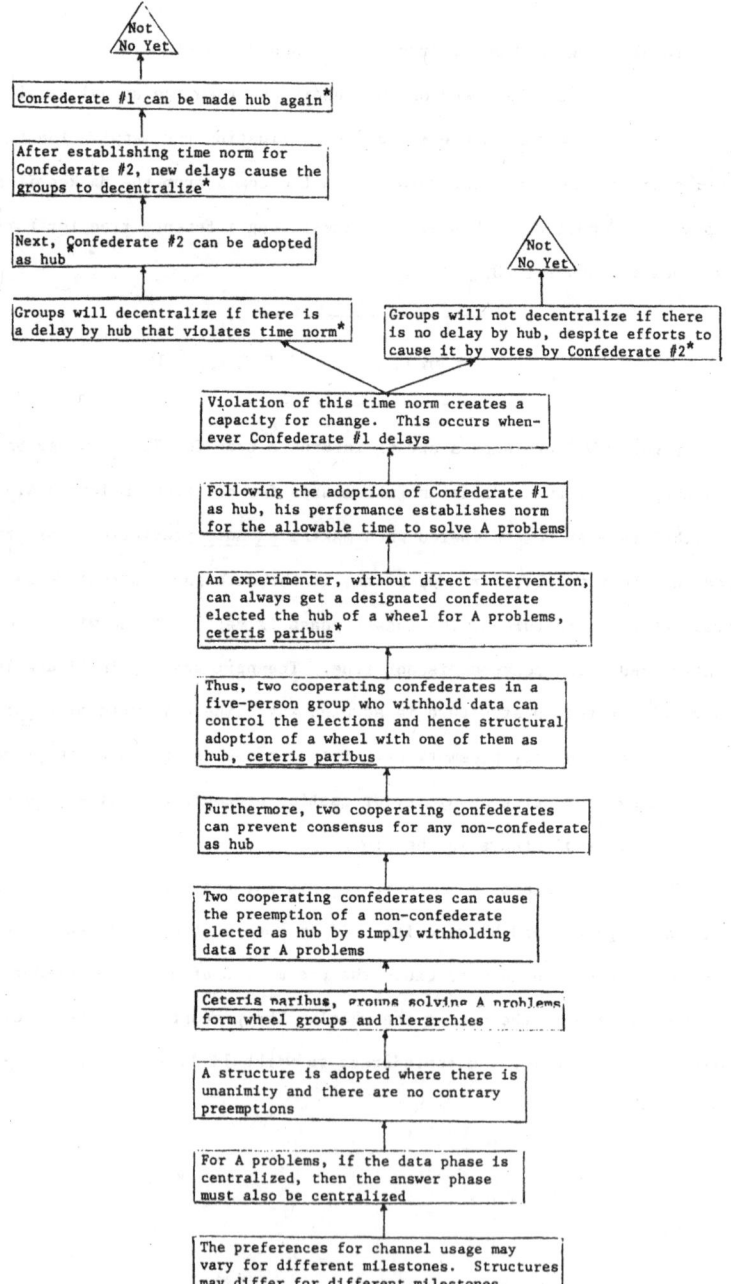

FIGURE 17.8 PART G OF THE STRONG INFERENCE TREE OF FIGURE 17.1. PART G REPRESENTS REASONING FOR HOW TO EMPLOY CONFEDERATES TO CONTROL GROUP STRUCTURES FOR A PROBLEMS

Because the problem cannot be solved unless all of the data are known by
at least one member, the withholding of data can prevent the group from
arriving at a solution. Withholding data can preempt any adopted wheel
structure. The two confederates in a group of five can also prevent attainment of consensus for any non-confederate as hub. Therefore, ceteris
paribus, two confederates in a five-person group can control elections
and thereby control the adoption of a wheel with one of the confederates
as its hub. Specifically, an experimenter, without direct intervention,
can always get a designated confederate elected the hub of a wheel, ceteris
paribus. Data do not reject yet this conclusion.

If the experimenter can cause the election of one confederate as hub,
he should also be able to cause the removal of that confederate and the
election of another. The process is as follows: The performance of Confederate #1
on the first few problems establishes a norm for the allowable time for
solving A problems. This time norm is explained in Chapter 6 under maximum
span of control. The time norm can be violated by Confederate #1 if he
merely delays sending out the answer. By definition, this delay in a
centralized group creates a capacity for change. This causes a change
in variable $X_7(T)$ in the mapping function. The prediction of the mapping
function is that, under these conditions, the delay by Confederate #1 will
result in the group decentralizing. If there is no capacity for change,
the mapping function predicts that the structures will not decentralize.
This pair of predictions is not yet rejected by the data from Chapter 15.

The whole procedure can be repeated. First, the experimenter can cause

the election of Confederate #2 as the new hub. After establishing the
time norm, a delay creates a capacity for change and causes the decentralization
of the structures. Following the "dumping" of Confederate #2, if the theory
is correct, the experimenter should be able to cause the reelection of
Confederate #1 as hub. These manipulations were attempted. These data
do not yet reject the theory because of successful predictions.

PART H   AXIOM OF CONSUMMATION, STRUCTURAL CHANGE, AND HOSTILITY

Part H grows out of the left hand side of Part G. Part H uses the
manipulations employed in Part G in order to make another attempt to validate
the behavioral constitution of Chapter 7. One of the axioms is C2, which
reads: An adopted structure will be consummated. Consummated means utilized,
implemented, or actually occurring. Axiom C2, then, states that if a
structure is adopted it will actually be employed by a group. Suppose,
however, that Axiom C2 represents a norm of a group. The violation of
this axiom, if it is in fact a norm, should initiate frustration-hostility
processes directed at first towards the violator. One can imagine a control
group having a similar sequence of messages where the structure has not yet
been adopted. Attempts to alter the structure when it is not yet adopted
are not violations of C2. The confederate's non-violation should not have
the same response from the group in the control condition even though his
behavior is identical to that when he is in the main experiment.

The main experiment of Part H is the left hand side branch and the
control experiment of Part H is the right hand side branch. Data for
Part H come from the Mackenzie-Beynon experiment reported in Chapter 16.

The strong inference tree for Part H is presented in Figure 17.9.

Refer To Figure 17.9 (Page 472)

The experiments require the concept of an impasse in a hostility formation process. The analysis of hostility formation sequences is presented in Chapter 16. Briefly, when two parties recognize that they have incompatible positions, that only one can win and the other must lose, they are said to be in conflict. They will interact. If one states his position, receives a reply that ignores it, he may state it again. If it is then ignored again, the first person has been _impassed_ by the second. There are other types of 4-message sequences such as resolution and holding sequences. The level of interpersonal hostility is defined in terms of the number of these 4-message sequences in Equation (16.9)

An impasse is likely to occur earlier in situations where there is clear conflict than in situations where the presence of conflict is ambiguous. A behavior which results in a violation of a strongly held norm is more likely to result in a clear conflict than the same behavior if it does not violate a strongly held norm. Thus, if the Axiom of Consummation, C2, is a strongly held norm, its violation should trigger early first impasse with the violator. Furthermore, the "violator" should be able to behave the same way and not trigger first impasses if the axiom is not violated. I seek thus to use the timing of occurrences of first impasses to validate at least one part of the behavioral constitution of Chapter 7. The underlying

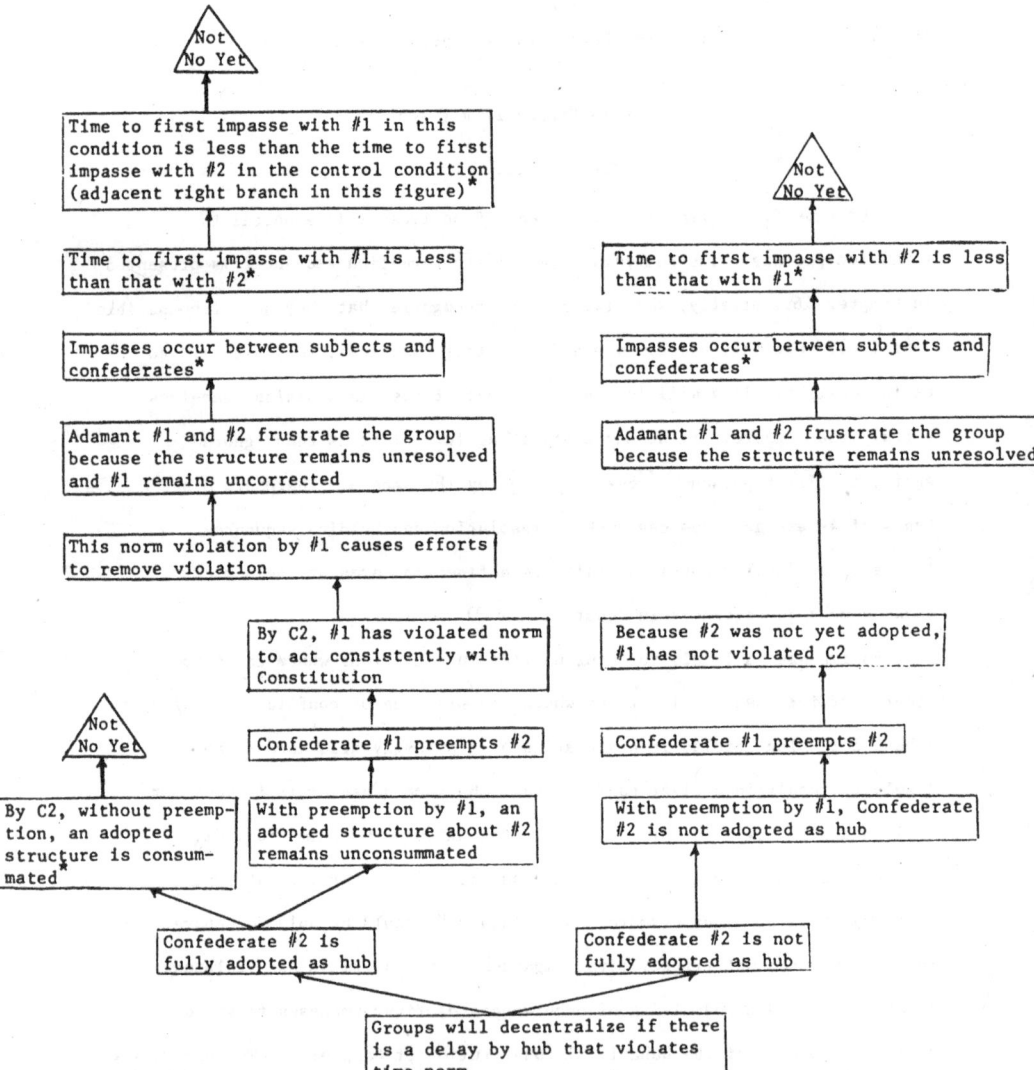

FIGURE 17.9 PART H OF THE STRONG INFERENCE TREE OF FIGURE 17.1. PART H REPRESENTS EXPERIMENTS FOR THE VALIDITY OF THE BEHAVIORAL CONSTITUTION BY THE PROVOCATION OF INTERPERSONAL HOSTILITY WHEN IT IS VIOLATED.

belief is that the behavioral constitution which describes the "as if" behavior of subjects represents a codification of social norms. Hence, any violation of it is a norm violation and such norm violations create conflicts that in turn can generate hostility. Turning this about, we say that C2 is a norm if violations of this norm can create the predicted events.

The experiments for Part H begin like those in Part G. After Confederate #1 delays, the group goes about selecting a new hub. In the main experiment (the left hand side branch of Figure 17.9), Confederate #2 is fully adopted as the hub. In the control experiment (the right hand side branch), Confederate #2 is not fully adopted as hub. Without preemption in the main experiment, a wheel is consummated with Confederate #2 as its hub. However, a preemption by the first confederate is a violation of C2 in the main experiment and not so in the control.

After the preemption, both confederates (who are both "contending" to be hub) are adamant and refuse to give in. In both experiments the subjects become frustrated because the issue of structure remains unresolved. An unresolved structure means, in this case, that the group can make no progress. In the main experiment there is an additional problem in that the norm violator (Confederate #1) has not yet been corrected. In both experiments impasses occur between subjects and confederates. I predict that the time to first impasse will be less towards #1 than #2 in the main experiment and that the opposite timing will occur in the control. Furthermore, the time to first impasse with #1 in this experiment will be less than the time to first impasse with #2 in the control experiment. Data do not yet permit the rejection of these hypotheses. Hence, we cannot yet reject the hypothesis that the Axiom of Consummation C2 is a widely held group norm.

SOME LIMITATIONS OF THIS WORK

The preceding summary of the empirical checks for the theory of group structure presented in the first ten chapters of this work has been completed. It would appear that one is not yet able to reject it. The very phrasing, however, suggests that it should be possible to create a rejection. It may be useful in this regard to examine some of the obvious limitations of this work. The theory, measures, models, data, and results of this book represent one view. Experiments by their very nature deal with specific instances rather than generalities. Models and theories are simplifications designed to see relationships among the "main" features of phenomena. Data are inherently biased and limited by the sequence of transformations made explicitly or implicitly by the experimenter as he proceeds from a universe of potential observations to statistical or other types of results.

The theory of group structures and the results of empirical work are, of course, limited. The optimistic viewpoint expressed in Chapter 11 of long term advances of human knowledge and its attendant benefits of shedding of inadequate theory does suggest that the theory of this book must meet the same fate. Examination of the strong inference trees of this chapter can suggest many new investigations. Every limb of any of the Figures

(17.2-17.9) can yield new experiments to reject the theory. The logic behind the upward and outward movements in these strong inference trees can only be reexamined for logical flaw or possible correctness within a very narrow range of situations. In addition to this type of analysis, one can also examine the omissions in this work.

The major omission is no changes in membership are considered. The membership was always kept constant and I attempted to study changes and effects of changes in the relationships between the members. Any change in membership necessarily changes the relationships in the structures. While it was possible that these changes are similar to the ones studied with respect to the theory, there may be some new and interesting processes of change.

There appear to be three types of membership change that are possibly interesting. The first is a reduction in membership by member departure. Members can depart by quitting, moving, being promoted or transferred. Members can partially depart, as in the case of illness, vacation, and emotional disturbances that affect performance. The second is an increase in membership by acquiring a new member. A group can grow for many reasons, each one of which implies different processes for structural change. The third type of change in membership is the "simultaneous" loss of one member and the gain of another. All three types of changes in membership are subsumed under the rubric of "employee turnover" in organization theory.

All three types of changes involve actions whereby role sets are altered. In the case of departure, one whole row of the role matrix is suddenly unfilled. Assuming that at least some of these behaviors are necessary, the remaining members have to decide how to accomplish these. They will create processes to cope with these changes. It is very possible that very simple changes can result in enormous difficulties depending upon the contingencies reached by the group. Groups may form structures to cope with disturbances. Disturbances may trigger subsequent disturbances. There may be interesting processes for reducing disturbances.

The incorporation of a new member will be relatively easy to the extent that it involves new activities rather than the reallocation of previous activities without previously agreed upon rules. In addition to disturbance processes such as some mentioned above, there may arise special processes designed to indoctrinate the new member into the group's norms and to assure his compliance.

The switching of members may be quite different in effects depending upon the type of switch. A simple replacement of a departing member by an arriving one should be easier for a group to manage than the departure of one member from one role and the arrival of another to fill a different role.

The basic theory of structural change should apply to changes in membership. I suspect, however, that we shall encounter several new processes and that these new processes will change our current theory. Basically, there is the task process graph, the milestone structures, and the role matrix. All changes can be viewed in terms of changes in these quantities. I suspect that for efficiency-minded groups having a stable structure before the disruption, the groups will react to the disruption by attempting to minimize its effects.

Another basic omission is not using problems or circumstances that do not favor efficiency. These were avoided, because I felt that it would be more difficult to guess at what needs were being satisfied and that it would be easier to work with data if there could be one major need such as having money. Certainly, we need to reexamine the theory for other types of problems and incentives. The maximum span of control and the mapping function depend heavily on the need for efficiency. There may be analogous processes for other types of needs.

The method of answer control employed in every experiment is only one of many possible methods. The requirement that all must submit a correct answer and that a subject could submit only one answer until a decision was announced by the experimenter definitely affected the processes. Any number of other methods could have been used. Changing the method of answer control alters the task process graph and the perceived instrumentality of specific acts, and hence, could alter the structures. It would be interesting to determine whether groups alter structures to adjust to the method of answer control and payments.

The range of experimental situations is restricted. Face-to-face groups should be tried as well as groups of different size and different types of memberships. All of the reported experiments involve five-person groups from a college population who interact via written messages. No explicit use of personality variables are employed. There is no reason why one could not introduce personality variables.

Throughout this work I have attempted to express my reservations with a particular idea, technique, model, and result. There are many questions concerning details. Overall, however, it is clear that it is useful to conceptualize group structure in terms of possible substructures. It is also clear that structures can change and should not be thought of as static. A theory of structure becomes essentially a theory of structural change. Structural changes do not appear to be particularly exotic or basically different from other types of change. The rules differ and there are different processes, but the change processes can apparently be easily controlled to some extent. Certainly, the changes induced by the various experiments are convincing evidence that structural change can be subjected to control.

The most significant tool presented in this book is the concept of task process and the derived measure for the degree of hierarchy. The strength of the correlations between the degree of hierarchy and efficiency and some effectiveness measures across a wide set of experiments is very encouraging.

I hope that the method presented in this book for attacking the formulation of a theory for ill-defined problems is a prototype paradigm. The method of strong inference with its heavy emphasis on clarity and counter-example seem particularly appropriate for ill-defined problems such as developing a theory for group structures. I also believe that the reported results demonstrate how the apparently negative procedures of strong inference are actually more efficient in producing positive results than methods relying on more eclectic procedures.

I believe that the research methods, the theoretical tools developed, and the empirical findings constitute major steps out of the morass into which studies of group structure have fallen. Hopefully, a few years hence the field will be revitalized and honest authors won't have to divorce theories about structure from "facts" about structure. Such a division is wrong and it is wasteful of talent. I hope that this work may serve to revitalize inquiry into this class of important human problems.

REFERENCES

Allen, R. D., Francis, D. W. and Zeh, R. "Direct test of the positive gradient theory of pseudopod extension and retraction in amoebae," Science, 1971, 174, No. 4025, 1237-1240.

Allen, R. D., Zeh, R., Condeelis, J. and Francis, D. W. "Reply to Jahn and Votta and to Kirby, Rinaldi and Cameron," Science, 1972, 177, No. 4049, 638.

Allen, V. L. "Situational factors in conformity," Advances in Experimental Social Psychology (L. Berkowitz, ed.), Vol. II. New York, N.Y.: Academic Press, 1965, 133-176.

Arrow, K. J. Social Choice and Individual Values. New Haven, Conn.: Yale University Press, 1963.

Bain, J. S. Industrial Organization. New York, N.Y.: Wiley, 1959.

Bales, R. F. Interaction Process Analysis. Cambridge, Mass.: Addison-Wesley, 1951.

Bales, R. F. and Borgatta, E. F. "Size of group as a factor in the interaction profile," Small Groups (A. D. Hare, E. F. Borgatta and R. F. Bales, eds.). New York, N.Y.: Knopf, 1955, 396-413.

Barron, F. H. and Mackenzie, K. D. "A constrained optimization model of risky decisions," Journal of Mathematical Psychology, 1973, 10, No. 1, 60-72.

Bass, B. M. Leadership, Psychology, and Organizational Behavior. New York, N.Y.: Harper & Row, 1960, Chapters 17-21.

Bass, B. M. and Norton, F. T. M. "Group size and leaderless discussions," Journal of Applied Psychology, 1951, 6, 397-400.

Bavelas, A. "A mathematical model for group structures," Applied Anthropology, 1948, 7, 16-30.

Bavelas, A. "Communication patterns in task-oriented groups," Journal of the Accoustical Society of America, 1950, 22, 725-730.

Berkowitz, L. "Some factors affecting the reduction of overt hostility," Journal of Abnormal and Social Psychology, 1960a, LX, 14-21.

Berkowitz, L. "Repeated frustrations and expectations in hostility arousal," Journal of Abnormal and Social Psychology, 1960b, LX, 422-429.

Berkowitz, L. Aggression: A Social Psychological Analysis. New York, N.Y.: McGraw-Hill, 1962.

Berkowitz, L. "A re-examination of the frustration-aggression hypothesis," Roots of Aggression (L. Berkowitz, ed.). New York, N.Y.: Atherton Press, 1969, 1-27.

Bernhardt, I. and Mackenzie, K. D. "Measuring seller unconcentration, segmentation, and product differentiation," Western Economic Journal, 1968, 6, No. 5, 395-403.

Bernhardt, I. and Mackenzie, K. D. "Acceptance of change: A theory with models," Management Science in Planning and Control, (J. Blood, Jr.). New York, N.Y.: TAPPI, 1969, 321-350.

Bernhardt, I. and Mackenzie, K. D. "Some problems in using diffusion models for new products," Management Science, 1972, 19, No. 2, 187-200.

Birch, D. and Veroff, J. Motivation: A Study of Action. Belmont, Calif.: Brooks/Cole, 1966.

Bolton, G. M., Gray, L. N. and Mayhew, Jr., B. H. "An experimental examination of a stochastic model of dominance," Social Forces, 1970, 48, No. 4, 511-519.

Boulding, K. E. Conflict and Defense: A General Theory. New York, N.Y.: Harper Torchbooks, The University Library, Harper & Row, 1962.

Boyle, R. P. "Algebraic systems for normal and hierarchical sociograms," Sociometry, 1968, 30, 99-119.

Brams, S. J. "Measuring the concentration of power in political systems," American Political Science Review, 1968, 62, 461-475.

Bridgman, P. W. Dimensional Analysis. New Haven, Conn.: Yale University Press, 1963.

Byrne, D. "Attitudes and attraction," Advances in Experimental Social Psychology (L. Berkowitz, ed.), Vol. 4. New York, N.Y.: Academic Press, 1969, 36-90.

Carroll, J. D. and Chang, J. "Analysis of individual differences in multidimensional scaling via an N-way generalization of 'Eckart-Young' decomposition," Psychometrika, 1970, 35, No. 3, 283-319.

Carzo, Jr., R. and Yanouzas, J. N. Formal Organization: A Systems Approach. Homewood, Ill.: Richard D. Irwin and The Dorsey Press, 1967, 291-323.

Caves, R. American Industry: Structure, Conduct, and Performance. Englewood Cliffs, N.J.: Prentice-Hall, 1964.

Chomsky, N. and Miller, G. A. "Introduction to the formal analysis of natural languages," Handbook of Mathematical Psychology, Vol. II. (Luce, Bush, Galanter, eds.). New York, N.Y.: Wiley, 1963, 269-321.

Coleman, J. S. "The mathematical study of small groups," *Mathematical Thinking in the Measurement of Behavior* (H. Solomon, ed.). Glencoe, Ill.: The Free Press, 1960, Part I.

Coleman, J. S. *Introduction to Mathematical Sociology*. Glencoe, Ill.: The Free Press, 1964a.

Coleman, J. S. *Models of Change and Response Uncertainty*. Englewood Cliffs, N.J.: Prentice-Hall, 1964b.

Coleman, J. S. "Loss of power," *American Sociological Review*, 1973, 38, No. 1, 1-17.

Coleman, J. S., Katz, E. and Menzel, H. *Medical Innovation: A Diffusion Study*. New York, N.Y.: Bobbs-Merrill, 1966.

Collins, B. E. and Guetzkow, H. A. *A Social Psychology of Group Processes for Decision Making*. New York, N.Y.: Wiley, 1964.

Collins, B. E. and Raven, B. H. "Group structure: Attraction, coalitions, communication, and power," *The Handbook of Social Psychology* (Lindzey and Aronson, eds.). Reading, Mass.: Addison-Wesley, 1969, Vol. 4, Chapter 30, 102-204.

Cronback, L. J. and Furby, L. "How we should measure 'change'--or should we?" *Psychological Bulletin*, 1970, 74, 68-80. (See also Errata, *Psychological Bulletin*, 1970, 74, 218.)

Cushman, D. and Whiting, G. C. "An approach to communication theory: Towards consensus on rules," *The Journal of Communication*, 1972, 22, 217-238.

Cyert, R. M. and Grunberg, E. "Assumption, prediction, and explanation in economics," *A Behavioral Theory of the Firm* (R. M. Cyert and J. G. March). Englewood Cliffs, N.J.: Prentice-Hall, 1963, 298-311.)

Cyert, R. M. and March, J. G. *A Behavioral Theory of the Firm*. Englewood Cliffs, N.J.: Prentice-Hall, 1963.

Davis, J. A. and Leinhardt, S. "The structure of interpersonal relations in small groups," Dartmouth College (mimeo), 1967.

Davis, J. H. and Restle, F. "The analysis of problems and prediction of group problem solving," *Journal of Abnormal and Social Psychology*, 1963, 66, No. 2, 103-116.

Debrue, G. *Theory of Value: An Axiomatic Analysis of Economic Equilibrium*. New York, N.Y.: Wiley, 1959.

Deutsch, M. and Krauss, R. M. *Theories in Social Psychology*. New York, N.Y.: Basic Books, 1965.

Dodd, S. C. "Testing message diffusion in controlled experiment: Charting the distance and time factors in the interactance hypothesis," American Sociological Review, 1953, 18, 410-416.

Dodd, S. C. "Diffusion is predictible: Testing probability models for laws of interaction," American Sociological Review, 1955, 20, 392-401.

Dollard, J., Doob, L., Miller, N., Mowrer, O. and Sears, R. Frustration and Aggression. New Haven, Conn.: Yale University Press, 1939.

Doreian, P. "A note on the detection of cliques in valued graphs," Sociometry, 1969, 32, 237-242.

Entwisle, D. R. and Walton, J. "Observation on the span of control," Administrative Science Quarterly, 1961, 5, 522-533.

Ervin-Tripp, S. M. "Sociolinquistics," Advances in Experimental Social Psychology (L. Berkowitz, ed.). New York, N.Y.: Academic Press, 1969, Vol. 4, 91-166.

Faucheux, C. and Mackenzie, K. D. "Task dependency of organizational centrality: Its behavioral consequences," Journal of Experimental Social Psychology, 1966, 2, No. 4, 361-375.

Fawcett, J. (ed.). Dynamics of Violence. Chicago, Ill.: American Medical Association, 1972.

Feather, N. T. "A structural balance approach to the analysis of communication effects," Advances in Experimental Social Psychology, Vol. 3 (Berkowitz, L., ed.). New York, N.Y.: Academic Press, 1967, pp. 100-166.

Feldman, J. and Kanter, H. E. "Organizational Decision Making," Handbook of Organizations, (J. G. March, ed.). Chicago, Ill.: Rand McNally, 1965, 614-649.

Festinger, L. "The analysis of sociograms using matrix algebra," Human Relations, 1949, 2, 153-158.

Fischer, P. H. "An analysis of primary groups," Sociometry, 1953, 16, 272-276.

Fishbein, M. "The search for attitudinal-behavioral consistency," Perspectives in Consumer Behavior (Kassarjian, H. H. and Robertson, T. S., eds.). Glenview, Ill.: Scott, Foresman and Co., 1968, 210-220.

Flament, C. Applications of Graph Theory to Group Structure. Englewood Cliffs, N.J.: Prentice-Hall, 1963.

Ford, Jr., L. R. and Fulkerson, D. R. Flows in Networks. Princeton, N.J.: Princeton University Press, 1962.

Forsyth, E. and Katz, L. "A matrix approach to the analysis of sociometric data: Preliminary report," Sociometry, 1946, 9, 340-347.

Frye, R. L., Sprvill, J. and Stritch, T. M. "Effect of group size on public and private coalescence, efficiency, and change," *Journal of Social Psychology*, 1964, 62, 131-139.

Gebbard, A. "Manipulation of voting schemes: A general result," *Econometrica*, 1973, 41, No. 4, 587-601.

Gergen, K. *The Psychology of Behavior Exchange*. Reading, Mass.: Addison-Wesley, 1969.

Gibb, C. A. "An interactional view of the emergency of leadership," *American Psychologist*, 1954, 9, 502 (Abstract).

Glanzer, M. and Glazer, R. "Techniques for the study of group structure and behavior, I. Analysis of structure," *Psychological Bulletin*, 1959, 56, 317-322.

Glanzer, M. and Glazer, R. "Techniques for the study of group structure and behavior, II. Empirical studies of the effects of structure in small groups, *Psychological Bulletin*, 1961, 58, 1-27.

Griliches, Z. "Hybrid corn: An exploration in the economics of technological change," *Econometrica*, 1957, 25, 501-522.

Gustafson, H. W. *On the Frequency Distribution of Participation in Small Group Discussions*. Ph.D. Thesis, University of Utah, 1955.

Guttman, L. "Measurement as structural theory," *Psychometrika*, 1971, 36, No. 4, 329-347.

Harary, F. "Status and contrastatus," *Sociometry*, 1959, 22, 23-43.

Harary, F. "Demiarcs: An atomic approach to binary relations and group dynamics," *Journal of Mathematical Sociology*, 1971, 1, 195-205.

Harary, F. and Havelock, R. "Anatomy of a communication arc," *Human Relations*, 1972, 25, No. 5, 413-426.

Harary, F., Norman, R. Z. and Cartwright, D. *Structural Models: An Introduction to the Theory of Directed Graphs*. New York, N.Y.: Wiley, 1965.

Harary, F. and Ross, I. C. "A procedure for clique detection using the group matrix," *Sociometry*, 1957, 20, 205-215.

Hare, A. P. "Interaction and consensus in different sized groups," *American Sociological Review*, 1952, 17, 261-267.

Hauron, M. D. and McGrath, J. E. "The contribution of the leader to the effectiveness of small military groups," *Leadership and Interpersonal Behavior* (B. M. Bass and L. Petrillo, eds.). New York, N.Y.: Holt, Rinehart, and Winston, 1961.

Heider, F. The Psychology of Interpersonal Relations. New York, N.Y.: Wiley, 1958.

Hempel, C. G. Philosophy of Natural Science. Englewood Cliffs, N.J.: Prentice-Hall, 1966.

Henderson, J. M. and Quandt, R. E. Microeconomic Theory: A Mathematical Approach. New York, N.Y.: McGraw-Hill, 1958.

Herzberg, F., Mausner, B. and Snyderman, B. B. The Motivation to Work. New York, N.Y.: Wiley, 1959.

Hofshi, R. and Korsch, J. F. "A measure of an individual's power in a group," Management Science, 1972, 19, No. 1, 52-61.

Hogan, R. and Henley, N. M. "Nomotics: The science of human rule systems," Law and Society Review, 1970, 5, 135-145.

Hollander, E. P. Leaders, Groups, and Influence. New York: Oxford University Press, 1964.

Hollander, E. P. and Julian, J. W. "Contemporary trends in the analysis of leadership processes," Psychological Bulletin, 1969, 71(5), 387-397.

Hubbell, C. H. "An input-output approach to clique identification," Sociometry, 1961, 24, 377-399.

Indik, B. P. "The relation between organization size and supervision ratio," Human Relations, 1964, 17, 301-342.

Ipsen, D. C. Units, Dimensions, and Dimensionless Numbers. New York, N.Y.: McGraw-Hill, 1960.

Jahn, T. L. and Votta, J. J. "Capillary suction test of the pressure gradient theory of amoeboid motion," Science, 1972, 177, No. 4049, 636-637.

Katz, L. "A new status index derived from sociometrix analysis,"Psychometrika, 1953, 18, 39-43.

Keller, J. "Comment on 'channels of communication in small groups,' American Sociological Review, 1951, 16, 842-843.

Kendall, M. G. "Further contributions to the theory of paired comparisons," Biometrics, 1955, 2, 43-62.

Khinchin, A. I. Mathematical Foundations of Information Theory. New York, N.Y.: Dover Publications, Inc., 1957.

Kirby, G. S., Rinaldi, R. A. and Cameron, I. L. "Capillary suction test of the pressure gradient theory of ameoboid motion," Science, 1972, 177, No. 4049, 637-638.

Komorita, S. S. and Chertkoff, J. M. "A bargaining theory of coalition formation," Psychological Review, 1973, 80, No. 3, 149-162.

Laird, A. K. "The dynamics of growth," Research/Development, 1969, 20, 28-31.

Lancaster, K. "A new approach to consumer theory," Journal of Political Economy, 1966, 74, 132-157.

Landau, H. G. "On dominance relations and the structure of animal societies, I and II," Bulletin on Mathematical Biophysics, 1951, 13, 1-19 and 245-262.

Lazarsfeld, P. F. and Henry, N. W. "The application of latent structure analysis to quantitative ecological data," Mathematical Explorations in Behavioral Science. (Massarik, F. and Ratoosh, P., eds.). Homewood, Ill.: Irwin-Dorsey, 1965, 333-348.

Leavitt, H. "Some effects of certain communication patterns on group performance," Journal of Abnormal and Social Psychology, 1951, 46, 38-50.

Luce, R. D. and Perry, A. D. "A method of matrix analysis of group structures," Psychometrika, 1949, 14, No. 1, 95-116.

Luce, R. D. and Raiffa, H. Games and Decisions. New York, N.Y.: Wiley, 1957.

Mackenzie, K. D. "Structural centrality in communications networks," Psychometrika, 1966a, 31, No. 1, 17-25.

Mackenzie, K. D. "The information theoretic entropy function as a total expected participation index for communications network experiments," Psychometrika, 1966b, 31, 249-254.

Mackenzie, K. D. "Decomposition of communication networks," Journal of Mathematical Psychology, 1967, 4, 162-172.

Mackenzie, K. D. "The structure of a market," Management Science in Planning and Control (J. Blood, ed.). New York, N.Y.: TAPPI, STAP, No. 5, 1969, 167-216.

Mackenzie, K. D. "A set theoretic analysis of group interaction," Psychometrika, 1970a, 35, No. 1, 23-42.

Mackenzie, K. D. "Some effects of status upon group risk taking," Organizational Behavior and Human Performance, 1970b, 5, 517-541.

Mackenzie, K. D. "An analysis of risky shift experiments," Organizational Behavior and Human Performance, 1971, 6, No. 2, 283-303.

Mackenzie, K. D. "A datum are a system," Research Methodology in Accounting, (R. R. Sterling, ed.). Lawrence, Ks.: Scholars Book Co., 1972, 91-94.

Mackenzie, K. D. "Organization theories: State of the art for the problem of bureaucracy," *Manpower Planning Models* (D. J. Clough, C. G. Lewis, and A. L. Oliver, eds.). London, U.K.: English Universities Press, 1974a, 3-24.

Mackenzie, K. D. "Organizational change," *Contemporary Management: Issues and Viewpoints* (J. W. McGuire, ed.). Englewood Cliffs, N.J.: Prentice-Hall, Inc., 1974b, Chapter 9.

Mackenzie, K. D. "Measuring a person's capacity for interaction in a problem solving group," (to be published by *Organizational Behavior and Human Performance*, 1974c).

Mackenzie, K. D. and Barron, F. H. "Analysis of a decision making investigation," *Management Science*, 1970, 17, 4, B-226-B-241.

Mackenzie, K. D. and Frazier, G. D. "Applying a model of organization structure to the analysis of a wood products market," *Management Science Series B*, 1966, 12, B-340-B-352.

Mann, R. D. "A review of the relationships between personality and performance in small groups," *Psychological Review*, 1959, 56, 241-270.

Mansfield, E. "Technical Change and the rate of imitation," *Econometrica*, 1961, 29, 741-766.

March, J. G. and Simon, H. A. *Organizations*. New York, N.Y.: Wiley, 1958.

Marschak, J. and Radner, R. *The Economic Theory of Teams*. New Haven, Conn.: Yale University Press, 1972.

Maslow, A. H. "A theory of human motivation," *Psychological Review*, 1943, 50, 370-396.

McKeachie, W. J. "Research on teaching at the college and university level," *Handbook of Research on Teaching* (N. Gage, ed.). Chicago, Ill.: Rand McNally, 1963, 1118-1172.

McNeil, E. B. (ed.) *The Nature of Human Conflict*. Englewood Clifss, N.J.: Prentice-Hall, 1965.

McPhee, W. N. *Formal Theories of Mass Behavior*. New York, N.Y.: The Free Press, 1963.

McWhinney, W. H. "Isolating organization dynamics in a small group experiment," *Sociometry*, 1963, 26, 354-372.

Meier, R. L. "Information input overload: Features of growth in communications-oriented institutions," *Mathematical Explorations in Behavioral Science*, (F. Massarik and P. Ratoosh, eds.). Homewood, Ill.: Irwin, 1965, 233-273.

Mitchell, T. R. and Biglan, A. "Instrumentality theories: Current uses in psychology," *Psychological Bulletin*, 1971, 76, No. 6, 432-454.

Mitroff, I. and Betz, F. "Dialectical decision theory: A meta-theory of decision making," *Management Science*, 1972, 19, No. 1, 11-24.

Moreno, J. L. *Who Shall Survive? A New Approach to the Problem of Human Interrelations*. New York, N.Y.: Beacon House, 1934.

Nemeth, C. "A critical analysis of research utilizing the prisoner's dilemma paradigm for the study of bargaining," *Advances in Experimental Social Psychology*, Vol. 6 (L. Berkowitz, ed.). New York, N.Y.: Academic Press, 1972, 203-234.

O'Connor, Jr., E. F. "Response to Cronback and Furby's 'How we should measure "change"--or should we?'" *Psychological Bulletin*, 1972, 78, No. 2, 159-160.

Parsons, T. and Shils, E. A. (eds.). *Toward a General Theory of Action*. New York, N.Y.: Harper Torchbooks, 1962.

Pearce, W. B. "Consensual rules in interpersonal communication: A reply to Cushman and Whiting," *The Journal of Communication*, 1973, 23, 160-168.

Pepitone, A. *Attraction and Hostility*. New York, N.Y.: Atherton Press, 1964.

Platt, J. R. "Strong Inference," *Science*, 1964, 146, No. 3642, 347-353.

Popper, K. R. *The Logic of Scientific Discovery*. London, U. K.: Hutchinson and Co., 1959. New York, N.Y.: Basic Books. Harper Torchbooks, 1968.

Rapoport, A. "Outline of a probabilistic approach to animal sociology," *Bulletin of Mathematical Biophysics*, 11, 1949.

Rogers, E. *Diffusion of Innovations*. The Free Press, 1962.

Rosenthal, R. *Experimenter Effects in Behavioral Research*. New York, N.Y.: Appleton-Century-Crofts, 1966.

Russett, B. M. "Probabilism and the number of units affected: Measuring influence concentration," *American Political Science Review*, 1968, 62, 476-480.

Sabidussi, G. "The centrality index of a graph," *Psychometrika*, 1966, 31, 581-603.

Samuelson, P. A. "A note on the pure theory of consumer's behavior," *Economica*, 1938, 5.

Savage, L. J. *The Foundations of Statistics*. New York, N.Y.: Wiley, 1954.

Sen, A. K. "Behavior and the concept of preference," *Economica*, 1973, 40, No. 159, 241-257.

Shaw, M. E. "Group structure and the behavior of individuals in small groups," *Journal of Psychology*, 154a, 38, 139-149.

Shaw, M. E. "Some effects of problem complexity upon problem solving efficiency in different communication nets," *Journal of Experimental Psychology*, 1954b, 48, 211-217.

Shaw, M. E. "Communication networks," *Advances in Experimental Social Psychology* (L. Berkowitz, ed.). New York, N.Y.: Academic Press, 1964, Vol. 1, 111-149.

Shaw, M. E. *Group Dynamics: The Psychology of Small Group Behavior*. New York, N.Y.: McGraw-Hill, 1971, 137-147, 233-288.

Shubik, M. "Game theory and the study of social behavior: An introductory exposition," *Game Theory and Related Approaches to Social Behavior* (Shubik, M., ed.). New York, N.Y.: Wiley, 1964, 3-78.

Siegel, S. *Nonparametric Statistics for the Behavioral Sciences*. New York, N.Y.: McGraw-Hill, 1956.

Silcox, A. C. *Influencing Group Structure by Direct Intervention into Group Decision Processes*. MaSc Thesis, Department of Management Sciences, University of Waterloo, 1972.

Simon, H. A. "The proverbs of administration," *Public Administration Review*, 1946, 6, 53-67.

Simon, H. A. "Causal ordering and identifiability," *Studies in Econometric Method* (Hodd and Koopmans, eds.). New York, N.Y.: Wiley, 1953 Chpater 3.

Simon, H. A. "How big is a chunk," *Science*, 1974, 183, No. 4124, 482-488.

Singer, J. L. (ed.). *The Control of Aggression and Violence: Cognitive and Physiological Factors*. New York, N.Y.: Academic Press, 1971.

Slater, P. E. "Contrasting correlates of group size," *Sociometry*, 1958, 21, 129-139.

Starbuck, W. H. "Organizational growth and development," *Handbook of Organizations* (J. G. March, ed.). Chicago, Ill.: Rand McNally, 1965, 451-533.

Starbuck, W. H. (ed.). *Organizational Growth and Development*. Baltimore, Md.: Penguin Modern Management Readings, Penguin Books, 1971.

Stephan, F. "The relative rate of communication between members of small groups," *American Sociological Review*, 1952, 17, 482-486.

Stephan, F. and Mischler, E. G. "The distribution of participation in small groups: An exponential approximation," *American Sociological Review*, 1952, 17, 598-608.

Stieglitz, H. "Optimizing span of control," *Management Record*, 1962, 25-29.

Stigler, G. J. *The Organization of Industry*, Homewood Ill.: Irwin, 1968.

Suojanen, W. W. "The span of control--fact or fable," *Advanced Management*, 1955, 5-13.

Swinth, R. L. "Organizational joint problem solving," *Management Science*, 1971, 18, No. 2, B-68-B-79.

Tannenbaum, P. H. "The congruity principle revisited: Studies in the reduction induction, and generalization of persuasion," *Advances in Experimental Social Psychology*, Vol. 2 (Berkowitz, L., ed.). New York, N.Y.: Academic Press, 1967, 272-320.

Taylor, M. "Influence structures," *Sociometry*, 1968, 31, 490-502.

Thalen, H. A. "Group dynamics in instruction: Principles of least group size," *Scholastic Review*, 1949, 57, 139-148.

Thomas, E. J. "Effects of group size," *Psychological Bulletin*, 1965, 60, 371-384.

Thomas, E. J. and Biddle, B. J. "Basic concepts for classifying the phenomena of role," *Role Theory: Condepts and Research* (Biddle and Thomas, eds.). New York, N.Y.: Wiley, 1966, 23-45.

Thompson, R. E. "Span of control--conceptions and misconceptions," *Business Horizon*, 1964, 49-58.

Tuddenham, R. D. "Fame and oblivion," *Science*, 1974, 183, No. 4129, 1071-1072.

Tukey, J. A remark attributed to Tukey in a footnote by H. Raiffa in *Decision Analysis: Introductory Lectures on Choices Under Uncertainty*. Reading, Mass.: Addison-Wesley, 1971, 264.

Tversky, A. "Elimination by aspects: A theory of choice, *Psychological Review*, 1972, 79, No. 4, 281-299.

Vroom, V. H. *Work and Motivation*. New York, N.Y.: Wiley, 1964.

Wald, A. *Statistical Decision Functions*. New York, N.Y.: Wiley, 1950.

Walster, E., Berscheid, E. and Walster, G. W. "New directions in equity research," *Journal of Personality and Social Psychology*, 1973, 25, No. 2, 151-176.

Warner, W. K. and Hilander, J. S. "The relationships between size of organization and membership participation," *Rural Sociology*, 1964, 29, 30-39.

Wedderburn, H. G. *Group Preference for a Centralized Structure is Independent of Initial Structure*. MaSc thesis, University of Waterloo, Waterloo, Ontario, 1972.

Weyrauch, W. O. "The 'basic law' or 'constitution' of a small group," _Journal of Social Issues_, 1971, _27_, No. 2, 49-63.

White, H. C. _An Anatomy of Kinship: Mathematical Models for Structures of Cumulated Roles_. Englewood Cliffs, N.J.: Prentice-Hall, 1963.

Zajonc, R. D. "Cognitive theories in social psychology," _The Handbook of Social Psychology_, 2nd Ed. (Lindzey and Aronson, eds.), Vol. 1. Reading, Mass.: Addison-Wesley, 1969, Chapter 5, 320-411.

AUTHOR INDEX, VOLS. I & II

Allen, R. D.   5, 6n
Allen, V. L.   258
Arrow, K. J.   147
Bain, J. S.   16, 149
Bales, R. F.   119, 119n
Barron, F. H.   41, 148
Bass, B. M.   119n, 120
Bavelas, A.   1, 16
Berkowitz, L.   403
Bernhardt, I.   27, 48, 100, 198n, 208, 379
Berscheid, E.   146
Betz, F.   6n
Biddle, B. J.   64
Biglan, A.   147, 245
Birch, D.   147
Bolton, G. M.   100
Borgatta, E. F.   119
Boulding, K. E.   403
Boyle, R. P.   100
Brams, S. J.   101
Bridgman, P. W.   247n
Byrne, D.   433
Cameron, I. L.   6n
Carroll, J. D.   195n
Cartwright, D.   15, 37
Carzo, Jr., R.   231
Caves, R.   31
Chang, J.   195n
Chertkoff, J. M.   151
Chomsky, N.   16
Coleman, J. S.   16, 100, 119n, 200
Collins, B. E.   2
Condeelis, J.   6n
Cronback, L. J.   195n
Cushman, D.   154
Cyert, R. M.   142
Davis, J. A.   100
Davis, J. H.   120
Debreu, G.   147
Deutsch, M.   16
Dodd, S. C.   119n
Dollard, J.   403
Doob, L.   403
Doreian, P.   99
Entwisle, D. R.   120
Ervin-Tripp, S. M.   154
Faucheux, C.   27, 91, 263, 278

Fawcett, J.   403
Feather, N. T.   37
Feldman, J.   16
Festinger, L.   99
Fischer, P. H.   119n
Fishbein, M.   154
Flament, C.   16
Ford, Jr., L. R.   35
Forsyth, E.   99
Francis, D. W.   5, 6n
Frazier, G. D.   69
Frye, R. L.   120
Fulkerson, D. R.   35
Furby, L.   195n
Gebbard, A.   147
Gergen, K.   146
Gibb, C. A.   119n
Glanzer, M.   1
Glazer, R.   1
Gray, L. N.   100
Griliches, Z.   200
Grunberg, E.   65n
Guetzkow, H. A.   2
Gustafson, H. W.   119n
Guttman, L.   195n
Harary, F.   15, 35, 99, 100
Hare, A. P.   120
Hauron, M. D.   120
Havelock, R.   100
Heider, F.   152
Hempel, C. G.   152, 267
Henderson, J. M.   30
Henley, N. M.   154
Henry, N. W.   16
Herzberg, F.   148
Hilander, J. S.   120
Hofshi, R.   101
Hogan, R.   154
Hollander, E. P.   379, 394
Hubbell, C. H.   99
Indik, B. P.   123, 124
Ipsen, D. C.   247n
Jahn, T. L.   6n
Julian, J. W.   394
Kanter, H. E.   16
Katz, E.   200
Katz, L.   99
Keller, J.   119n

Kendall, M. G. 99
Khinchin, A. I. 52
Kirby, G. S. 6n
Komorita, S. S. 151
Korsch, J. F. 101
Krauss, R. M. 16
Laird, A. K. 200
Lancaster, K. 150
Landau, H. G. 100
Lazarsfeld, P. G. 16
Leavitt, H. 1, 16
Leinhardt, S. 100
Luce, R. D. 99
Mackenzie, K. D. 16, 21, 27, 29, 41, 41n, 48, 49, 52, 53, 54, 69, 88, 91, 100, 127n, 128n, 142, 151, 198n, 208, 260, 263, 278, 379
Mann, R. D. 36
Mansfield, E. 200
March, J. G. 16, 142, 244
Marschak, J. 147, 148
Maslow, A. H. 148
Mausner, B. 148
Mayhew, Jr., B. H. 100
McGrath, J. E. 120
McKeachie, W. J. 119n
McNeil, E. B. 403
McPhee, W. N. 16
McWhinney, W. H. 231
Meier, R. L. 142
Menzel, H. 200
Miller, G. A. 16
Miller, N. 403
Mischler, E. G. 119n
Mitchell, T. R. 147, 246
Mitroff, I. 6n
Moreno, J. L. 99
Mowrer, O. 403
Nemeth, C. 151
Norman, R. Z. 15, 37
Norton, F. T. M. 120
O'Connor, Jr., E. F. 195n
Parsons, T. 16
Pearce, W. B. 154
Pepitone, A. 403
Perry, A. D. 99
Platt, J. R. 4, 46, 266
Popper, K. R. 152
Quandt, R. E. 30
Radner, R. 147, 148
Raiffa, H. 147
Rapoport, A. 100

Raven, B. H. 2
Restle, F. 120
Rinaldi, R. A. 6n
Rogers, E. M. 198n, 379
Rosenthal, R. 4
Ross, I. C. 99, 100
Russett, B. M. 101
Sabidussi, G. 22
Samuelson, P. A. 150
Savage, L. J. 147
Sears, R. 403
Sen, A. K. 150
Shaw, M. E. 1
Shils, E. A. 16
Shubik, M. 16
Siegel, S. 388
Silcox, A. C. 375, 385
Simon, H. A. 16, 121n, 152, 244
Singer, J. L. 403
Slater, P. E. 120
Snyderman, B. B. 148
Sprvill, J. 120
Starbuck, W. H. 119n
Stephan, F. 119n
Stieglitz, H. 122
Stigler, G. J. 30
Stritch, T. M. 120
Suojanen, W. W. 121n
Swinth, R. L. 261
Tannenbaum, P. H. 37
Taylor, M. 101
Thalen, H. A. 119n
Thomas, E. J. 64, 119n, 120
Thompson, R. E. 122
Tuddenham, R. D. 153
Tukey, J. 6n
Tversky, A. 148
Veroff, J. 147
Votta, J. J. 6n
Vroom, V. H. 16, 245
Wald, A. 147
Walster, E. 146
Walster, G. W. 147
Walton, J. 120
Warner, W. K. 120
Wedderburn, H. G. 346
Weyrauch, W. O. 154
White, H. E. 154
Whiting, G. C. 154
Yanouzas, J. N. 231
Zajonc, R. D.
Zeh, R. 5, 6n

SUBJECT INDEX, VOLUMES I AND II   Page z

A-Activity Role Matrix Segment   156

A Problems (Minimum List of Symbols
   Problem)   85, 91, 280, 451, 459,
   463, 468

Absolute Controller   159, 239, 240,
   443, 444

"Act as if" Explanations   65, 144, 445

Active Process   209

Active Process Behavioral System   211

Active Process Paradigm   211

Adopted Structure Consummated   472

Adoption and Consummation Processes
   182-184, 264, 462-466

Adoption Experiments   375-394

Adoption of Entry   182

Adoption of Hub   472

Adoption of Issue   237

Adoption of Milestone Role Matrix   182

Adoption of Role Matrix   182

Adoption of Structure   203-208, 240,
   294-497, 375, 462, 468

All-channel Graph   50, diagram 51, 454

Amendments   159

Arc Matrix   19

Axioms for Behavioral Constitution
   163, 177, 184

B Problems (Network Decomposition
   Problem)   87, 91, 280, 451, 463

Ballot   157, def. 235

Basic Intellectual Commitments   2

Behaviorial Constitution   154-186,
   187, 235-241, 375, 444, 459, 463

Axioms for Constitution
A1 Axiom of Preemption   163
A2 Axiom of Redundancy   163
A3 Axiom of Recall   163
A4 Axiom of Final Vote   163
A5 Axiom of Resolution   164-165

Axioms for Milestone Voting
B1 Axiom of Milestone Preemption
    177
B2 Axiom of Milestone Vote
    Redundancy   177
B3 Axiom of Milestone Pattern
    Recall   177
B4 Axiom of Final Milestone
    Vote   177
B5 Axiom of Milestone Resolution
    177
B6 Axiom of the Dominance of the
    Critical Milestone   181

Axioms for Consummation
C1 Axiom of Favorable Elections
    184
C2 Axiom of Consummation   185,
    474, Experiment, 419

Changes in Timely Role Set
Addition   156
Deletion   156
Election   156
Recall   157

Berkeley Channel-Renting Experiment
   317-325
   Method   317-320
   Results   320-323
   Discussion   323-325
   Strong Inference Tree   318
   Summary   447-449

Berkeley Eight-Hour Wheel Experiments
   299-314
   Method   301-304
   Results   304-313

z + 1

Berkeley Eight-Hour Wheel Experiments, continued
  Strong Inference Trees   302, 303, 314, 461, 462

Bridge Principles   267

Capacity for Change   214

Carnegie-Mellon Channel-Renting Experiments   325-344
  Method   329-331
  Results   332-344
  Strong Inference Tree   318
  Summary   447-449

Centrality   35, 48, 52, 54, 55, 111, 256
  Calculations from Experiments   325, 357, 362, 374

Centralization, Noncentralization   459, 463

Centralized Structure   def. 213-217, 222, 223, 241, 242, 252

Chain Graph   def. 50, diagram   51, 451

Channel   225, 444, 448, 451, 463, 468

Channel Renting   259, 448

Circle Graph   def. 50, diagram 51, 451

Coding Scheme   45, 59

Compacted Timely Group Role Matrix $\hat{R}_T$ 96, 228

Compacting the Timely Role Matrix   69-74, 96

Consummation   237, 398-436, 470-474
  Consummation Axiom   184

Contrary Milestone Votes   174

Control Set of A   156, def. 235

Controllers with Respect to A   156, 235

Cousin Relationship   76, 110, 229

Critical Milestones   178

Data, D   39, 269

Data for Hypothesis Testing, D_{HT} 40, 269

Dependent Milestones   181

Diffusion Model   207, 243, 244, 377, 463, 468

Diffusion of Innovation   198, 200, 201

Efficiency   def. 81-85, 459

Efficiency and Effectiveness   230, 290

Efficiency and Hierarchy   116-118, 229, 290, 292, 300, 307, 374

Efficiency, Index for Calculating   229

Elected   156

Eligible Voter   157

Entry in Role Matrix   182

Experiment, Concept of   43, 269

Experimental Universe of Potential Observations, Ω_E 59, 269

Exploration   def. 43, 269

External Vote   159, 235

Father-Son Relationship   76, 110

Faucheux-Mackenzie Experiment   280-279
  Experimental Design   278-279
  Method   280
  Theory   280-285
  Results   285-299
  Strong Inference Trees   286, 314

Faucheux-Mackenzie Problems   91-97

Favorable Election   183, def. 184, 237
  Axiom of Favorable Elections   184

z + 2

Favorable Recall   184

Favorable Vote   183, 237, 463, 464

Feasible Structure   216

Final Vote
  Axiom of the Final Vote   163
  Axiom of the Final Milestone Vote
    177

First Pass Group Milestone Role
  Matrix, R_{A_m} def. 68-69, 96, 227

First Pass Group Role Matrix, R
  def. 68, 74, 93, 227

Four-Message Sequences   405-412, 471
  Resolution   407
  Holding   407
  Impasse   407-408

Graphic Sum   20

Gross Adoption Rate   def. 379, 381
  388, 390, 463, 465

Group Milestone   48, 91-93, def. 225
  442

Group Milestone Role Matrix   59, 182

Group Milestone Structure   74

Group Role Matrix R^* 73

Group Structure   8, def. 15-37, 38, 59,
  62, 63-64, 74, 226, 234, 262, 280,
  442-443, 444, 451, 454, 458, 459,
  463, 468

Half-Channel   168, def. 225, 239, 443,
  444
  Open, def. 50
  Closed, def. 50

Hierarchy, Calculations in Experiments
  324, 338-339, 357, 359-361, 362, 374

Hierarchy, Concept of   102-118, 350
  Pure Hierarchy, Properties of
    103-105, 228-229

Hierarchy, Efficiency, and Effectiveness
  265, 290-291, 300, 324, 458-460

Hierarchy Formation   234, 260-261, 281,
  482, 285-293, 299-301, 468

Hierarchy, Index for Measuring   102-
  116, 229, 459
  Hierarchy Equation   111

High Status Differential with Delay
  Experiment   385-394

Hostility   264, 398-436, 470-474
  Hostility Model   404-420
  Hostility Measure   414-417

Hostility Experiment (Mackenzie-Beynon
  Experiment)   398-436
  Method   419-424
  Results   424-436
    Strong Inference Trees   402, 418
  Questionnaire   437-438

Identical Content of Votes   174

Immediate Superior   75

Immediate Superior Matrix   228

Immediate Superior-Subordinate
  Relationship   228, 261

Impasse   407-417, 471, 472

Implicit Preemption   159

Influence Attempts   235

Insertion   159

Interaction   def. 225

Internal Principles   267

Investigation   def. 43, 44-47, 269

Isocracy   112

Learning Models   231-233, 306-314,
  459, 460, 462

Levels   75-81

Life History of a Group   7, 10, 225

Limitations of the Study   474-479

Low Status Differential with Delay
  Experiment   385-394

Mapping Function   209, 212, 213-223,
  241-243, 263-264, 297-299, 375-394
  446, 462, 463

Maximum Span of Control   119-125, 125-
  143, 230, 241-242, 444, 446, 463
  Procedure for Estimating   130-142

Measures, M   40, 269

Measures of Effectiveness   230, 265

Message   def. 224
  Message Content   9, 59, 224
  Message Identification   9, 59, 224

Methodology   def. 43

Milestone   def. 58, 58-74, 91-97,
  213, 225, 281, 442, 444, 459, 461,
  463, 468
  Axioms for Milestone Voting   177

Milestone Elections   172

Milestone Votes   172
  Identical Content Milestone Votes   174
  Contrary or Contradictory Milestone
    Votes   174

Miscellaneous Group Milestones   93

Multi-Dimensional Graph Concept of
  Structure   28-29, 293

Multiple Issue Voting   170

Need-Satisfaction   8, 240, 255, 262,
  263, 280-281, 289-290, 443, 444

Network   209

No-Delay Experiment   385-393

Non-Disjoint Behaviors   106-116

Obnoxious Confederate   250-252, 328-
  329, 332, 448, 449

One-Dimensional Graph Concept of
  Structure   18-20

One-Dimensional Stochastic Concept
  of Structure   24-28

Organizational Level   75-81

Passive   210

Passive Stimulus-Response Paradigm
  211

Passive Stimulus-Response Process
  209

Pattern of Entries   170

Preemption   159, 177, 472
  Preemption Axiom   163

Preference or Utility Function
  245-248, 315-317, 345, 443-446,
  454, 463, 468
  Experiments   248-263, 315-344
  Summary   447-450

Problem Complexity   230

Process Passive   210

Rate of Adoption   243, 244, 264

Raw Data, D_R 40, 269

Reached Milestone   61, 63, 64, 225
  459

Recall Vote   157, 177, 236, 255
  Axiom of Recall   163

Redundancy Axiom   163

Redundant Behavior   def. 62, 227

Redundant First Pass Group Role
  Matrices   69, 74

Redundant Vote   163, 174, 177

Relationship   def. 225

Resolution Event   def. 404

Results, R   40, 269

Role, Concept of   64-66

Role Matrix   def. 182

Scalar Measures   48-49

Search Heuristic   44-47

Second Pass Group Role Matrix R^* 74, 228

Second Pass Timely Group Role Matrix R_T^* 74, 94-95, 228

Self-vote or Preemption   159, def. 236

Simple Decomposition Problem   21

Simple Recomposition Problem   21

Slash Graph   def. 50, diagram 51

Solution Time Per Problem   231-234

Stimulus-Response Model   8

Stimulus-Response Paradigm   210

Strong Inference   3, 4-6, 46, 267-277, 278-279

Strong Inference Trees   286, 302, 303, 314, 318, 351, 381, 402, 418, 441, 445, 448, 451, 454, 459, 463, 468, 472
 Generating a Strong Inference Tree   271, 274-275
 Strong Inference Tree of the Whole   441, 445, 448, 451, 454, 459, 463, 468, 472

Structural Change   210, 213-223, 235, 238-243, 281, 285, 462-466
 Measure for Change   188-198
  Absolute Change   191, 192
  Relative Change   191, 192
 Change Models   203-208, 231, 243-244
 Theory of Change   202-208

Structure Preference   345-374
 All-Channel and Wheel   252-256, 261-263, 345-353
 Chain and Circle   256-260, 353-357, 357-362
  Summary   450-453

Structure Preference, continued
 Effects of Prior Consensus   362-374
 Summary   453-457

Structural Switches   262, 353, def. 366, 457
 Extreme Switch   def. 366
 Intermediate Switch   de. 367
 Zero Switch   def. 367

Structure and Satisfaction   291

Superior-Subordinate Matrix   81

Surrogate Concept of Structure   30-32

Task-Oriented Activities   225-228

Task Process Graph   def. 60, 226, 281, 459

Timely First Pass Group Milestone   74

Timely Group Milestone   def. 62

Timely Group Milestone Matrix   69, 227

Timely Second Pass Group Role Matrix   73,

Transformations of Data   39-43, 66, 269
 Choice of Experimental Universe   39
 Recording Data   39
 Converting Data to Raw Data   39-40
 Converting Raw Data to Measures   40
 Converting Measures to Data for Hypothesis Testing   40
 Hypothesis Testing   40

Trigger Event   def. 404

Unanimity   164, 236, 345, 454, 463, 368

Uncle-Nephew Relationship   76, 107, 229

Unfavorable Election   183, 237

Unfavorable Recall   184, 237

Unfavorable Vote   183, 237, 244, 463, 464

Unfeasible Structure   216

Unit Relative Complexity   def. 136

Untimely Behavior   def. 62, 227, 229, 459

Untimely First Pass Group Role Matrix   74

Untimely Group Milestone   62, 227

Untimely Group Milestone Matrix   69, 227

Untimely Role Matrix   69

Vector Concept of Structure   32-33

Vote   157, def. 235, 444, 459, 463

Vote Content   158, 236
   Consistent Vote   236
   Contradictory or Contrary Vote   236
   Redundant Vote   163, 236

Voting Rules   236

Voting Sequence   157-158, 236

Waterloo Circle Experiment   353-362
   Method   353-354
   Results   354-357
   Strong Inference Tree   351

Waterloo Lutheran Chain Experiment   357-362
   Method   357-358
   Results   358-362
   Strong Inference Tree   351

Waterloo Lutheran Channel-Renting Experiment with Prior Consensus on Structure Required   362-374
   Method   364
   Results   364-274
   Strong Inference Tree   351

Waterloo Structural Adoption Experiment (Mackenzie-Silcox Experiment)   380-394
   Method   380-387
   Results   387-394
   Strong Inference Tree   381
   Confederate's Answer Sheet, Normal and Delay Times, Lists of Persuasion Messages   395-397

Weighted Measure of Change   197

Wheel Graph   def. 50, diagram 51, 451, 454, 468

Wheel Structure   282

Y Graph   def. 50, diagram 51